THIRD EDITION

Business Behavior

Allien R. Russon
Professor of Management
College of Business
University of Utah

SOUTH-WESTERN PUBLISHING COMPANY

CINCINNATI   CHICAGO   DALLAS   BURLINGAME, CALIF.   NEW ROCHELLE, N.Y.

K 40

Copyright © , 1964
by
SOUTH-WESTERN PUBLISHING COMPANY
Cincinnati, Ohio

≡ PREFACE

We are living in what might be described as an *instant* society. Travel between cities is now completed in minutes instead of hours or days. Complex business problems are solved by computers in seconds instead of days or weeks. Happenings on the other side of the globe are reported on the ten o'clock news the same day. Is it any wonder that this *instant* factor should spill over into the way we react to people?

In the modern business world, no one has time to smooth the rough edges of a beginner's personality. Not only does the employer hope for instant efficiency, he also hopes that the newly hired employee will fit instantly into the business team. This puts a heavy burden upon the young employee. Put yourself in his place. Because everyone expects you to be at ease in the new situation, you become even more nervous and worried. Because you try too hard to please, you are unable to keep calm when your superior reprimands you. Because you let your emotions show, someone says you are lacking in poise.

There is, of course, no easy road to an attractive personality. The rewards that come to the businessman or woman with efficiency plus personality, however, make the journey worthwhile, no matter how difficult. The first step is the biggest one. You must want to improve. You must be willing to face yourself, "warts and all," as Abraham Lincoln said to his portrait painter. When you are able to appreciate your good points, you will be more willing to accept those on the other side of the ledger.

Just what is personality? You might say it is the sum total of what the other person sees and hears, plus empathy. This sum total can be improved a little at a time by working on your personality *traits*. Traits are a lot smaller and easier to handle. In this book you will be given specific activities that will help you improve one trait at a time. Each trait that you improve helps you build the whole of your personality.

What the other person sees, your appearance, is a big part of your personality. What kind of picture do you present? Are you dressed appropriately? Are you well groomed? What the other person hears, your voice and diction, these are also important parts of your personality. How does your voice sound to others? Do you know? Have you ever heard a recording of your own voice? Are you a good conversationalist? Are you able to thank someone or give him a word of praise without embarrassment? Empathy, or feeling with another, is intangible, more difficult to define. Part of empathy is made up of the other person's reaction to your attitudes, your habitual way of looking at life. This part of your personality is tremendously important.

You will be the kind of person others like if you get rid of negative feelings and attitudes. The old saying, "Laugh, and the world laughs with you; weep, and you weep alone," is only too true. Many of you may be blaming your unhappiness on events in your life. Yet everyone knows men and women who are cheerful in spite of misfortune. Much of the unhappiness complained about comes from negative habits of mind.

In this book I have made suggestions to help you build an attractive, positive personality. Take the first step. Start working on just one part of the *you* the other person perceives. If your appearance, your way of speaking, and your attitudes begin to improve, you will find that road to success a much smoother one.

ALLIEN R. RUSSON

CONTENTS

PART 5

GETTING THE JOB YOU WANT

APPENDIX

PART 1 THE NINETY PERCENT FACTOR

Chapter 1

Success — Ninety Percent Personality

Everyone wants to be a success. Some observers say that Americans are *too* concerned with material success, that our values are weighted too heavily in the direction of status symbols. But there is another side to this picture. What about the kind of success that means satisfaction with your work? Success on the job defined in this way is something else altogether.

SUCCESS IN BUSINESS

Success in business is based not only on your abilities and how you work, but also on your *attitude* toward your work. Success is based on your knowledge and skill, but it is also based on how you look, how you talk, and how you act. In other school courses, you will build skills and acquire a background in literature, art, science, business, economics. But this is not enough. If you want to be a success in business, you must have the kind of personality that fits into the office team. You must get along well with other workers in business. Developing your business personality will be the purpose of this course.

There are two sides to business success: efficiency and satisfaction of needs. The first, efficiency, is foremost in people's minds. If you are efficient in your work, you are doing well; you are a success. The other side is satisfaction of needs, and it is less well known.

Everyone has basic physical needs: to have shelter from the cold; to have food when hungry; to be safe from harm.

The need to share with others, to be part of a group, is a strong human need. The need to achieve and to acquire possessions is present in most of us, as is the need to have others recognize our achievements. These needs must be met if we are to be happy in our work.

You may be a success in your work, then, if you work efficiently and if your basic needs are met. It is quite likely that these two sides will work together. When your efficiency improves, this improvement may cause you to feel more secure. And when you feel more secure, you may find yourself working still more efficiently.

HOW SUCCESS IS ACHIEVED

If you are convinced that you should develop your personality, how do you go about it? If you should analyze the personal traits that make up a good personality, you might include a smile, a pleasant voice, a friendly attitude, the use of tact. These would certainly be some of the signs of a good personality, but what is underneath these surface signs? A personality can grow only when such growth is based on deeper habits of mind and heart.

A genuine liking for other people is an important habit of heart. If you like someone, you will want to put him at ease; and, presto, you will forget your own ill-at-ease feelings. Self-confidence is an important inner trait. To develop self-confidence, it is wise to do your best to excel. You will then have a reason to be assured, to forget your inadequacies. Naturalness is another habit, a habit of mind. To be natural, you must keep out anxiety, for anxiety causes you to think of yourself, how you look, how you walk, how you talk. This makes you self-conscious — the very opposite of being natural.

Building the inner and outer habits of personality is not an easy matter, but it is a task that will bring rich dividends. Personality is not achieved by picking up a few tricks, nor can it be gained by memorizing facts. To build desired traits, you must *want* to improve; you must *believe* that you *can* improve. With knowledge and belief as the foundation, you can do the right things with a positive aliveness, and your personality will grow. The following steps will help you reach this goal:

1. Determine the type of personality you wish to possess and decide to develop within yourself those habits, attitudes, and traits that will best express that personality.
2. Keep constantly before you the image of the kind of person you wish to become. This mental picture must be so clear and so constantly present that your mental processes and your ways of conduct will bring satisfaction only if they stand approved by this mental personality.
3. Analyze yourself. Discover and acknowledge the weaknesses in your makeup. Face these facts squarely and decide to remove the objectionable factors and substitute new strength for any weakness that stands in the way of your reaching your objective.
4. Exercise the traits of the personality you wish to possess. Only the constant practice of the acceptable conduct will encourage the development of desirable traits and a pleasing personality.

Positive Work Attitude

One of the important factors in success is your attitude toward your job. A positive work attitude can be the difference between success and mediocrity. If you like your work, you will have a positive attitude; if you dislike it, your attitude will be negative. No one likes to be around a negative person. This is just as true in business as it is in personal relations. If you complain, if you say it can't be done, you will be defeating yourself.

Every beginner has a lot to learn; but if your attitude is favorable, you will learn faster and your learning time will be excused by others. How does a positive work attitude manifest itself?

Enthusiasm. A good work attitude includes enthusiasm, both for the work and for the firm that employs you. Enthusiasm is actually nothing more than positive energy. When you are enthusiastic, you accomplish seeming miracles. And the best part of enthusiasm is that it is "catching." If you are enthusiastic, a co-worker may find his "down-in-the-dumps" feeling has disappeared. Enthusiasm is a trait that contributes a major share to what goes into success.

Willingness to learn. A beginner does have a lot to learn. People expect it. They do not expect the learning process to go on forever, though. The beginner who needs to be told something only once is considered a paragon, and the one who learns the new routines and facts without being told is rare, indeed. Everyone makes mistakes, but the beginner with a good work attitude seldom makes the same mistake twice.

Getting along with people. Perhaps the most important factor in a positive work attitude is getting along with people; this involves understanding yourself, the other person, and the way you choose to influence the other person. Where do you begin? Begin with the most difficult part — understanding yourself. You may wonder why understanding yourself is more difficult than learning how to influence others. The answer lies in the years that have been devoted to self-deception. We look at ourselves through rose-colored glasses. We can see the faults of others, but we cannot see our own. Or, if we do see them, we "rationalize" — find excuses for the unattractive sides of our personalities and our characters. So the first step is to take a good look at yourself. Some of the tools for doing this will be discussed in Chapter 2.

The next step is to look for something to like in that person with whom you wish to get along. Liking *something* in others must precede having the other person like you. It may seem an oversimplification, but much of getting along with people consists of just such "turnabouts." If you want to be liked, you must like others. If you want to be *interesting*, you must be *interested* — in the other person's ideas, problems, and suggestions. If you want others to adjust to your wishes, you must first learn to adjust to theirs. Others will overlook your failings more readily if you develop tolerance toward their failings.

Having a goal. Another factor that helps you achieve a positive work attitude — and success — is having a goal. Your grandparents believed you should "hitch your wagon to a star." This belief is not accepted universally now, however, as it frequently involves the choosing of stars too high in the heavens. If you choose a goal that is closer to you, your chances of reaching it increase greatly. If you reach your goal, you will have a feeling of success. This feeling is the greatest spur to ambition that has ever been discovered. The old saying "Nothing succeeds like success" is still true.

The goals which you set for yourself must be realistic in terms of your own ability, interests, aptitudes, training, work habits, and personal qualities. For instance, a boy who has difficulty passing his high school mathematics courses would be foolish to decide to become an engineer because he thinks the profession a glamorous one. Positions of responsibility may require longer hours of work — frequently without any increase in salary and certainly not "time and a half."

Goals must be flexible. A person who decides to become a personnel manager cannot entirely control his destiny. He can do much to achieve this objective, but he cannot be certain that he will become a personnel manager. Certainly many other people aspire toward the same goal, and not all who compete can succeed. Therefore, even though he obtains the necessary education and works in personnel offices, even though he studies and develops attractive personal traits, elements of chance may not enable him to become a personnel manager. His goals must be flexible enough that he will not be frustrated. He must consider that he still has his training and the knowledge that he has acquired; that he is utilizing this preparation, if not in the capacity in which he wants to use it, in a worthwhile form of service; that he has contributed his best ability in the position in which his business placed him. Anyone who can say these things of his career has reason to hold his head high. However, in obtaining the preparation for personnel director, he acted as wisely as he could. By obtaining such training, he increased his chances of reaching his goal. Because training and work cannot assure success, do not withdraw from the competition. To withdraw is certain defeat. To run well in the race is a noble feat.

Plan your goals carefully in terms of the investment of time and work which you want to make. The goals which you set will have great influence on your life. Happiness and success may not be synonymous terms for you. Weigh them in the balance. Try to reconcile the conflict if one exists.

In setting goals and planning their attainment, you cannot always be definite or specific. You can decide only the direction in which you wish to move. You can be prepared. Many opportunities you must seek for yourself. The opportunities which you will find cannot be anticipated with exactness. Some element of chance necessarily exists although you can do much to control that element of chance by training, a good record, habits of industry, and desirable personal traits. New avenues of opportunity may open to you, opportunities that you cannot now even imagine. If you have the necessary training and personal qualities, you may find employers will compete to obtain your services.

Read the life stories of men who succeeded. You find few accounts of sudden fame, power, or wealth. You read of their long, hard struggles and of their overpowering desire to win their fight. Although success is not assured through hard work, you cannot name any person who has reached his goal in life who has not left a trail of hard work behind him.

Importance of Hard Work

Just as there is no royal road to learning, so is there no smooth way to success. That road has not yet been paved. Every man who has traveled on it has learned how to take the bumps, how to make the grade. A survey was made in New Orleans to determine success factors. One hundred sixty-one local business leaders were questioned, and the findings of the study showed that the rules that hold good for becoming a success in one field applied in all other fields. A man needs to expend energy in becoming a successful retailer or a successful banker. He needs to possess an understanding of men if he is a broker or a manufacturer. Note the facts in the following table.

TO WHAT DO YOU ATTRIBUTE YOUR SUCCESS?

Energy	103	Impartial mind	29
Perseverance	100	Instinctive recognition of values	27
Health	91	Visualize results	26
Self-confidence	86	Had money to invest	25
Endurance	85	Enjoy authority	23
Knowledge of business	73	Cultivation of mutual understandings	22
Understanding of men	66		
Intelligent and understanding wife	51	Able assistance	20
Good memory	45	Family connections	20
Judgment	44	Social position	17
Desire to be helpful	41	Physical strength	16
Possessed traits needed	35	Fluent speaker	15
Sense of humor	33	Social contacts	14
		Luck	1

Note that "Energy" receives top rating. One hundred three men out of the one hundred sixty-one (sixty-four per cent of those who were questioned) acknowledged this trait as the factor that most greatly influenced their success. "Perseverance," "Health," "Self-confidence," and "Endurance," which follow immediately, all indicate that hard work lies back of accomplishment.

You are planning your life, your business career. There are set before you examples of men who have planned and achieved. Your desire is to follow paths that will lead to goals as high as those that others have reached. The urge for improving your condition in life is a natural desire. It is one of the dominant characteristics of normal behavior, just as the possibilities for achievement are ingrained in the democratic way of life. The strong desire to find expression of self through your own accomplishments causes you to pursue your ambitions in spite of handicaps and hardships. The human race would know no progress were this motive power lacking.

Telling you to work hard in your field of employment is speaking in generalities. Help must be given with more specific instructions. Assuming that you have the desire to work hard, in what directions will you spend your energies? The following advice will be helpful, provided that you do more than read it, for unless practice follows the reading, you will not have added much to your equipment.

1. *Discover Your Own Ability.* In reading the life stories of successful men, you may decide that there is little you hold in common with such famous people. These men and women seemingly had special abilities that they developed. They made use, however, of what they had.

You, too, have individual talents. Discover them; employ them; develop them. Of what use are your own special gifts and talents if you ignore them? Of what use is a course of training if you do not employ the lessons it would teach? Do not blame fate if you do not make use of the power and the ability that have been given you.

2. *Find Your Job.* Be sure that it is a job that stimulates your ambition. Is it one that is worthy of your best endeavors? Will it keep you working in a field for which you are fitted mentally, physically, and emotionally? Your first job may not offer the opportunity you seek, but eventually you must locate employment where you can best express yourself. Do not expect by any sudden jump to leap from poverty to riches, from obscurity to fame; but by working in a field in which your interests lie, you will find deep satisfactions. If you keep fighting obstacles constantly, in spite of handicaps and hardships, in spite of disappointments and

discouragements, you will discover that you are climbing, little by little, the pathway leading to success.

3. *Have Courage.* Your mental attitude is of greater value than your mental capacity. Just at the time when you think you have exhausted all your resources, there comes a deciding moment demanding more of you than you think you possess. If you fail to meet the test, if you stop trying, you lose the prize. A belief in yourself is essential to success; there must be such a sense of self-confidence and self-assurance that failure, no matter how often repeated, cannot get you down. The strength of will of the individual determined to succeed is the deciding factor in measuring his success.

Do not expect that success will come quickly and easily; rather be prepared to build it carefully and slowly. Profit by your unpleasant experiences, interpret them as opportunities for broadening your outlook, for displaying your own inner powers of resistance, and "keep on keeping on." Believe in yourself, in your ability, in the sureness of the final outcome.

FOLLOW-UP ACTIVITIES

1. Outline the type of personality you would like to have.

    What objectionable habits that you now possess must you eliminate?

    What agreeable habits that you do not now possess must you acquire?

2. If you are an employee wishing to succeed at your first job, you must:

    (a) Know yourself.

    (b) Know the job.

    (c) Use all the abilities you possess.

    (d) Acquire new knowledge, skill, and business information needed on the job.

    (e) Develop the personality traits and behavior patterns for which the job calls.

    (f) Analyze the requirements of the job ahead.

    (g) Analyze your qualifications for meeting these requirements.

(h) Prepare for the job ahead if you believe you would find satisfaction in it.

Select a job for which you might be preparing and discuss (e) in the outline above, telling what personality traits and behavior patterns you need to develop.

3. By what outward signs do you judge people when you first meet them?

4. What opportunities does your community afford for furthering your progress in business through additional educational advantages? If no such opportunities are afforded, what are your plans, once you are employed, for additional schooling?

5. For what reasons, other than educational ones, can you expect promotion in business?

6. In the book, *Why We Don't Like People,* by Donald A. Laird,[1] there are listed "Traits Which Make Us Liked" with the explanation:

In the traits we have enumerated, the average man holds the key to the attitude toward him of his fellow average man.

The higher your score by this self-analysis, the better liked you are in general. Each "No" answer should be changed through self-guidance into a "Yes" answer. The highest possible score is 81. About 10% of people have this score. The lowest score made by a person who was generally liked was 56. The average young person has a score of 64. The average score of a person who is generally disliked is 30. The lowest score we found was 12. It is encouraging to note that the average young person has a score closer to that of the average-liked person than to that of the average-disliked person.

Give yourself a score of 3 for each of these questions you can answer "Yes":

1. Can you always be depended upon to do what you say you will?

2. Do you go out of your way cheerfully to help others?

3. Do you avoid exaggeration in all your statements?

4. Do you avoid being sarcastic?

[1]Donald Laird, *Why We Don't Like People* (New York: A. L. Glaser & Co., Inc., 1933), pp. 30-32.

5. Do you refrain from showing off how much you know?
6. Do you feel at ease with your associates?
7. Do you keep from reprimanding people who do things that displease you?
8. Do you refrain from bossing people not employed by you?
9. Do you avoid making fun of others behind their backs?
10. Do you keep from domineering others?

Give yourself a score of 2 for each of these questions you can answer "Yes":

11. Do you keep your clothing neat and tidy?
12. Do you avoid being bold and nervy?
13. Do you avoid laughing at the mistakes of others?
14. Is your attitude toward the opposite sex free from vulgarity?
15. Do you avoid finding fault with everyday things?
16. Do you let the mistakes of others pass without correcting them?
17. Do you loan things to others readily?
18. Are you careful not to tell jokes that will embarrass those listening?
19. Do you let others have their own way?
20. Do you always control your temper?
21. Do you keep out of arguments?
22. Do you smile pleasantly?
23. Do you avoid talking almost continuously?
24. Do you keep your nose entirely out of other people's business?
25. Do you have patience with modern ideas?
26. Do you avoid flattering others?

Give yourself a score of 1 for each of these questions you can answer "Yes":

27. Do you avoid gossiping?
28. Do you refrain from asking people to repeat what they have just said?
29. Do you avoid asking questions in keeping up a conversation?

30. Do you avoid asking favors of others?
31. Do you avoid trying to reform others?
32. Do you keep your personal troubles to yourself?
33. Are you natural rather than dignified?
34. Are you usually cheerful?
35. Are you conservative in politics?
36. Are you enthusiastic rather than lethargic?
37. Do you pronounce words correctly?
38. Do you look upon others without suspicion?
39. Do you avoid being lazy?
40. Do you avoid borrowing things?
41. Do you refrain from telling people their moral duty?
42. Do you avoid trying to convert people to your own beliefs?
43. Do you avoid talking rapidly?
44. Do you avoid laughing loudly?
45. Do you avoid making fun of people to their faces?

CASE PROBLEMS

1. One Step at a Time

The placement department of the Whittier School placed Don Hardwood as a general clerk with the Atlas Trucking Company. Don was well qualified for the work; the salary was good, and the boss was fair. After a month, however, Don left the company. He told the placement director that he could have stayed on the job forever and never had a chance to do anything but what he had done every day for a month — routing, checking, and keeping routine records.

The placement director called to check with Mr. Hardy, the self-made owner of the Atlas Trucking Company, to see what was wrong. Mr. Hardy said: "Too anxious to be vice-president. Don told me he didn't see how he could get anywhere in this business. He wanted to get ahead too fast. He couldn't see the chance that was right here waiting for him."

1. What should Don's attitude be toward "getting ahead"?
2. How long does it take in a new position before an employee is worth his salary?
3. Do you think there is drudgery in all vocations and professions?
4. What should be a beginner's attitude toward routine work?

2. Detour

Frank Davis majored in accounting in college. After graduation, he tried for several weeks to find a job for which his training qualified him. Finally, he found a job as a bookkeeper for a large life insurance company. He has been there over a year and is reported to be doing excellent work. His salary, though not large, is satisfactory for the type of work he is doing. The physical conditions in the office are extremely good. He feels that the routine work he is doing will not lead to a more responsible job. As he has not had a chance to use his accounting, he fears he will soon be out of touch, especially with the current laws and developments that affect accounting practice.

1. Put yourself in Frank's place. What are some of the possible solutions to this problem?
2. After evaluating the solutions, which one would you take?

3. To Speak or Not to Speak

Marilyn Clark's employer has had a bad day. He has given reprimands to several of the employees and discharged one salesman. When Marilyn answers his ring to take dictation, he reproves her for being late. He had sent Marilyn on an errand a few minutes before, and she could not have returned earlier. When he says, "Why don't you ever get here promptly? I always have to wait for you," it is too much for Marilyn. She answers, "Because I had gone to the filing room to find those papers you wanted!" Her employer then says coldly, "You may go back to your more important work. I'll dictate to one of the others."

1. Evaluate Marilyn's handling of this situation.
2. What would you do in a similar case?
3. Is it helpful to fix the blame? Why or why not?

4. Short- or Long-Term Goals?

Patrick Hyde had always wanted to be a lawyer. Both his father and grandfather had been attorneys, and Patrick had always been certain of his career. After three years of college, however, he was told that his grades were not high enough for him to be accepted by the School of Law. Patrick's schoolwork slipped badly after this news, and his counselor, Mr. Cannon, called him in for an interview. During the interview, Patrick told Mr. Cannon that he had no other interests. He added, "If I can't be a lawyer, I won't be anything." At this point Mr. Cannon asked about the other courses Patrick had taken in high school and college. Among other things, Patrick mentioned that he had taken typing and shorthand in high school and had reached a high level of skill in both subjects. Mr. Cannon then suggested that Patrick find a part-time job as a stenographer in a law office while taking a reduced load in college.

1. What advantages to Patrick do you see in this suggestion?
2. Will firsthand knowledge of legal work give Patrick a more realistic idea of his goal?
3. What effect do you think working part-time will have on Patrick's grades in college? Why?
4. Do you think working as a legal stenographer may help if he is later accepted in a school of law?

Chapter 2

The "U" in Human Relations

Just as everyone wants to be a success, so does everyone want to be liked. No one who watches television or reads a popular magazine can doubt this statement. To many young people being popular is the most important goal in their lives. Frequently, however, this desire is coupled with an utter lack of knowledge of how to achieve popularity. That is why each new mouthwash, perfume, hair style, or fashion is adopted so rapidly by so many people. They are seeking some way to escape from their sense of loneliness, of being shut away from the love and recognition and acceptance they would like to have. There is an approach you can use, but first it is important to understand how the mechanism of self-improvement works.

NEEDS AND MOTIVATION

The person who wants to be liked must first learn to look away from himself. You have heard the word *outgoing*, and this means just the opposite of *self-centered*. If you can learn to be outgoing, this one ability will solve many of your problems. Everyone knows the devastating effects of self-consciousness. You may be happy and relaxed until someone asks you to stand up and speak before a group. Immediately, you wonder what to do with your hands; you worry about the way you stand; your voice sounds strange to your ears. Why can't you think about the audience and forget yourself? The reason is that certain needs must be filled first.

Psychologists tell us that all individuals work their way through several stages of needs. First, everyone must satisfy his physical needs. He must have food when he is hungry, water when he is thirsty, shelter from the cold. Until these physical needs are met, no one can think of anything else.

Second, everyone needs to feel safe from harm. If you fear that an earthquake may engulf you at any minute, the need to be safe from this danger would take precedence over a need to be popular. It is useless to sell a man a "hyacinth for his soul" when he is starving for bread, and a man trapped in a burning building wants nothing but to be rescued. In our country, these two needs are largely met. When this is true, each person begins to experience intense feelings of loneliness. When the first two needs are taken care of, you are ready for the third.

The third need is to belong, to establish social relationships, often called interpersonal relations. You have seen this in certain grades in school. In junior high school, for example, teenagers may join a gang to become a member of a group. With this need to belong comes a desire to dress as others do, to become such a conformist that the slightest deviation from what "everyone does" cannot be tolerated.

When you suddenly find that you want to be liked, admired, recognized for your true worth — then you will know that you have reached the fourth stage in this category of needs. In this stage you may go too far: you may antagonize others in your determination to gain recognition. The fourth stage, however, is the one demanding an *outgoing* personality. When you have reached it, your self-improvement campaign can begin.

One interesting aspect of categories of needs is that most people stop at the third stage. They may daydream about achieving some kind of recognition, but they do not take the first step up the ladder. So, if you are bothered and unhappy about your own inadequacies, take heart. You are a member of the minority that is beginning to rise to the top.

In Chapter 1 the "turnabout" method of getting along with people was mentioned. This same "turnabout" can be a part of finding esteem — both the esteem of others and self-esteem. No one is proud of his own actions and accomplishments all the time. In fact, the more renowned an individual may be, the more likely he will be striving to achieve still more. Also, the more you know about the goal you are trying to reach, the farther you will seem to be from reaching it. Remember this: Every person of high position was once in your shoes. Everyone has had to work his way through a jungle of self-doubt.

Accentuate the Positive

You have probably already learned that negative statements should be avoided when you write or speak to others. The main thing that is wrong with a negative attitude or statement is that negatives are contagious. You know, yourself, that you can get up in the morning with a feeling of well-being. Yet, if you meet four or five friends during the day who tell you of depressing happenings, who complain about their lot, or — worst of all — who criticize you and call attention to your mistakes, your mood of happiness will soon disappear. The other side of the coin is just as contagious, however. Although you may be tired and discouraged, your mood changes when you meet someone who gives you a sincere compliment or who greets you with a smile.

The step to take, then, is to accentuate the positive and eliminate the negative. Being negative is actually nothing but another of those habits discussed in Chapter 1. Just to prove this, you might try an experiment. On the left side of a folded sheet of paper, write "Negative Statements"; on the right side, write "Positive Statements." Choose an hour of the day that is about average for you. Avoid five o'clock in the afternoon, for this is a low period for most of us. Now keep track of the negative and positive statements you make during that hour. Don't try to be different from the way you normally talk, but make a record of each positive and each negative statement. Did you have more negative or more positive statements at the end of the hour? You will be quite unusual if your positive statements outnumber the negative ones. This is because our culture encourages negativism. Most of us tend to say nothing about the good things in our lives. We may go so far as to say, "What a beautiful day," but we are more likely to complain about life's irritations than to give praise.

The next step, after you have found your score, is to start a "Let's be more positive" campaign. Watch yourself. When you start to complain about a teacher, an assignment, the weather, or your financial state, stop. See if you can twist your statement around so that it will be positive. For example, if you get a test paper back with a C- on it, you may start to say, "How awful! I'm below average." Instead, just for this experiment, say, "How about that! I passed!" This may seem ridiculous to you, but it is guaranteed to have a remarkable effect on your moods and emotions. With concentrated effort, you can all but eliminate negative thoughts — with their destructive effects — from your life.

No More Self-Pity

Besides being more positive in what we say, we must get rid of another bad habit — self-pity. Let's wipe out once and for all the "poor little me" feeling. You have heard the old proverb about the man who had no shoes and complained until he met a man with no feet. This is the way to erase those self-pitying thoughts that will — unless we are on guard — creep into our minds. There is too much self-pity in the world, and in its train comes an even more destructive emotion — resentment.

One way to cure resentment is through action. Don't just sit there and brood. Do something! Any kind of positive action will help eliminate resentment, but the best cure is action that you enjoy. Perhaps you have done poorly on a test and you deeply resent the fellow who got the top grade. Thinking about your resentment — nursing it to keep it warm — will not help; neither will additional study while

you are in a resentful mood.   Instead, do something you
enjoy that is active.   Play tennis, join a square dance group,
paint scenery for the drama club — anything that is fun for
you.

YOU, TOO, CAN!

You have seen the ads, "YOU, TOO," can play the piano,
paint a landscape, write a novel. For your self-improvement
campaign, let's borrow this phrase. You, too, can improve.
It's guaranteed. What you must do first, though, is look at
this year's model very carefully.   Imagine yourself as a
product — this year's model. Put yourself on the drawing
board; analyze the product in every detail.   What are the
good points? (Remember to start with the positive, always.)
List them. You will find that this activity is self-propelling,
too, because as you write down one good point, it will remind
you of another. After you have exhausted your plus qualities,
see if you can group them into three or four categories.   For
example, you might use a breakdown for appearance, mental
abilities, and emotional qualities.

Now, take up the emotional category list and check the
"Room for Improvement" traits that you have.   It is best to
start here because, believe it or not, you can talk about your
emotional difficulties more objectively than you can about
your looks or your brains. Somehow they seem more flexible,
more capable of being changed. Because of this, you feel less
resentment about these faults. If you have a tendency to put
off until tomorrow what should have been done today, you
may look upon this trait somewhat indulgently. You cannot
be complacent, however, about being covered with freckles
or having a long, pointed nose. These "born-with" traits
must be left until we build up our objectivity.

Your Improvement Campaign

Beginning with the emotional category, let's label it
Attitudes — a more neutral word.   Now, from your list,

select the trait that has the most references that are considered negative. If you have listed procrastination, you may find you have also listed failing to take care of your clothes properly, forgetting to return library books, losing things, and so on. All of these faults might be lumped under the heading *Procrastination*. You put off giving attention to doing things as you should. This trait, then, is the one with which you begin your improvement campaign.

Take up another sheet of paper. There is a reason for this suggestion. We impress upon our minds the importance of an action or thought much more completely when we write it down than when we merely think about it. Thoughts are the most elusive phenomena we have. You may have a brilliant idea and think: "That's good. I must remember that." But what happens? You *don't* remember it! It fades away almost immediately unless it is captured on paper. In a similar way, writing down a list of things to be done is one step toward doing them.

On a piece of paper, then, write the title, "To Be Done Thursday," or whatever the next day happens to be. The best time to write this list is just before retiring. Below the title, list numbers 1 through 5. It is better to start with not more than five things to be done. Remember, we are encouraged by success, so make it easy for you to succeed the first time.

After you have written your column of numbers, write opposite No. 1 the most difficult, most disagreeable job you have to do tomorrow. Beneath that, write the next most important job, and so on down to number 5. Think hard about your list; visualize yourself doing these things, perhaps in more than one way. Then place the list where you will be sure to see it the first thing the next morning.

When you awake the next morning and are ready for the day, start on that first job. *Do not* do all of the short, easy jobs first. You may think that you will finish the easy jobs first so that you will have nothing else on your mind and can concentrate on the big job. This is a fallacy. When you finish the short, easy jobs, you will have *nothing* on your mind. You will be tired and will probably decide to wait until tomorrow to get at that hard job.

After item No. 1 is finished, begin No. 2, and upon completion of that task, begin the next one. You may not finish all the items on the list, but that is all right. The most difficult job has been finished, and you should give yourself the heartiest of congratulations. Forget the items at the bottom of the list that you did not reach, and just add them to the next day's list. Concentrate on what you *did* do, not what you *did not* do.

Personality Tests

Although there is still some controversy about the effectiveness of personality testing, you will probably derive some benefit from taking such a test. In fact, one benefit that comes from completing a personality test is the feeling that a lot of people must be troubled with the same problems as you. Taking such tests also pinpoints areas that the author of the test considers important. This may help to clarify your thinking as to the relative merits of certain personality traits.

"Armchair psychologists" are everywhere today, and you may have spent quite a bit of time analyzing friends, teachers, and acquaintances. But have you analyzed yourself? The following self-analysis test should, perhaps, be considered an attitude test rather than a personality test. You may, too, consider it too idealistic and therefore old-fashioned. But remember that many businessmen are just as old-fashioned. They were brought up on a greater measure of "character-building" training than you were. It is quite likely that they will rate you in their minds on a scale similar to the one on pages 24 and 25.

A perfect score is, of course, 100; but few are likely to score at that level. Consider a score above 90 as excellent;

Self-Analysis Rating Scale

Score each statement in the scale as follows:

4 points — (always) — excellent
3 points — (usually) — good
2 points — (sometimes) — fair
1 point — (rarely or never) — poor

1. I am intelligent. I grasp instructions quickly and accurately. I comprehend directions instantly.	
2. I possess initiative. I attempt work beyond that required. I volunteer contributions to class or school activity. I am a leader in extracurricular affairs.	
3. I am dependable. I am reliable at all times; I do routine duties without being told; I am on hand when I am needed. I am reticent about confidential matters entrusted to me.	
4. I am punctual. I complete assignments on time and keep appointments on time.	
5. I am obedient. I observe the rules of my school, of my employer, and of my community.	
6. I cooperate with others. I work harmoniously in group activities. I consider the interest of the group of paramount importance.	
7. I possess good judgment. I have good common sense. I distinguish the important from the unimportant in class work. I consider all phases of a situation before deciding on a course of conduct. Others ask my opinions and advice.	
8. I am tactful. I say and do the right thing when dealing with others. I never give offense to others.	
9. I am neat and clean. My person and attire are neat and clean. I keep my surroundings for which I am responsible neat and clean.	
10. I display good taste in attire. My grooming is in the best of taste.	
11. I have habits of good posture. When I walk, sit, or stand, I create a favorable impression because of my bodily postures.	

12. I speak well. The words I speak and my enunciation create a favorable impression.	
13. I show consideration for others. In making decisions, I am mindful of the effect my future conduct will have on others.	
14. I am well mannered. I show a refinement of manner and a natural grace in my contact with others.	
15. I am healthy. I am practically never ill.	
16. I have tireless energy. Even after a day's work, my energy is not exhausted.	
17. I am accurate. I get information correctly. I keep records properly in order.	
18. I am speedy. I lose no time in doing my work. I get my work done quickly.	
19. I am honest. I do not tell falsehoods. I do not steal money, time, supplies, or ideas.	
20. I am adaptable. I turn from one task to another. I am not confused by changes. I adjust myself to people, places, and things.	
21. I have a good memory. I remember the names of persons, telephone numbers, addresses. I remember facts and incidents that have a bearing on a question of the moment.	
22. I am industrious. I am happy when I am busy. I find work to do at all times.	
23. I am loyal. I feel strongly the ties that bind me to ideals, institutions, and to people, both those who depend upon me and those upon whom I depend.	
24. I have executive ability. I plan work with system and with efficiency, and I assign tasks to others with understanding. I manage people, and they like to work for me.	
25. I have businesslike attitudes. I realize the importance of the work to be done. I am not a "clock watcher." I realize the value of time and the importance of giving a day's work for a day's pay.	
TOTAL SCORE	

from 80 to 89 as very good; from 70 to 79 as fair; and from 60 to 69 as poor. Now, go back to your ratings and check the items you marked with a (2) or a (1). These are the areas where you can begin to work.

In item 8, for example, assume that you marked this with a (2), indicating that you are sometimes tactful in dealing with others. This can be a starting point: improving your use of tact. For one week, look for opportunities to practice the trait of tactfulness. Use the following score sheet, or you may type one with more lines on a sheet of paper. In the middle column, "Opportunities for Practice," describe the situation that occurs.

Perhaps your first opportunity to be more tactful occurs on Monday morning when a friend asks to borrow your new cashmere sweater. You don't want to acquiesce because this particular friend is extremely careless with clothes. Before answering, think of a tactful response. For instance, you might offer another sweater instead, giving a good reason for wearing the cashmere yourself. Now observe the reaction of your friend and give yourself a score (from 4, excellent, to 1, poor) as in your Self-Analysis Rating. Continue working with this one trait until you consistently rate yourself with 3's and 4's.

Now choose another trait on which you need improvement and start looking for opportunities to practice improvement in the same way. You will find a positive approach to trait improvement just as helpful as it is in other situations. Instead of saying to yourself, "I'm hopeless. There is no use in my trying to improve," think: "I'm going to look for opportunities to improve, and I feel sure that it will be easier as I go along." You can help yourself if you want to, and *wanting to* is the beginning of any kind of personality improvement.

BASIC BUSINESS TRAITS

Each person is an individual, different in many ways from everyone else. That is why a Self-Analysis Rating Scale is

PERSONALITY TRAIT _____

	Opportunities for Practice	Score
MONDAY		
TUESDAY		
WEDNESDAY		
THURSDAY		
FRIDAY		
SATURDAY		
SUNDAY		

given, so that you might see just how you rate as an individual. There are some business traits, however, on which there is agreement as to their value in business. Only two will be discussed in this chapter, industry and loyalty.

Industry

What is industry? Is it busy work? Most of you have had all you want of this kind of activity. Or is it rather a drive within yourself to get things done? How can you acquire this drive if you do not possess it now? Review the discussion of needs and motivation at the beginning of this chapter and you will see that as needs change, the spark that motivates you will change also. Right now, you may be working for grades — a passing grade or a high one. Or you may be interested in the approval of someone whose opinion is important to you. Or you may aspire to the honor roll. All of these motivating influences are what we call "external" or "extrinsic" ones. This means that the spur to achieve comes from the outside. In time, this external motivation may be partly replaced by "internal" motivation, the kind that comes from within, with the satisfaction that comes from doing a good job.

When you are internally motivated in most things, you will find accomplishment much easier. Most of us, however, never quite reach the point where we care nothing for the praise or commendation of others. This stage of need fulfillment is sometimes called "self-realization." Consider it an ideal that, some day, you may attain. In the meantime, try to find some motivating influence that will work for you, that will help to keep you from wasting time, from making excuses to yourself — in short, from lacking in industry.

Loyalty

The second trait every worker must possess is loyalty to his firm. In some government agencies this one trait supersedes all others in importance. If you are loyal, you can be taught what you do not know, but no amount of ability, skill, or personality can make up for disloyalty. Think of some company you have always admired. Imagine that you are hired by this firm. In what ways could you practice loyalty to this company? One important way is never to repeat a word that is told to you in confidence. Nothing should ever be said to *anyone* about information you overhear, for example. Another way to express loyalty is to cooperate with other workers in your department. You should be eager for your firm to succeed; you should work shoulder to shoulder with everyone else in the business — because you are loyal.

Another important part of loyalty is showing respect for the men and women who are at the head of the organization. You do not say disrespectful things about them; neither do you listen to criticism of them made by your co-workers. You trust them to make wise decisions for the firm; after all, they know much more about the business than you do. If you should ever find yourself in a position where loyalty to your employer and to your firm is impossible it would be wise for you to find another job.

FOLLOW-UP ACTIVITIES

1. *Meeting New People.* One of the most difficult ways of becoming more outgoing is taking the initiative in meeting new people. To help you overcome this universal tendency toward "inwardness," you are to meet, entirely through your own efforts, 5 men and 5 women (of any age). Exactly four weeks from today you are to report the results of the project in the following form:

1. *Name*	*Short Biography*	Situation: *How we met*	Opener: *What I said*

Remember, you must have ten names and *you* must make the first move. No one else may introduce you. The short biography should contain at least four items of information about each person.

2. *Learning to Be Positive.* As a follow-up of the project described on pages 19 and 20, keep a list of all the positive statements you make during one hour. Time the project so that it is on the same day of the week and the same time of day. If your new number of positive statements is the same (or fewer) than before, try the experiment again the next day. Keep doing this until you form the habit of the positive approach.

3. As has already been said, you should possess the ability to estimate "the other fellow" so that you may determine what line of conduct you are to follow in order to please him. Remember, however, that "the other fellow" is sizing you up and evaluating your personality through your appearance, words, and conduct.

How do you think an employer would estimate you on the following list of traits, and on what outward evidence would he base his opinion?

muscular coordination . . . . clumsy muscular reaction
persistent. . . . . a quitter
sociable. . . . . unsociable
careful. . . . . careless
accurate . . . . inaccurate
industrious. . . . . lazy
enthusiastic . . . . indifferent
self-confident. . . . . inferiority complex
ambitious. . . . . satisfied to "get by"
punctual. . . . . dilatory
adjustable . . . . obstinate
optimistic. . . . . pessimistic
patient . . . . impatient
thrifty. . . . . spendthrift
modest . . . . vain

4. Write an experience you may have had in which the application of one of the principles given on the following page was made in a business situation.

Principles Underlying Business Behavior

a. Recognize your abilities and limitations. Prepare yourself for employment in a field of activity where you will find opportunity to use the special gifts and talents which are yours.

b. Cultivate health habits which will protect your most priceless possession, your body. Include in your personal regimen those practices which will tend to add to your attractiveness in grooming and in general appearance.

c. Show that you possess desirable traits and habits by exercising them consistently. Actions register with your business associates with greater force than do words.

d. Let a conscientious desire to give efficient service motivate your conduct and prompt your reactions in business situations. Acceptable business behavior is based on sincerity, not on sham.

e. An unselfish spirit, a courteous attitude, and the ability to adjust yourself to the spoken and unspoken wishes and instructions of those you contact will influence your business associates to like you.

f. Show an interest in people. Have a genuine liking for other people. Success is possible only through other people. Cultivate their liking for you by showing an honest interest in them.

g. Have an interest not only in the duties of the immediate job but in the bigger job which is just ahead. Be prepared to meet opportunity — rather, be prepared to make opportunity.

h. Receive suggestions for improvement gladly and accept reprimands impersonally. You show the ability to grow in the right direction when you display an understanding of the business point of view.

i. Cultivate a sense of humor. Applying a ready wit in good spirit, in appropriate time and place, will serve you well in the process of getting along with people.

j. Work hard. Make every moment of the day count. Although success is not assured through hard work, the dominant motivating force in the lives of others who have achieved fame and fortune has been found expressed in terms of zealous, determined, untiring application to the task at hand.

CASE PROBLEMS

1. Running Away

Max Nelson has been very happy and successful as a junior accountant with Patterson and Lee, Tax Accountants. One afternoon in April his superior, Mr. Mitchell, could not find an important document connected with a case on which Max had been working. He called Max to his office and accused him of losing the document. Ordinarily a quiet man, Mr. Mitchell began a tirade of accusations and threats against Max. Max tried to remain calm but continued to insist that the document was clipped with the others when he had placed them on Mr. Mitchell's desk that morning. In utter dejection, Max returned to his office. Just before closing time Mr. Mitchell came into Max's office and told him that the document had been found. Apparently Mr. Mitchell had enclosed it with some other papers that he sent to another company. It had just been discovered by one of the mailroom employees. Mr. Mitchell apologizes sheepishly and promises to avoid such a display in the future. Max goes home and thinks the matter over. He has been unusually conscientious in his work and his pride has been hurt deeply. He decides to leave the firm and calls the senior partner, Mr. Patterson, the next morning and resigns.

1. What do you think of Max's actions? Discuss particularly his calm when accused by Mr. Mitchell, his decision to resign, and his call to Mr. Patterson.

2. What was Max's motivation for resigning from his position? On what stage of need fulfillment was he operating?

3. What other alternatives can you suggest in this case? Which of the alternatives, including Max's decision, would you choose?

2. The Perfectionist

Betty Varner is a private secretary in the firm of Strong Electronics, Inc. She has been working four years, after graduating from an excellent junior college. Betty's parents were very strict, and she has always been a perfectionist. Her superior, Mr. Bartlett, was a kind, fatherly man, and Betty has worked happily and well. Two weeks ago, however, Mr. Bartlett was transferred to San Francisco and Betty was assigned to his replacement, Mr. Kearny. The new man is brilliant and efficient, but he is somewhat short on patience. He speaks crisply and concisely to everyone. In Betty's anxiety to please, she finds herself making many errors. This fact in itself distresses Betty, but when Mr. Kearny criticizes her work rather sharply, Betty bursts into tears. Mr. Kearny takes her tears in stride, but he becomes extremely irritated with Betty's continued apologies for her previous errors. Finally, he asks the personnel manager to transfer Betty to another office.

1. Put yourself in Betty's place. Is there anything you can do to eliminate this overly sensitive attitude? Can you detect any causes for perfectionism that are not particularly praiseworthy?
2. What should a beginning worker's attitude be toward criticism? How about the experienced worker? Do you think being able to "take it" will increase or decrease further criticism?
3. If you were the personnel manager, would you tell Betty the reason for her transfer?
4. What suggestions, as personnel manager, could you give Betty to help her overcome her desire for perfection in everything?

3. Getting the "Lay of the Land"

Walter Newman has just started in his first job as a salesman in the men's furnishings section of a large department store. One of the older employees, Mr. Parker, asks Walter to lunch at the end of his first week in his new job. During lunch the older man talks freely and critically about the head of the department, the management policies of the store, and how hard it is to inject any new ideas. Walter agrees with Mr. Parker, adding that he has found it rather hard to work with Mr. Green, the head of the department. "He seems to know all the answers," Walter says, "and doesn't respect the ideas of others. I guess he's afraid they might be better than his own."

The next day Walter is called to the general manager's office and berated for criticizing the department manager. Walter immediately realizes that his luncheon companion has reported Walter's comments. He is very angry and decides he will be less friendly with the older employees in the future.

1. What do you think of Walter's solution to the problem? Can you suggest another solution that might be more effective?
2. What should a new employee's attitude be toward early friendship with other employees?
3. If you had been Walter, how would you have answered Mr. Parker when he criticized the policies and management of the store? Why?

Chapter 3

Problem Solving in Human Relations

One of the reasons that 90 percent of an individual's success in business depends upon his personality is that wherever he goes he will encounter different types of people. There has never been an office worker who has not had to cope with an overly sensitive colleague, a "set-in-his-ways" supervisor, or a blustering boss. Because this is true, part of your preparation should include techniques for meeting and coping with problems with people.

PROBLEMS WITH PEOPLE

The first thing you must decide is that you are likely to have problems with your co-workers, with your supervisor, with your superior, and with *his* superior. In addition to these problems, however, you will very likely have the same kinds of difficulties with the people in your personal life. Your roommate may be hard to get along with; your fiance(e) or mate may be demanding; later on, your children will present problems. There will never be an end to problems with people, but you can arm yourself with a helpful way of handling the ones that come up in your life.

You Can't Change Others

The most frustrating aspect of human relations is discovered when you try to change someone else. Your best friend mispronounces words. So, with the best of intentions, you correct him. Is your friend grateful? Does he thank you for your interest in his self-improvement campaign? No, he is not grateful and he does not thank you. He resents your meddling, and he resents it deeply.   Furthermore, just to show you who is boss, he does not improve. Or say you are a newly married husband. You see that your wife is not an economical shopper, so you give her a lecture on how to buy. What happens? Your wife flies into a tantrum, bursts into tears, and presents you with the job of buying groceries from now on. Or perhaps you fancy yourself as a crusader; you imagine the thrills of redeeming lost souls and with true reforming zeal marry a man who is charming but shiftless. You know that love will conquer all and that you can turn your playboy into a captain of industry. Alas, before many months have passed you must admit your mistake. Your playboy will never change because *you* want him to. If he changes, it will be because *he* has decided to reform himself.

Don't Fight the Problem

Another fallacy in this wilderness of problems with people is the belief held by many that you can talk the problem away. You can say, "This should not be," and all may agree with you; but it still *is*. So, when you are up for promotion and possess all the needed abilities and skills only to have the boss's nephew get the promotion, don't try to fight the problem. Bosses' nephews will continue, no doubt, to be promoted. Fighting the problem should be avoided; it will not alter the situation.

What you should do when the other fellow is obviously wrong and you are obviously helpless is to let it go. Chalk this one up to experience. Do something else for awhile, something that is enjoyable for you. Let your resentment out of your system through some kind of positive activity. In almost every language there is a proverb to the effect that we should change what we can change but accept what we cannot change.

Try to Change Yourself

So far, problems with people as a topic has taken on a rather negative hue. If we can't change others and can't fight the problem, what can we do? There is one thing left. There is one person you can make fun of without having an organized group send you scathing telegrams. There is one person you can "get tough with" without fear of reprisal. There is, in fact, one person whom you *can change* — yourself.

The mere changing of your own attitudes is a remarkably enlightening experience. If you have been having trouble with your supervisor and he has been criticizing you at great length and in graphic detail, you — being human — have probably retaliated in some way. Perhaps you have been sullen; you may have answered abruptly; or you may have threatened to quit if he didn't like the way you were doing things. What would happen if, instead, you said sincerely, "I know I made a terrible error, Mr. Burns. You are absolutely right to tell me about it. Is there anything I can do to repair the damage I have done?" No matter how formidable Mr. Burns may be, he could hardly fail to respond in a reasonably positive manner. And, if he were really human beneath that cold exterior, he may say, "That's all right. We'll forget it this time."

Changing yourself is the best kind of reforming you can possibly do. But how should you start? What faults do we all have in common? Everyone is an individual. How can we draw up rules for self-improvement that will be applicable to everyone? Well, there is one trait that most of us can improve. We can all learn to have a positive attitude. Or do you think you already have a positive attitude? Perhaps you do; but you will be unique, indeed, if you do not occasionally say something disparaging about a co-worker or grumble and complain about (1) the weather; (2) your work; (3) your teacher or boss; (4) your grades or your pay, etc. Everyone is negative some of the time.

Eliminate the negative. At a lecture on human relations, the speaker was giving the audience some rules for living.

One of the rules was to stop expecting perfection in this world. One member of the audience immediately raised her hand. "What's wrong with being a perfectionist?" she snapped. The speaker smiled, "Your tone of voice when you asked that question, for one thing," she answered. Negative feelings, negative attitudes, negative words — all are depressors of the spirit. They all take us — and our hearers — down instead of up. We are all climbing toward happiness or, at least, we would like to think we could do so. If happiness could be envisioned as lying at the top of a long stairway while unhappiness or misery lay at the bottom, each negative thought or word would take us one step down. Each positive, cheerful, helpful thought or word would take us one step up.

How can you tell if you need to work on this negative habit? Let's try an experiment. Take an ordinary three-hour period when you are free to say what you think. From six to nine in the evening is usually a time of relative freedom, or from three to six on a Sunday afternoon. Arm yourself with a scratch pad and a pencil. Every time you think or say something negative, write it down. This means *everything*, including, "Is it hot enough for you?" and "I wish Miss J. would wear something besides that blue dress." Just plain, ordinary negative things that all of us say and think. At the end of the three-hour period, read them over. You will be surprised at the number of items you have written. You will wonder when you had time to say or do *anything* positive, which may explain why some of us don't do more things of a positive nature.

Accentuate the positive. A negative attitude usually creeps up on us because it is so easy to be negative. It takes no effort to let a feeling of self-pity steal over you. There are disappointments in every day. The easy way is to let them engulf us. It does take effort to replace negative thoughts with positive ones, but it is time and effort well spent. The way to start is to take the first steps:

Customers like the man
with a smile.

H. Armstrong Roberts

1. *Smile.* If you make yourself turn the corners of your mouth up instead of down, it will be easier to think of something positive to say. A gloomy expression is another habit that is easy to acquire. Make a real effort to look pleasant and interested in what is going on around you. You know, under the stimulation of your interest, those around you may become interesting!

2. *Say something pleasant once every hour.* This step is not intended to be funny. There are many people in the world who never say anything pleasant. So, for your second step, think of something positive, good-natured, or complimentary to say to someone once each hour. This will do wonders to those around you, but it will also keep you so busy thinking of positive things to say that you won't have time to be negative.

3. *Change your negative statements to positive ones.* The third step is to change your negative statements in midstream. Say your roommate reaches into the closet and knocks your best coat on the floor. Without thinking, you start to say, "Why can't you watch what you're doing?" But you catch yourself before you get that far. You say, "Why can't — I help you find what you want?" At first, this kind of thing may strike you with a hollow, insincere ring. Your roommate may think you have lost your mind. But keep it up for at least a week. You may be surprised at the way your relationships with people improve.

4. *Change a negative problem into a positive situation.* After you have practiced on positive statements for a week, you are ready to attack a negative problem. Look around you for some negative situation. Is there a co-worker you dislike? Is there a friend who rubs you the wrong way? Whatever it is, try the positive approach. Remember, you are not to be the culprit; you are to be the victim. But you will still try to change the situation by being positive Let's say there is a friend who gets on your nerves. He talks about himself all the time. He boasts about everything -- his car, his job, his school. You think that, without a doubt, he is the most conceited person you ever met. You may think, "What can I say that is positive that he hasn't already said over and over?" That doesn't matter. Say it anyway. You meet him at lunch and you don't even have time for a greeting before he starts right in to tell you about a test on which he knew all the answers. Why not say, "Jerry, I wish I had your confidence." If you keep out the sarcasm and say it sincerely, this may cause Jerry to stop and think a minute. He probably doesn't have too much confidence, and his bragging is in the way of whistling in the dark. He may say, "To tell you the truth, I have always thought you were the confident one." If something like this should happen, the hostility on both sides will begin to evaporate. You say, "But how do you know this is the way it would go?" No one knows

exactly how a conversation will go. We know, however, that this kind of approach results in a positive reply nearly all of the time.

Your campaign to become more positive will get you over a big hurdle. When you learn to look at problems with a positive attitude, you can begin to solve them more easily.

SOLVING PROBLEMS WITH PEOPLE

The following method of solving problems with people is not new. Scientists use the scientific method to solve their problems. Management consultants use the case approach to solve their problems. Our method, then, is merely an adaptation of the logical way to attack a problem. The difference in this approach is that the emphasis is placed upon the human relations aspect of the problem.

State the Problem Clearly

The first step in solving a problem is to state it clearly and concisely. This may sound easy, but there is nothing more difficult. You may know something is wrong — but you don't know exactly what. Someone has said that a problem well stated is a problem half solved. How should you state the problem? One way is to ask a question. Care must be taken, however, not to give judgments in the statement of the problem. Be objective; do not favor anyone. Just state the problem in specific terms.

For example, assume that you have been working in an accounting department for two years. The supervisor, Mr. Phillips, suddenly retires because of ill health and you are promoted to his position over the head of John Tyler, a veteran of the company and the person who expected to be made supervisor. John is polite to you but noncooperative. He does his job and that's all. Worse still, the other workers in the division — consisting of 22 workers — are beginning to take sides. How would you state this problem? It is *not*: Why should John Tyler act like this? It is *not*: Should a junior accountant be promoted over the heads of those who have been in the firm longer than he? The problem is concerned with what you should do about the situation as it is. It could, of course, be stated in more than one way, but one possibility is the following: What steps can I take to improve the morale and production of this accounting division in light of the resentment felt over a newcomer's being made supervisor? You will notice that there is no question of right or wrong in this statement of the problem. Neither is there any attempt at a solution, which should be the last of the steps and not the first. This statement is also objective, another necessary feature.

State the Facts

The second step in solving human relationship problems is to gather the facts and state them. It is important that this step be done carefully and that the facts be stated without bias. For instance, it is not a fact if you say John Tyler is acting like a spoiled child. A statement of this kind implies a judgment of the facts rather than a statement of them. An objective statement of the same implication would be that John Tyler does not cooperate to the extent he did before the promotion. The facts, then, should be stated without emotional coloring. It is also helpful, after the facts have been gathered, to arrange them in a rough arrangement according to their importance.

State an Appropriate Rule or Principle

The third step is to see if there is a principle, rule, or axiom of business or living that would apply to the situation. If there is not one readily at hand, you may wish to state your main goal, your most important purpose. There are, however, many principles that have been worked out in psychology and in management that would prove helpful. One example from management is that one person should be in charge of an activity. Another is that promotion is a function of management. Your main goal would probably be the best good for the company. Step three, then, means finding the best rule, principle, or purpose to guide you in solving your problem. If no one rule seems to cover your problem, you may state more than one. The following would apply in this problem: (1) morale is improved when standards for promotion are known to all; (2) all workers want to feel appreciated; and (3) the good of the company is of paramount importance.

Set Up Alternate Solutions

Step four is to devise as many solutions to the problem as possible. One way of clearing the way for a good solution is to write down the extreme solutions first. Extreme solutions are seldom the best ones. In our problem, such solutions would be: (1) fire John Tyler; (2) resign from your job as supervisor; (3) resign from the company. Now the way is clear to devote your attention to constructive solutions, those which would take into consideration the complex human relation factors involved, yet would be forward looking in terms of getting the work of the division done well.

Choose the Best Solution

The last step is to choose the best solution. One standard for determining the best solution is this: (1) It must take care of the important facts. That is, it must solve the situation as it stands as far as the important elements are concerned. (2) It must be in line with the principle or principles we have chosen to guide us.

In the problem under discussion, the best solution might have a number of parts. There would be, first, the solution in terms of John Tyler, the resentful employee. It might be well to ignore his negative attitude and begin to build a better feeling between the two of you. This could begin by asking him, without making too much of it, to take charge of some project. This could be followed by commendation for any good work that he does. The best solution for you, as a new, inexperienced supervisor, would be to give yourself time to grow into the job. One fact of life in any kind of work is that authority cannot be maintained on an equality basis. In other words, there must be some distance between the one in authority and the ones over whom such authority exists. You must not expect to be liked by all of the workers under you. Because you have been chosen by your superiors to do a job, however, you should do all you can to make that job a success. An impersonal attitude toward negative feelings of others, plus a sincere determination to merit your workers' respect, will go a long way toward bringing about the needed change in their attitudes. If you keep your attention on getting the work done, while you are fair and positive toward those who work under you, you should expect the morale of the division to improve in time.

This, then, is a method of solving the problems with people that come up in every possible kind of work. One reason for the success this method brings is the mental attitude you need in order to follow the first three steps. You cannot state the problem, list the facts objectively, or find an appropriate rule until you become impersonal about the problem. When emotions are shelved temporarily and your mind is in charge, you will find that the correct solution sometimes appears to you before you get to step four. The secret of problem solving is the use of mental judgment rather than the emotional pitfalls of "getting even," "showing who is boss," and so on. Following these five steps will help you to improve and develop good judgment.

FOLLOW-UP ACTIVITIES

1. Each Monday afternoon, make a list of the negative statements you make during a three-hour period. Try to keep the time of day the same each week. Also, after you have become more proficient, make a list of the negative state-

ments you change to positive ones. and finally a list of the positive statements you make. Try to eliminate the negative habit in six weeks.

2. Deliberately choose the most difficult person you know, and begin a campaign to improve your relationship with him or her. Once a week, write the extent of progress you have made. Be sure to date each progress report.

3. Quick judgments are sometimes made without knowing all of the facts of the case. Make a list of negative statements made to you by others. Opposite the statements, write what you believe may have caused the person to be negative. See if you can find a reason other than dislike for you.

4. Describe a human relations problem that exists among those of your acquaintance. Go through the five steps given in this chapter, from stating the problem to choosing the best solution. Try to be completely objective. Submit your problem for evaluation.

5. If you were given a job requiring cooperation, how would you rate on the points given on the following pages?

Rate yourself against these positive and negative characteristics. Place a check after either one of each pair to indicate your attitude on a job requiring cooperation with others. Add the number of checks in each column and multiply each total by 4. The product of the positive column is a plus quantity, that of the negative column is a minus quantity. A perfect score is plus 100.

You may find in the results of your checking an explanation for your success or lack of success. Of course, all cooperative jobs do not require the practice of all the positive traits; some jobs may call for the use of a negative one; for instance, on a beginning job, the employee is expected to be a routine worker rather than to show ingenuity. In the final analysis, the situations surrounding the particular job, the dispositions of the employer and of the other workers, dictate those attitudes which will serve

WORK ATTITUDES

POSITIVE	CHECK	NEGATIVE	CHECK
1. Interested		Indifferent	
2. Industrious		Lazy	
3. Persistent		A quitter	
4. Thorough		Haphazard	
5. Orderly		Disorderly	
6. Adaptable		Set in your ways	
7. Speedy		A slow worker	
8. Responsible		Irresponsible	
9. Punctual		A shirker	
10. Loyal		Disloyal	

MENTAL ATTITUDES

11. Alert		A drifter	
12. Ingenious		A routine worker	
13. Intelligent		Slow to comprehend	
14. Accurate		Inaccurate	
15. Careful		Impulsive	
16. Self-confident		Fearful	
17. Honest		Dishonest	
18. Forceful		Inane	

SOCIAL ATTITUDES

POSITIVE	CHECK	NEGATIVE	CHECK
19. Friendly		Shy	
20. Cheerful		Gloomy	
21. Stable		Excitable	
22. Polite		Discourteous	
23. Tactful		Tactless	
24. Considerate		Inconsiderate	
25. Personally neat		Untidy	
TOTAL			

you best. The list might be lengthened to include other characteristics that help or hinder you when you are placed on a job requiring you to work with others. In its present form, it lists those positive attitudes that are generally approved for successful cooperative performance and those negative ones that make for inability to get along with others. Although a perfect score of plus 100 might be considered impossible to reach under all circumstances, it is a goal worthy of your best endeavors.

6. Why is initiative not always required of beginners in business?

7. Study pictures of good posture in magazines, in motion pictures, and on the television screen.

CASE PROBLEMS

1. Getting Even

Jean Miller had worked a year in a large company that employed 20 regular typists in a typing pool. During this time some of her friends had received promotions as stenographers to various supervisors and executives. Jean felt that she was as efficient as those who were advanced. Every time a girl was promoted from the typing pool, Jean showed her resentment by sulking for a week. She knew, of course, that she should not show these negative emotions; but she wanted Miss Share, the supervisor, to know how she felt. She had disliked Miss Share's crisp manner from the moment she had seen her. She was sure that Miss Share returned the feeling and was doing everything she could to prevent Jean from being promoted. You are a friend of Jean's. You have not wanted to interfere before this, but you now believe that something must be done. What would you say to Jean? Give the conversation, with the replies you believe Jean would probably make.

2. Negative vs. Positive

John Lockyer has been working for the Maurice Clothing Store for more than two years. He is an excellent salesman and has many regular customers. He has felt that his opportunities are very good, as the other salesmen are much older and John appeals to the college fellows. At the end of John's second year, an older salesman, Mr. Adams, retires; and Mr. Anderson, the owner, hires Bill Reese, a young man with many of the same abilities and advantages as John. At the first sight of Bill — a handsome, cheerful fellow — John decides to make it so unpleasant for him that he will quit his job. He is sullen to Bill, refuses to tell him about Mr. Adams' former customers, and is generally unpleasant. Bill recognizes John's dislike at once. Instead of quitting his job, however, he resolves to win John's friendship.

1. Do you think this is possible?
2. What steps should Bill take to reach this goal?
3. Why is John behaving as he does?

PART 2 PERSONALITY IS WHAT YOU SEE

Chapter 4

Your Health Shows!

Someone has said that all a young person needs is good parents and good health. Let us assume that all of you have good parents. At least, parents usually do the best they can. But the health of a young adult depends, unfortunately, upon him — unfortunately, because good health is seldom appreciated until it is in danger of slipping away.

Do you have endurance? Can you stand up under long hikes? Do you play tennis? Do you swim? It may be that *you* do these things, but far too many of our young adults have, seemingly, never been out of a car in their lives! They ride to school; they ride to meetings; their fathers drive them around their paper routes. It is to be expected that their muscle tone may leave something to be desired.

Whatever your present state of health, you should resolve at once to maintain it or, if need be, to improve it. Improving your health will be like opening a door to greater vitality and enjoyment of life, so do it gladly.

HEALTH HABITS

First of all, good health is the result of good health habits. If you smoke too much, skip meals, take sleeping pills to go to sleep and pep pills to wake up, there can be only one ultimate conclusion: Your health will break down. Of course, the opposite is true. To build up your health, you must develop the kind of health habits that increase your general well-being.

Stand Up Straight!

The first habit to develop is good posture. You can work at this habit anytime, anywhere. It is not necessary to invest in expensive equipment for practicing good posture. Neither is it essential to set aside 15 minutes a day for such practice. All you have to do is say to yourself, several times an *hour,* "Stand tall," "Sit tall," — and then do it!

Good posture does not mean throwing your shoulders back; it means stretching your ears upward. Imagine you are trying to reach the ceiling with your ears. This is the way to start. Just reach up with those ears and the rest of your body will automatically follow suit. You will find yourself slumping now and then, of course. But back you will go into good posture if you remember to stand tall, to reach upward.

The second part of good posture is *abdomen in.* This can be practiced while walking, standing, or sitting; and it takes a good bit of practice to develop a strong muscle tone that keeps a flat abdomen all the time. Just keep practicing. After you have learned to stand tall, it will be much easier to keep your abdomen pulled in.

Another part of good posture is good walking position. Feet should be pointed straight ahead — not pointed out and not pointed in. If you walk in this manner, stretching tall, your arms will fall naturally at your sides; and you will probably realize another dividend, better relaxation. Many of us are tense partly because we stand or sit in a tense "shoulders-up" position. Remember, the shoulders should not stretch up — just the ears.

Fun and Games

Another part of good health is recreation. Every young adult — and older ones, too — should have some plain fun now and then. The choice, however, must be left to each individual. Do you like organized sports? If you do, your problem will be solved quickly. Bowling, golf, tennis, basket-ball, football, baseball, hiking, swimming, skiing — the list goes on and on. If you like sports, see that you play your favorite game at least once a week, and more often if you can spare the time.

What if you don't like sports? The important point is that participation is the key to recreation. You do not get the same benefit from merely watching a basketball game on television. You must be active in the game or sport if you are to get the greatest benefit from it.

The healthiest people are involved in something they *enjoy*. So — get involved. Are you stagestruck but lacking in acting experience? Then volunteer to help paint scenery, sell tickets, sweep out the stage. Would you like to write on the school paper but have no background in this sort of work? Then offer to sell advertising, act as a reporter, or type other people's stories. Participation is the great advantage that comes from working in extracurricular activities. There is always room for someone who is willing to work and who will start at the bottom. If your recreation is relatively sedentary, however, you must get your exercise in some other way. Walking, especially if done at a good clip, is excellent exercise. Another method of exercise available to all is calisthenics. Even five minutes a day, done regularly and with vigor, will do wonders for you. If you exercise in no other way, this type is a must.

You Are What You Eat

If you ever pick up a home magazine, you know what you should eat; but do you? Are you one of the skip-breakfast, grab-a-donut-at-ten, skip-lunch, have-a-candy-bar-at-four kind of people? There is a very good chance that you are. If so, now is the time to reform. No one can function at anywhere near his best without good food.

At the risk of repeating what you have heard many times before, an adequate diet includes protein (meat, fish, eggs, milk), whole grain cereals, and fresh fruits and vegetables *every day*. You don't need as many starches as many of us eat. Most of us eat too many sweets. The quickest way to get into a vicious circle, by the way, is to overeat sweets. This creates insulin, which demands more sweets, which creates more insulin — and away we go. The carbohydrate habit can be broken, however, mainly by making sure that your diet is adequate in the whole grains that provide the B vitamins.

If you will try a balanced diet for one month, you will be convinced. Clear eyes, clear complexion, abundant energy — all of these will be natural by-products. Why not try it?

Do You Get Your Eight Hours?

Perhaps you don't get enough sleep. In these days of frantic overdoing, it is quite likely that the adage "Early to bed and early to rise" is seldom followed. But good sleep habits can be developed, just as can good eating habits. If you have formed the habit of staying up late — to watch the late-late show, let us say — you may find it impossible to get to sleep if you go to bed at 10:30.

The thing to do, then, is to taper off gradually. If midnight has been your retiring hour for quite some time, make it 11:45 for a week or two. Then, when you get into bed, imagine that your hands are made of heavy pieces of lead. Think "Heavy, heavy, heavy. My hands are heavy, heavy." Repeating these words to oneself seems to help many people drop off to sleep. After you have learned to go to sleep at 11:45, cut it back to 11:30, and so on until you can go to sleep in time to get seven to eight hours of sleep a night.

While you are working on this project, you may find that taking "catnaps" of ten minutes now and then through the day helps you to get the rest that you need. Even if you do not go to sleep, relaxing completely in an easy chair for ten minutes or so will soon become a most refreshing pause.

MENTAL HEALTH SHOWS, TOO

The word "psychosomatic" has become a part of the general vocabulary of most readers in the last few years. It means the interrelationship of mind and body. In its customary usage, it designates those bodily ills which are

A well-balanced diet provides for
necessary vitamins and minerals.

Seeing your dentist twice a year is as
essential as it was when the expression
was first coined.

Good posture is important both
for health and for appearance.

Exercise and play are good for both
physical and mental health.

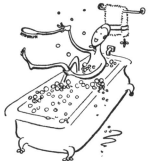

A daily bath is necessary for all
people.

Adequate rest makes you alert and
efficient during working hours.

Educational Service Department, Bristol-Myers Company

psychologically caused. Ailments that were once regarded as imaginary or dismissed as "nerves," are now considered by many to be bodily symptoms caused, at least in part, by mental conflicts.

Some of these conflicts come from our wishes vs. our tendency to conform to the "shoulds" of life. We want to be a "good girl" or "good boy," and this wish comes in conflict with some of the things we want to do or be. One of the "shoulds" that may cause trouble is the one relating to our feelings toward our parents, our brothers and sisters, our friends, our mates. We should love them; everyone knows this. But some of the time we just don't. This gives rise to a real conflict; and the greater the desire to be "good," the greater the conflict.

EMOTIONS AND MENTAL HEALTH

To be able to feel deeply the good things of life is a real blessing. Positive emotions make our lives worth living. But what about the negative emotions? What do they do to us? When you are seized with anger, hatred, jealousy, fear, worry, can you handle your usual tasks with efficiency and skill? In most cases, you cannot. The destructive emotions are just that. They destroy peace of mind, well-being, and often physical health. Is there anything we can do to control the destructive emotions?

How to Control Emotions

In order to control any emotion that may be a problem to you — jealousy, worry, fear — you must first identify it, describe it, state what it is. In Chapter 3 you learned to state the problem as the first step in the problem-solving process. You should do the same thing with a destructive emotion: define the emotion. What is worry, for example? You might say that it is a nameless dread for which you can find no real cause.

Step two in our campaign to control destructive emotions is to write down what the emotion does, what its manifestations are. In the case of worry, you might say it causes sleeplessness or, in some cases, sleeping too much; lack of appetite or overeating; headaches; mental blocks; lack of physical coordination, so that you drop objects that you attempt to grasp or drive a car in an erratic manner; poor memory for facts that you know. Excessive and prolonged worrying may cause you to become depressed.

Step three is to give an example, in your own life or in the life of someone you know, of what the emotion has brought about. This serves as a dramatic object lesson, showing vividly why it is wise to learn to control this emotion. In the case of worry, there is hardly a student anywhere who has not had the experience of worrying over an examination to such an extent that he is unable to think at all. If he could have relaxed, the knowledge he actually possessed would have been at his disposal, but he could not relax. This kind of experience shows the destructiveness of worry better than any number of abstract statements.

Step four consists of writing down all of the possible *actions* that might help to control the destructive emotion. In the case of worry, the list might include the following:

1. Set aside a certain time of day, or day of the week, for worrying. Then, when a worrisome thought enters your mind, just file it away to be worried about on Thursday!

2. Do something about the cause of the worry. If you worry about finances, start a budget; if about failing a course in school, study an extra half hour a day; if about being an old maid, have a party and invite several eligible men. This way of controlling emotions is an excellent one because it gets behind the emotion itself to one of its possible causes.

3. Invent some mental process that will automatically take place whenever the tendency to give in to the emotion arises. In the case of anger, you might think of something beautiful — a lovely lake you have seen, a strain from your

favorite musical selection, a line from a favorite poem. In the case of worry, one of the best devices is a slogan. Some of these are old, old saws, but they are still around because they have proved their effectiveness through the centuries. Such slogans as "Take one step at a time," "Rome was not built in a day," "What will it matter in a thousand years?" and the slang slogans, "So what!" and "To heck with it!" might help in the case of worry.

4. Forget the past. This is an important rule in the case of most of the destructive emotions. We get angry at a best friend and rake up old resentments from the past, and we find we no longer have a best friend. This is a particularly vicious habit in the case of married or engaged couples. It is almost impossible to hear someone rebuke us for a past action without retaliating in kind. Too frequently words are spoken that cause wounds that can never be healed. Whatever the emotion you are working on, forget your past failures. The past is gone; nothing can be done about it; so let it go.

5. Do or say something positive in line with the emotion. If you hate someone or dislike someone intensely, the best way to get rid of this emotion is to do something positive, something considerate, for that person. It is almost impossible to dislike someone for whom you have just done a kindness. The magic does not work, however, if you expect *any* kind of reward for your good deed. Don't expect to be thanked. The kindness should be done merely because it is good for *you* to do it. There will be intangible benefits, but don't look for a reward. In fact, the best way to accomplish this is to do something considerate anonymously; this is guaranteed to take the sting of hatred away from that person.

What Emotions Say

Whatever our emotional difficulty — fear, anger, jealousy, hate, worry — there is a reason for its being there.

Sometimes the reason is the exact opposite of what the emotion appears to be. It may be the other side of the coin. If you are jealous of someone's affection, for example, this does not say that you love the person deeply. It says instead that you are insecure about your own worth. You cannot believe that you are worthy of love; therefore, you cling possessively to the person who is closest to you. If you hate someone, this emotion says that you feel unappreciated. You are filled with resentment because your talents, beauty, ability, or knowledge have not received recognition, while someone else's have. Then this person has had the effrontery to belittle you in some way! It is the belittling that triggers the dislike, but the lack of appreciation is the real cause.

Envy is another resentful emotion, but here we are not sure of our abilities; we would like to be brilliant or talented or beautiful, but we feel we are not. The envious emotions say that we are insecure and that we resent this insecurity.

Worry, the kind that has no known cause, comes from hostility that we refuse to admit. That is why it is important that we take a good look at worry and at ourselves. We must admit that we are not paragons of virtue, that we may have negative feelings toward those we should love.

What We Should Say to Emotions

No matter what the emotion may be that is making your life miserable, you must not let it have its say. Learn to control it. Listen to what it tells you; then do something to change the situation that brings the emotion about. This means that you should become more lovable instead of being jealous and possessive. It means that you should become more appreciative of the accomplishments of others. Sooner or later someone will, in return, become appreciative of your accomplishments. Don't waste your life waiting for people to come to you. Take the first step. Then, while you are appreciating the achievements of others, work hard to become an expert at one thing. Many of us try to be musicians, writers, actors, debaters, athletes, and school political leaders all at once. No one can succeed in so many different fields. Choose the one activity that gives you the most satisfaction and that you do reasonably well. Then concentrate on that activity. Be willing to start at the bottom. Be willing to work on the team. It will not be long before your worth is recognized.

FOLLOW-UP ACTIVITIES

1. Walk across the room. Hold your head high, chin in, your chest raised, your arms swinging from your sides.
Is there animation, alertness, and buoyancy in your walk?
Does your walk suggest self-confidence?
2. Walk to the front of the room and, assuming your best posture, pause for a moment to gain attention.
Is the weight of your body centered on the ball of the foot that is placed forward?
Is your chest expanded?
Is there expectancy and animation in your pose?
3. Place a chair alongside the teacher's desk. The teacher, representing your future employer, says, "Sit down," and you do so.
Do you "sit up"?
Are your feet on the floor?
4. The interview is concluded, and you rise to depart.
Are your muscular movements coordinated?
Do you get your balance without leaning on the chair or desk?
5. Make a list of the groups in your community that offer opportunities for regular exercise. Find out the benefits of each group you are eligible to join, the membership dues, the obligations, and other information.
6. Draw up a schedule showing the amount and the kinds of exercise you have had in the last two weeks. What plans have you for following a regular schedule of time for exercise?
7. Make a selection of lunches appropriate and accessible for a salesperson in a downtown store. Tell what foods

are to be avoided (a) if a person is overweight due to overeating, (b) if a person is underweight and under-nourished, and (c) if a person is of normal weight.

8. You are employed in a clerical position. Make up a menu for a week for your own use.

9. If you are worried about a test or an interview, how do you cope with your anxiety? Is some fear natural and normal?

10. In your schedule of time how much is allotted for sleep? Are you rested and ready to work in the morning?

11. If you complain of inertia, suggest for yourself a remedy. Do not suggest more sleep. Would you like to spend your time and your energy so completely that you would be physically and mentally exhausted at the end of the day? What would fill your days and your life so full of inter-esting activity that only sleep would recreate you for the next new day of excitement? Would it surprise you to find that thrill in business? Get an opinion on this sub-ject from a successful businessman.

12. "If your relations with people are all wrong," says Milton Wright in his book, *Getting Along with People*, "it is be-cause you have one or both of two faults. Either you are timid or lazy. Of course, you have a number of other faults too — conceit, faulty judgment, and the like — but they do not amount to as much as one might imagine. Timidity and indolence are your two greatest weak-nesses." Discuss this statement.

13. Check yourself against the following list of questions to see in what ways you are apt to reveal timidity:

   a. Do you look a person in the eye when you address him?
   b. Can you keep a conversation going?
   c. Do any nervous mannerisms betray your timidity?
   d. Does the thought of addressing a stranger terrify you?
   e. If you have a physical defect, do you worry about con-cealing it?
   f. Does adverse criticism depress you?

g. Do you question your own ability?

h. Are you timid to the point of self-effacement?

i. Do you think of intelligent questions to ask when called upon to ask questions?

j. Have you many friends?

k. Do you belong to any social or athletic clubs?

l. Do you despair quickly?

m. Do you make decisions without undue mental conflict?

n. Do you feel sorry for yourself?

o. Can you openly defend a cause you think is right?

p. Are you interested in people — their problems, their successes and failures?

q. Do you feel awkward?

r. Do you fear the opinions of other people?

s. Do you smile readily?

t. Does your voice betray your uneasiness?

14. List the ways in which one is apt to show indolence.

15. Take a destructive emotion, other than worry, that you have been or are troubled with. Describe it, show what it does to people, give an example, and then list as many ways of controlling it as you can.

CASE PROBLEMS

1. Nerves — Your Friend or Your Enemy?

Jane Allison has been working for Corliss Associates, a public relations firm, for three years and has done good work. In her ratings every six months there is only one negative criticism that can be made. Jane puts too much nervous energy into ordinary jobs; and, when one of high pressure comes along, she gets too nervous, works too fast, does work over, and generally does work below her usual standard.

The personnel manager is looking for a private secretary to the head of the firm, Mr. Harvey Corliss. Mr. Corliss wants a girl with energy and initiative, one who can take care of clients when he is away from the office. This is an important factor, as Mr. Corliss travels a good deal. In looking over the ratings of the girls in the office who might be promoted to the job as his private secretary, Mr. Corliss is impressed with Jane's credentials. She scored the highest of any applicant on the intelligence test that is given to everyone who is considered for employment; her skills are excellent; she is a graduate of a good junior college where her grades were all A's and B's. Mr. Corliss interviews Jane and is even more favorably impressed. He tells the personnel manager that he would like to have Jane as his private secretary. He adds that the vacancy will not materialize for two months and suggests that something might be done to help Jane overcome her nervousness. If you were the personnel manager, what would you do? Follow the problem-solving method given in Chapter 3 in arriving at your decision.

2. "Moonlighting"

Ray Benton works as a junior accountant in the accounting department of a large firm. Ray is ambitious and particularly anxious to make more money than his salary as a beginner pays him. To augment his salary, he keeps books for a number of small firms, doing the work at night and on weekends. He also makes out income tax returns for both these companies and the individuals working in them. Because he wants to keep up with his field, he reads the accounting periodicals at night before going to sleep.

All this activity naturally interferes with his rest; also, he has not taken a vacation in three years, preferring to catch up on his outside work during this period. There is an opening for a senior accountant, and Ray is being considered for the position. Mr. Henry, the controller, has noted Ray's tenseness, his look of fatigue, and his apparent lack of interest in his work. He asks one of Ray's friends if he knows of anything that could be wrong. The friend tells Mr. Henry that Ray is overworking. Unable to understand how this could be so, as Ray's work load in the company is only average, Mr. Henry calls Ray in and asks him what work he is doing. Ray tells him that he wants to make more money and what he is doing to earn it. What would you do if you were Mr. Henry? Follow the five-step problem-solving plan to arrive at your decision.

3. A Time for Decision

Sara Rice has been dating a college friend, Howard Andrews, whom she would like to marry. She has refused dates with other fellows because of the way she feels toward Howard. Her feeling is obviously not returned, however, as Howard goes out with a number of different girls and continues to treat Sara merely as a friend. This has been going on for a year, and Sara's work is beginning to suffer. There are also symptoms in Sara's looks and manner that indicate she is suffering from anxiety.

1. What does the term "mental health" imply?
2. Is emotional strain as harmful as physical strain?
3. Do you think Sara might work out a solution to reduce the conflict she feels?
4. Even if problems cannot be solved rapidly, can a plan of action be followed to prevent the ill effects of worry?
5. Have you discovered a way to reduce the anxiety you have felt at some time?

Chapter 5

Do Clothes Make the Man?

"Costly thy habit as thy purse can buy,
But not expressed in fancy; rich, not gaudy:
For the apparel oft proclaims the man."
—Polonius' advice to his son; from *Hamlet*, W. Shakespeare,
Act I, Scene 3.

Suppose you knew that you were going to be given the chance to appear in a play on Broadway as a young person in business. How would you prepare for your audition? What kind of clothing would you choose? You would be careful to avoid clothing that was too casual, just as you would avoid a too formal look. To make sure that you would be considered the right type or right for the part, you would try to dress the part.

This same care to dress the part should be practiced when you are playing the business role in real life. There are magazines to help you; in fact, some advertise this as their purpose. Large stores have departments devoted to the well-dressed look for business. All you need to do is become aware. Notice how the top business men and women in your town are dressed. You will notice an understated look, one in keeping with current fashions yet adapted to the individuality of the wearer.

Most young people who are just beginning in business have to watch their pennies. When this is true, it is wise to plan your clothes purchases in advance. Examine your present wardrobe and plan new items to fit with those you already possess. Of course, business clothing is more subdued than the clothing you have been wearing in school or college.

65

Simple lines and dark colors are most appropriate for business wear. It is wise to plan your wardrobe around a definite color scheme and to select accessories that harmonize. New effects can be produced by a change in accessories — handkerchief, belt, scarf, and the like.

Be sure that all clothing is kept immaculately clean. Clothes absorb body odors, so keep your body clean and avoid this hazard. Men's underwear may be sent regularly to a commercial laundry — or taken regularly to a laundromat — but women must form the habit of laundering underwear and hosiery daily. In addition to the daily bath, both men and women must use a deodorant as an extra precaution against giving offense. This is one phase of "social security" that *must* be maintained.

No book can tell you exactly what you should wear and how you should wear it. Much of the fine art of clothing selection and its wear depends on your own good taste. It is a fact that most young business people dress appropriately and well. It is seldom necessary to caution against mixing clashing colors or wearing a party dress to the office. However, the suggestions that are detailed in the following paragraphs should be used as a double check to be sure you will dress the part.

THE YOUNG EXECUTIVE LOOK

The young man in business will want to look the part of a man who is on his way up. This look might be called the "young executive look." You will consult magazines, read articles on clothing, observe the executives in your firm. Most articles of clothing for men are well standardized. But you will still have some opportunity to express your good taste. Although masculine colors are usually subdued, a touch of color in a tie, shirt, or handkerchief can be much more effective than larger areas of color. Carefully planned costumes will give you greater enjoyment for a longer period of time than will impulse buying for special occasions.

The "Young Executive Look"

H. Armstrong Roberts

You should follow conservative styles when selecting clothes for business hours. Hats are not so important as they once were when all men wore them on all occasions. Young men in business, however, are better dressed for the part they play when they wear appropriate headgear. You should purchase ties that emphasize your good points in coloring and that harmonize with your suits and your shirts. Shoes should be selected for comfort and wearing qualities. In fact, your entire wardrobe should be selected for its suitability to your work and your working conditions.

Style for Men

In matters of style, it is important that you develop an eye for the fitness of things. Wear business clothes during business hours and avoid the sweater-sport-shoes combination on the job. Extreme fashions and current fads in the cut and color of your clothes should be avoided; they are usually short-lived and often create an effect of cheapness. If you are heavy, you should not wear suits of plaid or wide-striped material. If you are short, you will find unbroken lines best.

Let the same conservative taste in clothes guard you from extremes in the selection of your shoes.

Fabric

Material for suits should be selected according to the season. The finish of the surface of some fabrics may give style to your suit but make pressing and cleaning a never-ending job. If your suit is one hundred percent wool, you will not be disappointed in the way it holds a crease or with its wearing qualities. Light-colored suits are popular and appropriate for summer wear but can be worn to work only one day after each cleaning. Dark colors in new summer fabrics are more practical.

Shirts for business hours may be cotton or a mixture of cotton and one of the synthetic fabrics. Many of the new fabrics keep their crispness after laundering without ironing. If all shirts are sent to the laundry, cotton may be your best choice.

Solid color knit ties are always fashionable as are reps, challis, or foulards in neat stripes, small prints, or solid colors

Shoes need not be the most expensive brand advertised, but they should be of good quality material. Plain toe, wing tip, or moccasin-stitched lace types are best for business. Loafers and sports shoes are, of course, considered unacceptable for business wear.

Comfort and Cleanliness

Accustom yourself to keeping your collar buttoned and your tie in place. In some offices custom does not require the wearing of a coat, and you would be conspicuous if you failed to conform to the accepted practice. As a general rule, however, business expects men to dress as gentlemen do; and if a coat will produce the desired effect, cultivate the habit of wearing one.

You should keep your ties cleaned and pressed. Be sure to discard them when they become unsightly. Avoid frayed and soiled ends on your collars and cuffs. Do not press your suit at home until you have removed all stains and spots. Shirts that are open at the neck may be appropriate for sport wear, but they are quite obviously inappropriate for business.

Jewelry is out of place on a man. You should use only those accessories that are appropriate, as anything else looks flashy. Buttons and service club pins may be effective if they are inconspicuous. A wristwatch and a tie clasp or tie tack are businesslike.

Color

In the matter of color, harmony of ensemble should be your goal. Tie, hat, shirt, shoes, and suit must have a color relation to one another. White shirts are always acceptable in business, but styles in shirt colors vary. If pastels or stripes are popular and accepted, you may want to wear them.

The chart on page 70 presents some recommendations for harmonizing color combinations. Gray, black, or natural pigskin gloves are appropriate for almost any business costume. A black and gray herringbone coat is a good choice, and it may be worn no matter how formal the occasion. Solid color coats of simple lines and unobtrusive patterns are always in good taste, also.

THE TOP-FLOOR LOOK

Just as there are offices with high skill requirements and offices with less stringent ones, so there are offices that demand more in the way of dress and appearance than others. These high-standard requirements have been called the "top-floor look." This is because in firms taking up an entire building, the top floor is usually reserved for the top executives. The best jobs for women are, therefore, on the top floor. A girl who wants to work on the top floor someday should dress "as if" she were working there already.

HARMONIZING COLORS IN MEN'S APPAREL

SUIT	SHIRT	TIE	SOCKS	SHOES	HAT
Gray Hues	White	Blue, Maroon, Gold, Olive, Gray	Same as Tie or Black	Black	Gray, Black, Heather
	Blue, Solid or Striped	Blue, Maroon, Gold	Same as Tie or Black	Black	Gray, Black, Heather
	Gray, Solid or Striped	Blue, Maroon, Gold, Olive, Gray	Same as Tie or Black	Black	Gray, Black, Heather
Clay or Olive Hues	White	Olive Hue, Heather	Same as Tie or Shoes	Black or Brown	Heather, Olive, Black
	Cream	Brown, Olive Hue	Same as Tie or Shoes	Black or Brown	Heather, Olive, Black
	Tan, Solid or Striped	Brown, Olive Hue	Same as Tie or Shoes	Black or Brown	Heather, Olive, Black
	Olive, Light Solid or Striped	Olive Hue, Heather	Same as Tie or Shoes	Black or Brown	Heather, Olive, Black
Brown Tones	White	Maroon, Olive, Blue, Brown	Same as Tie or Brown	Brown	Brown, Heather, Olive
	Cream	Maroon, Olive, Blue, Brown	Same as Tie or Brown	Brown	Brown, Heather, Olive
	Tan, Solid or Striped	Blue, Gold, Brown	Same as Tie or Brown	Brown	Brown, Heather, Olive
	Blue, Solid or Striped	Blue, Gold, Brown	Same as Tie or Brown	Brown	Brown, Heather, Olive
Black	White	Gray, Blue, Gold, Maroon	Same as Tie or Black	Black	Gray, Black
	Blue, Solid or Striped	Blue, Gold, Maroon	Same as Tie or Black	Black	Gray, Black
	Gray, Solid or Striped	Gray, Gold	Same as Tie or Black	Black	Gray, Black
Blue	White	Blue, Maroon, Gold, Gray	Blue or Black	Black	Gray, Black
	Blue, Solid or Striped	Blue, Maroon, Gold, Gray	Blue or Black	Black	Gray, Black
	Gray, Solid or Striped	Blue, Maroon, Gold, Black	Blue, Dark Gray, or Black	Black	Gray, Black

Courtesy: The H. A. Seinsheimer Company

The "Top-Floor Look" brings
assurance

H. Armstrong Roberts

Style for Women

Styles for women change from year to year, yet there are certain classic styles that never seem outdated. The shirt-waist dress, for example, is perennially in fashion. You may have a favorite dress or suit that you have worn for years and may continue to wear for years to come. If you were to analyze these classic styles, you would find them to be simple in cut, carefully fitted, and well made in good quality fabrics. These three factors — simplicity, cut, and quality — should be considered in all clothing that you plan to buy for business wear.

Fabric

The smart business girl selects fabrics that can be cleaned or (preferably) washed frequently. One of the true basics of any wardrobe is the ever-popular knit. Knit suits and dresses are ideal for office wear because they need little upkeep and always look appropriate and attractive. If the fabric requires drycleaning, it should be worn with dress shields and, of course, a deodorant. Wool suits and dresses are also popular for business wear.

For summer wear, fabrics such as cotton and synthetics are a good choice. It is important that washable materials be chosen and that these light dresses be washed after each wearing. Drip-dry fabrics make this a simple matter. With the wealth of new materials on the market, the business girl can always be clean, neat, and attractive.

When buying articles made of the newer materials, it is wise to read the labels carefully before you buy and to consult the salesgirl regarding washing instructions. Some of the cotton-appearing materials are machine washable; others require careful hand laundering. Be sure you buy the dress or suit that you will be able to keep up with a minimum of expense.

Comfort and Cleanliness

One side of fashion seems to be evolving toward a more sensible approach — footwear fashions. The medium or low heel is now fashionable. When buying shoes for business, however, you should choose a tailored rather than a sports look. The difference is in the leather, the color, and the design of the shoe. Anything approaching tennis "sneakers" should be avoided for business wear. Comfort, quality, and good looks should be your three-cornered goal when buying shoes for business.

There is one situation where you must sacrifice comfort for appearance. This is in the matter of foundation garments. Every woman in any business job should wear a girdle — regardless of stringbean figures — and a properly fitting brassiere. Girls who are very slender may choose the lighter-weight fabrics; girls with more figure to control will need heavier materials. But you should never appear in the business world without these important parts of your wardrobe. Another important part of your wardrobe is a number of slips of varying opaqueness to supplement the dress or suit you wear. Be sure to buy a non-clinging slip to wear under knits.

One of the nicest things about washable clothing is the wonderful feeling you get when your dresser drawers are filled with clean, fresh lingerie and closets with crisp, starched blouses. When you wear these items, you will have a corresponding feeling of assurance.

Your suits and winter dresses will have to be dry cleaned frequently. Although undergarments, hosiery, and dress shields must be laundered daily, the frequency with which you clean other clothing will depend partly on the weather and partly on the amount you perspire. If you detect any perspiration odor whatsoever, the garment should be washed or cleaned. Do not put any dirty clothing in the closet. Obviously any odor in the closet will affect clean clothing. Neatly arranged clothing in the closet will enable you to dress more rapidly each morning. An orderly arrangement of dresser drawers will also facilitate morning dressing.

It is a good idea to keep spot remover or cleaning fluid in a safe place, both at home and at the office. Always brush clothing thoroughly before it is worn. Some fabrics and colors do not show dandruff or lint as much as other fabrics. Perhaps this should be considered in selecting clothing. Always inspect your dress or suit carefully for lint or spots before you put it on.

Always observe the little niceties of careful dressing. These include slips that do not show, stocking seams that are always straight (or well-fitting seamless hose), shoulder straps that are always out of sight, and clothes that are mended. Furthermore, when adjustments are necessary, they should be made at home or in the lounge. Watch your shoes for run-down heel lifts. Keep shoes brushed, cleaned, and polished.

Jewelry does not have to be expensive to be in good taste, but it should be simple. Someone once stated that there should never be more than eleven different articles in sight when you have finished dressing. When you begin adding them up, you will see that you reach eleven rather quickly.

A purse, a pair of gloves, a belt, a pin at the lapel, a hat, a pair of shoes, a pair of hose, and a watch come to eight items already. This means you have only three left for whatever your costume consists of. The difference between being well-dressed and over-dressed may be that twelfth item. Usually you may add one more piece of jewelry (in addition to your wedding ring, of course). Avoid a combination of earrings, necklace, bracelets, *and* lapel pin. Choose one or two of the four — *not* all of them. Occasionally a necklace and a pair of matching earrings or a bracelet might be worn with a conservative blouse or dress.

THRIFT

We are living in what the economists call an affluent society; people do not like being reminded of hard times or future emergencies. Nonetheless, one should learn very early to practice *thrift*, which means economy or frugality, in all of his expenditures.

In Buying Clothes

Because one of the easiest ways to be a spendthrift is in buying clothes, a discussion of thrift is appropriate in this chapter.

One way to practice thrift is to take advantage of sales for buying staple items. Such articles as hose, underclothing, raincoats, shirts, blouses, and shoes do not show radical changes in style. Buying these articles at a reduced price is, therefore, a thrifty habit. It is not thrifty to buy extremes of color or style after the season of their popularity is past.

In Other Activities

Did you ever stop to think of the number of other ways in which you can be thrifty? One way is to be saving in the use of your employer's time and supplies. Typing accurately and making out sales slips carefully saves your employer money. Developing a speedy routine in handling repetitive jobs is another way of being thrifty.

There are a number of practices that should be avoided if you wish to develop the habit of thrift. These include such things as keeping people waiting on the telephone, making personal telephone calls during office hours, and spending too much time in the lounge. You should never take any supplies belonging to the office for personal use.

The final suggestion for developing the habit of thrift is a savings account. The first paycheck should start you on your saving habit. The first step is crucial: Take out a small sum for savings *first*, then pay your bills, make your purchases, and so on. If you wait until after you have taken care of these obligations, you will find you have nothing left for savings. If you have never saved any money, you may prefer to start by saving *for* something — a long vacation trip, for example. This kind of saving is less painful for the beginner. After you have established the habit of saving, you should begin to save for future security. When you have accumulated a reasonable amount, you may wish to invest some of your savings in safe bonds or interest-bearing securities. This kind of financial reassurance gives you greater poise and peace of mind; you will have purchased not only financial security but emotional security as well.

FOLLOW-UP ACTIVITIES

1. If you have not yet begun your career in the business world, what changes in your present wardrobe will you make when you go to work?
2. What will you wear when you are interviewed by a prospective employer?
3. What preparations for your appearance will you make the evening before an employment interview?
4. What sources of information regarding clothing, color, line, design, and fashion are available for study? Books? Magazines? Shops? Others?
5. What accessories should be worn with a tailored black suit?

6. What variations of accessories would you like to have to wear with the black suit?

7. What lines of costume are most becoming to a short, stout woman? What lines are most becoming to you? Have you noticed also the effect of the lines of a coiffure on the shape of your face?

8. What lines of costume are probably most becoming to a tall, slender man? Would the lines of a suit be influenced by the style of the day?

9. Jim Austin has light red hair and a fair complexion. He has just purchased a dark brown suit. What color should his ties and shirts be to harmonize with the new suit?

10. Make a checklist of duties that should be performed regularly in order to maintain a neat, clean wardrobe.

11. Frank Ross wears his shirts two days before sending them to the laundry. Dave Brown questioned this practice, but Frank said that he did not have enough shirts to wear a clean one each day. Is there a better solution than the one that Frank uses?

12. Hazel Abbott likes drop earrings and bracelets that jangle. Her employer mentioned that he finds them distracting. Hazel later tells you that she considers her clothing her own affair and does not welcome such criticism from her employer. What would you tell Hazel? Why should Hazel be concerned about her employer's statement?

13. Phyllis Foster wears tight sweaters and very short skirts to the office. Miss Milton, the office manager, mentioned that such clothes are not businesslike. Phyllis said nothing at the time, but later commented, "I want to be noticed. Nobody will notice Milton in her old, tailored black dresses." Should Phyllis adapt her costume in the way Miss Milton suggested? What type of attention is desirable attention?

14. Phillip Sturges observes that when working with other employees, they move a few steps from him. One of the

salesmen tells Phil that he has found a very effective deodorant and asks if Phil would like to try it. Phil replies that deodorants are for girls. "Anyway," he says, "I take a shower every day." Are deodorants only for women? Is a daily bath sufficient protection from perspiration odor? Are both deodorants and the daily bath sufficient protection if clean clothing is not worn every day?

CASE PROBLEMS

1. Drifting

There was not enough work in the real estate office to keep Elsie Marsh, a general clerk, busy all the time. During the dull hours she often sat and looked out the window, building air castles for the future. Her employer found her so occupied one day and severely reprimanded her for wasting time. She told him that she had all her work completed. He insisted, however, that Elsie find some constructive work. "Make a record of the supplies on hand," he said, "or a list of the telephone numbers we use frequently, or arrange our listings by streets. Use your time to some advantage."

1. Why should Elsie have had no idle moments in the office?
2. Suggest other activities for her.

2. Take Up the Slack

Lisa Brady and Marian Stuart are employed as billing clerks by a merchandising firm. When Lisa is asked for certain invoices, she has to rummage through her files before she can find them. She does, however, make out all invoices neatly and accurately. Marian, who occupies the next desk and does the same kind of work, uses a system. She makes notations about invoices that cannot be completed at once and is constantly trying to find shortcuts and timesaving devices.

Lisa is always joking with Marian about the latter's "efficiency." Lisa tells Marian that she really does not produce any more work than she, Lisa, does. However, Marian is promoted to the bookkeeping department to a position that has more responsibility. Lisa believes that favoritism is being shown.

1. What businesslike attitudes does Marian show that she possesses?
2. In what ways does Lisa show that she is not businesslike?

3. Wisdom in Spending

Margaret Grover is fortunate in obtaining summer employment in a large office. There is a possibility that if she makes good, she may obtain permanent work later in the same office. The other girls in the office dress better than Margaret does, and they spend more money for recreation and entertainment. Margaret has been trying to save for further study, but wonders if she should not spend more on her clothes to impress her employer favorably so that she may be considered for a permanent position.

1. If Margaret decides to spend all or most of her money now, how will she benefit?
2. If she decides to save her money, how will she benefit?
3. What would you do in this case? Why?

Chapter 6

Good Grooming is Important

Today there can be few persons in the United States un-aware of the necessity of good grooming. Advertising media are constant reminders of the importance of good grooming: the necessity of a daily bath or shower, proper oral hygiene, proper care of the hair, and the use of deodorants. In spite of this wealth of information, however, many people believe themselves to be immune to the problems of good grooming. This is a fallacy. Everyone should learn and practice *all* of the rules of good grooming.

BODY CLEANLINESS

Nothing makes one less popular either in business or in society than unpleasant odors. It is a fact of life, however, that we may be all too aware of the problem in others yet unaware that we, too, may be at fault. A daily shower or bath plus the use of a deodorant is usually adequate for safety; however, if special body odors are a problem, you should consult a doctor and follow his advice. Also, in this matter, you must be your own detective; truly, your best friend won't tell you. Sometimes more than one bath daily is required. Sometimes the problem is not body cleanliness but the habit of wearing a shirt or a blouse more than one day. Men in business can wear a shirt only one day; it must be laundered before it is worn again. The best policy for blouses is the same rule: wash after each wearing. Woolen over-blouses may be reworn if dress shields are attached and laundered after each wearing. Colognes and body powders are accepted during the working day but only if the fragrance is a light one.

Before putting away clothing that has been worn, expose it to fresh air. An outdoor clothesline is ideal for periodic airing. If such a luxury is unavailable, however, let clothing worn during the day air elsewhere.

Everyone is aware that soiled hands must be washed immediately. Fingernails must always be clean. The use of nail polish is approved, but light colors are much more fashionable and in better taste. The use of colorless polish is a wise decision. The absence of color eliminates the problem of chipped polish, yet the nails present a cared-for look. If you work with duplicating machines, or if your hands become smudged from carbon paper, special creams and liquids will remove all but the most stubborn stains.

Hair must always be clean, and this means frequent shampoos. The frequency of the shampoo may vary but should never be less frequent than every ten days. Most women prefer the weekly shampoo and set. Dandruff should be controlled by daily brushing and by the use of special shampoos. If you have special problems with your hair, such as excessive oiliness, dryness, or dandruff, it may be wise to consult a dermatologist.

The Skin

Nothing contributes so much to an attractive appearance as healthy, glowing skin. Such a state of affairs involves more than health. The avoidance of certain rich foods is necessary in many cases. Plenty of fresh fruits, exercise, vitamins — all of these will affect your skin — plus sufficient rest. In addition to these factors there is cleanliness. Your skin must be clean! This means the removal of all makeup before retiring. It means soap-and-water cleansing in some cases and cleansing cream plus astringents in others. Whatever your skin type, you should never permit an oily, smudged look. If your skin is oily, eliminate most fats from your diet and wash your face with special soaps several times a day and follow each washing with the use of an astringent.

If ordinary cleanliness, diet, and rest do not care adequately for your skin, consult a dermatologist. The time and money invested in such professional help will be worth it to you in improved appearance and freedom from worry. If you have acne, the help of a dermatologist is absolutely essential. Today even scars resulting from bad cases of acne can be helped.

If you possess a clear and attractive skin, count your blessings. Then start a regime that will keep your skin attractive. The same rules should be followed: adequate rest, sensible diet, perfect cleanliness, and exercise. One word of caution must be given: never squeeze a blemish that appears on your face. Wash your face carefully and cover the offending blemish with a medicated ointment. It will take care of itself in a short time, but any tampering with it may result in disaster.

The Hair

The importance of keeping your hair clean and shining has been discussed. No matter how beautiful the curl, how luxuriant the growth, or how modish the style, you cannot have attractive hair unless it is clean. One successful buyer in charge of ladies' ready-to-wear in a large shop said to the women employed there, "If your hair is clean, your face looks cleaner." The hair does create an illusion either of cleanliness or untidiness.

An old and tested way to care for the hair is to brush it one hundred strokes a day. At first, such brushing may make the hair oilier, and more frequent shampoos will be required. After a few weeks, however, you will notice a new shine to your hair, a cleaner look than you had before. Such brushing also improves the health of the scalp. Every day or so it is helpful to wash your brush and comb; a bit of ammonia in the water will make the task quick and easy. A clean brush and comb will help to keep your hair cleansed as it is brushed.

Hair styles for men are more or less standardized, with the shorter styles predominating. However, for men frequent haircuts are essential. Nothing spoils the well-groomed appearance like shaggy hair. Never postpone visits to the barber shop. Be sure, too, that you choose carefully the lotion applied in dressing the hair.

Women's hair styles do provide variety, but extremes of fashion should be avoided. It is advisable to consult a good hairdresser as to the most becoming hair style because hair arrangement can give illusions that change the shape of your face and that minimize or magnify either good or bad features. The way you wear your hair can also make you look taller or shorter. With the general features of a becoming style in mind, you can modify the hair style that is in fashion to suit you. It is unwise to go on wearing a favorite hair style long after it has passed into the out-of-date category.

Young girls will likely prefer simple styles that they can care for themselves. They do not need elaborate styles, permanents, and so on to look attractive. Hair that is clean and arranged in a simple style to show off a good feature is usually sufficient.

Women who do have permanents will probably continue with them about once every four months. A weekly visit to a beauty salon is no longer considered an extravagance, but careful brushing and (perhaps) resetting are necessary between such visits. One disadvantage with elaborate hair styles is the tendency to try to keep them intact for several days. A simple style that can be brushed each day is preferred.

Makeup

The best guides for up-to-date developments in cosmetics are fashion magazines. New ideas are constantly pouring forth, and these magazines are mines of information. Another possibility is the cosmetics counter in the better department stores. For an expert opinion, you may want to consult a cosmetologist. Some of the latest discoveries in cosmetics are preparations that cover blemishes, scars, and birthmarks. Also most welcome are the "moisturizing" preparations that reduce the tendency of the skin to dry out as the years go by.

Like other fashions, styles in makeup change from year to year. One year heavy eye makeup will be fashionable. Another year may bring the bronzed look into vogue. Regardless of the current trend, the business woman should strive for the natural look. It must be admitted, however, that we become conditioned by what we see on all sides. A completely natural look does *not* look natural if we have grown accustomed to certain cosmetic aids. A case in point is eye shadow. A few years ago eye shadow worn during the day was considered to be in very poor taste. Now we see it on many women whether morning, noon, or night. Perhaps the key word in the use of cosmetics should be discretion. The woman in business should not look conspicuous — whether from too much or too little makeup.

The business woman should take the time to select the best shades and brands (for her) of foundation, powder, lipstick, and eye makeup. Books and magazines on grooming will prove helpful. Beauty salons and department stores frequently employ experts to help with these decisions. Many schools and colleges have classes in which the subject is studied. Some schools have style centers where individual help can be obtained. Some manufacturers of cosmetics provide free color charts indicating shades of makeup becoming to individuals with certain coloring. A little study and experimentation should provide the right answers. When a reliable and becoming brand has been chosen, it is wise to continue with it.

Applying makeup is an art, and skill in any art requires practice. It will pay you to take the time to master the lipstick brush, for example. Another skill requiring practice is the subtle use of an eyebrow pencil. Eyebrows should never be drawn on the face, although eyebrow pencil may be applied to darken brows or to emphasize their shape. Care should be taken to apply the pencil (sharpened to a fine point) in short hair-like strokes. If mascara is used, the lashes should then be brushed with a clean brush so they will not stick together and look spiky.

Lipstick, nail polish, and rouge must be harmonized with coloring, face makeup, and costume. Lighter shades of lipstick and rouge are more popular now. If rouge is worn at all, it should be placed high on the cheekbone and used sparingly. If a favorite brand of lipstick is drying, you might use lip foundation creams both at night and during the day.

TESTS FOR GOOD GROOMING

To simplify the grooming process, it may be helpful if one has some sort of yardstick to measure the extent to which one has achieved it. Just how well groomed should a young man or woman in business be?

Tests for Men — Brushed and Shined

If you are a young man planning to enter the business world, you should take the problem of grooming seriously. In some kinds of work, to be sure, the problem is not so crucial. Auto mechanics do not have to worry about how they look on the job. In business, however, everyone you meet will be judging you and your firm by your appearance. Your co-workers, too, will be affected by the care you take with grooming yourself for your job. Each day, therefore, you should mentally check off each of the following:

A man is well groomed when
    His body and his teeth are clean and free from odor
    His skin is clear, not oily, and he is freshly shaven
    His hands have a cared-for look
    His hair is neatly trimmed, clean, and combed
    His underwear is clean
    His shoes are shined

His socks are clean and not allowed to wrinkle around
    his ankles
His shirt is fresh daily
His suit is pressed; the trousers are well creased
No spots stain his clothing
His tie harmonizes with his shirt and suit
His clothing fits the occasion and is odorless
His hat is the sort that gentlemen wear

Tests for Women — The White Glove Look

A young woman who plans to work in business must be
extremely serious about the problem of grooming. Unfair
though it may seem, a man may be excused for certain viola-
tions of the "brushed and shined" look while a woman will
not. The reason may be that femininity is partially dependent
upon the grooming shown by a girl or woman. Whether you
have the money to spend on your wardrobe is not particularly
important. You *must* spend time and money on grooming,
however, if you are to succeed in business. Each day you
should check off the following statements:

A woman is well groomed when
    Her body and her teeth are clean and free from odors
    Her skin is clear and well-cared for
    Her hair is clean and attractively styled
    Her clothing fits properly and suits her personality
    Her clothing is appropriate for the business hours
    Her shoes give an air of refinement and comfort. They
        are dust free and polished. The heels are straight,
        and the toes unscuffed.
    Her makeup is not obvious; it is never applied in
        public
    Her clothing is clean, pressed, and free from odors
    Her underwear is fresh daily
    Her hosiery is fresh daily and free from runs or holes
    Her clothes are supported by adequate foundation
        garments

NEATNESS

Emerson once said, "I have heard with admiring submission the experience of a lady who declared that the sense of being well-dressed gives a feeling of inward tranquility which religion is powerless to bestow." Neatness and grooming are important, not only because they indicate orderliness and good taste, but also because of the feeling they give you. If you picture yourself and feel that others picture you as an example of a poised, well-groomed business man or woman, you will find it easier to play that role. The self-confidence that comes from feeling that your appearance is right makes it easier to give your entire attention to the tasks before you.

If your clothes are appropriate for office wear, if you do not wear the same ones every day, and if your shoes are polished and in good repair, you have attended to surface necessities only. Then get at the fundamentals. Your teeth are to be cared for; your skin and hair are to be kept in good condition; body odors are to be avoided; and your hands are to be well groomed. The cumulative effect should be one of good health, cleanliness, and tidiness. These matters are to be taken care of at home. In the store or the office, toilet articles are to be kept out of sight.

If you eat in the office, remove all evidences of the noon-day lunch from your desk. Tidiness demands that you keep your desk clear of all unnecessary papers, that you put away equipment and supplies you have used, and that you pick up papers which someone else may have dropped carelessly. Be careful to throw wastepaper *into* the wastebasket rather than *at it.* Place things where they belong in or on the desk or in the files. Perform such housekeeping tasks each morning as the office or the store regulations permit.

If your duties are clerical, you are to keep neat reports and records, to keep the files in perfect order, to fold letters and insert them into envelopes carefully, to arrange all material systematically before giving it to your employer, and to send out only typewritten work that is mailable — that is, letters that are attractively arranged and free from carbon smudges, fingerprints, and visible erasures.

A young woman, sent to interview an employer about a prospective job in the stenographic department, reported a successful termination of her call. After her employment she was told that she had been selected from many applicants because she displayed traits which the company thought important. During the interview when she was being considered for the position, the personnel director had dictated some letters for her to transcribe. When she went to the typewriter to transcribe, she removed the cover from the machine and hung it over the back of her chair. When she erased, she was careful to avoid erasure crumbs falling into the typewriter mechanism. She moved the carriage all the way to one side so that the crumbs fell on the desk where they could be brushed away. When she completed her transcription, she covered the machine and slid the chair close to the typewriter table.

"Because of these indications of neatness," her new employer told her, "I selected you."

FOLLOW-UP ACTIVITIES

1. Many department stores require that their salespeople dress in a prescribed way. For example, salesgirls may be asked to wear beige sheath dresses only, in order that their clothing will not distract attention from the merchandise. What would you consider a reasonable amount that would be required for maintaining such a wardrobe for one month? Would this make a difference in the salary you would consider adequate for such a job?

2. Suppose you have been hired to work as a dental technician. You must wear plain white uniforms for work, but they may be of any material you prefer. Investigate the cost, upkeep, and wearing qualities of three different fabrics commonly used for such uniforms. Which one would you choose? Why?

3. You are a young man recently hired as a clerk in a large office. It is necessary that you wear white shirts, a fresh one each day. Your salary is not large, and you find washing and ironing extremely burdensome. See if you can find a drip-dry shirt that looks as well as your regular cotton shirts. What is the difference in cost? Which would you purchase? Why?

4. Janet Wells has just taken a position as typist in a small office. The ventilation is inadequate and there is no air conditioning. Janet's superior is Mrs. Christensen, who has a desk very close to Janet's. On a particularly hot day, Mrs. Christensen has the janitor move her desk into another corner some distance away. Should Janet consider this a reflection on her grooming? If you were Janet, would you say anything to Mrs. Christensen? If so, what would you say?

5. Do you think a person's weight has any effect on his grooming requirements? If you were your present height and 30 pounds heavier, what additional grooming precautions would you need to take?

6. From your own experience, can you think of an application of the importance of neatness? Write the situation down and use it for class discussion.

7. You are a young man working in the data processing division of a large firm. All of the men in your division wear white shirts but remove their coats during working hours. What type of suit would you buy to wear to work? How often would you have it cleaned?

8. Do you take regular exercise? If you do, list the kinds and the frequency of each. In what ways could this list be extended? It is said that five minutes of exercise each day is better for you than two hours once a week.

9. Jerry Smith is a typist in the duplicating department. He has been working in this job for six months. Much of his work is with the fluid duplicator. Suddenly he notices a breaking out on his hands. He consults a

dermatologist who tells him that he has developed an allergy for either the carbon or the fluid and that he should discontinue this type of work. What steps should Jerry take to take care of this situation?

10. It has been said that "your best friend won't tell you" that you are troubled with body odor. To whom can you appeal if you honestly want to know?

CASE PROBLEMS

1. Samples From the Stock Room

Jim Thurman worked for the shipping department of Hogles Company. He hoped to become a salesman for the firm someday. After two years, however, he was neither given a raise nor promoted. Other men who were no older were transferred to the retail sales department. Finally Jim became discouraged and decided to quit. Before he left, he asked his employer why he had never been promoted. The answer was that when Jim reported to work his hair was not neatly combed, his shoes were not polished, his clothes were not pressed, and his nails were not clean. Jim left feeling that his employer should have told him previously that his appearance was not measuring up to the firm's standards. Yet he could not see why it should have been necessary for him to be neat in the shipping room.

1. Do you think Jim was right in thinking that neatness did not matter in the shipping room?
2. Do you feel Jim's employer should have mentioned Jim's lack of neatness when it was first noted?
3. Do you think a person's work can be predicted from his personal grooming?

2. Prepare for the Day

Sam Cohn and Donald Huff worked in the same office. Both were good workers and were looking forward to being sent out on the road to sell the products of the company. It was a big moment when they received a notice to report the following morning to the sales manager's office for an interview. Sam looked over his clothing that night and saw that everything was clean and well pressed. Donald was going out and did not have time to see about his clothes. The next morning he overslept and had to rush to be on time for his appointment. On his way to the office he noticed that his shoes were in need of polishing and that he had on the same shirt he had worn yesterday. He felt, however, that he would pass inspection. He was interviewed first, and the sales manager missed no detail of his grooming. Sam was interviewed next, and he received the promotion.

1. Do you think it was fair to judge Donald solely on his appearance?
2. Would Donald's attitude toward his appearance be indicative of his attitude toward his work?
3. What effect might Donald's appearance have had on his attitude during the interview?

3. Constructive Criticism

Lester McAfee was the bookkeeper for the Worth Mercantile Company. As he was working he would often run his hands through his hair, leaving it mussed and untidy. Lester's desk could be seen through a window by the customers as they came into the notions department. The head of this department, Mr. Cameron, although not connected directly with the bookkeeping department, spoke to Lester about his habit and told him how untidy it looked through the window. Lester replied, "I've had the habit for years. I do it without thinking when I'm working."

1. Was Mr. Cameron justified in criticizing a worker in another department?
2. Should Lester have paid any attention to Mr. Cameron, since he was in a different department?
3. How would you have reacted to this criticism if you had been Lester?
4. Mr. Cameron might have gone to Lester's superior with his criticism. Would this have been preferable? Why or why not?

PART 3 PERSONALITY IS WHAT YOU HEAR

Chapter 7

The Power of Words

Have you ever listened to a gifted actor or actress and thought, "What an attractive person." Later you may have seen this same person on the street and failed to recognize him or her. What was it that created the illusion of attractiveness? It may have been the beauty of the voice, or it may have been the beauty of the words that were spoken. Later in this chapter you will learn something about how to speak, but first you must learn what to say. There is no playwright at hand to furnish you with witty, wise, or sympathetic remarks. You must write your script yourself.

How can you tell if your knowledge of what to say is adequate? There is a simple test. When you speak, do people listen to you? When you write, do your letters command attention? Do people lean forward when you speak, afraid to lose a word of what you say? Or do they wait for you to stop speaking so they can say something? You have had these experiences. You have been stimulated and inspired by one person's speaking. You have also listened to another with half an ear while you planned what you were going to do the following day.

Written communication may be either exciting or dull. Some letters are dull and drab. They cannot persuade because they possess no stimulating words or phrases. Yet another letter covering the same subject might awaken you to action because of the appeal of its wording. Freshness of expression is in great demand, as words can sell everything from machinery to ideas. If you want to make a favorable impression on your business and social contacts, you need not be a spellbinder. But you must have the ability to attract people through your speaking and writing.

How Many Words Do You Know?

A recent newspaper article quoted a psychologist who had determined the value of word power in dollars and cents. Through a survey of thousands of business and professional workers he found that the greater the vocabulary, the greater the earning power. Johnson O'Connor, Director of the Human Engineering Laboratory of Boston, has conducted similar tests to determine the value of vocabulary in business. As an outgrowth of his testing, O'Connor concludes that:

1. A large vocabulary is an important key to success.
2. Persons who are shy and self-conscious can become better leaders by enlarging their vocabularies.
3. Anyone can enlarge his vocabulary and thus add to his chances of success.

As a matter of fact, you are judged consciously or unconsciously by your speech. A knowledge of words is important whether you are a beginner or the head of the firm. Promotion will depend partly on your ability to speak and write English correctly and effectively. Careless writing and poor speech habits are handicaps just as are unkempt appearance and boorish conduct, and they become greater handicaps every year. This is because of the tremendous increase of educational opportunities in the last twenty years. It has been said that a college education is now as essential as was graduation from the eighth grade two generations ago. The days are past when you can afford to take a chance on entering business only partially prepared.

You must not be lulled into the belief that a knowledge of words is not necessary in some office jobs. You may think that if you take dictation, you will be using the vocabulary of your employer and that a knowledge of his vocabulary will be sufficient. Aside from the fact that word knowledge aids transcription and helps you to get the thought of the dictator, you may be required to answer letters on your own. Your superior may say, "Tell this fellow 'No,' but make it sound like 'Yes'." How would you solve such a problem? Your confidence in your ability to solve this and other problems will be strengthened if you have a good vocabulary.

Telephone communication is another activity that demands a knowledge of words. It is embarrassing if you have to ask your party to spell an unfamiliar word. He would judge you unfavorably — and your firm as well. In all of the many roles you have to play in business you have your lines to speak. A knowledge of the words used by educated business men and women is a necessity.

You can improve your vocabulary. The gift of knowing the right word to use at the right time can be developed. The best method, of course, is by reading widely from literature, biography, and quality periodicals. This is the method that insures success, but it does take a long time. If you want to supplement this method with another that helps bring results more quickly, there is a way. Whenever you hear a word you do not know, look it up. You might have a little trouble finding new words at first, but practice will bring success. You will soon learn the possible spellings of a word that sounds a certain way. A good beginning is to write it down the way it sounds. Suppose you heard one of your superiors say to another, "What we need is a mnemonic device to help us." Perhaps you have never heard the word *mnemonic*. How would you look it up? The best way is to write it down phonetically: *nemonic*. Not finding it under the *n*'s, you might try the *p*'s. After all, *pneumonia* sounds like it starts with an *n*. The next thing to do would be to consult the pronunciation guide of your dictionary. If you cannot determine the spelling by referring to the pronunciation guide, then you should ask someone else in your office — or even in the public library. Librarians have such a wealth of knowledge and rarely have a chance to display it!

Remember, too, that words are tools of thought. To think precisely you must know the exact word needed. You must know the associations of words, the emotions they carry with them; for words convey feeling as well as thought. A vocabulary that is alive with pictures and with action gives power and interest to your speaking and writing. You can learn to choose the right word and thus paint a picture, sell yourself or your ideas, inspire others to action. There is a great need for this ability to express ideas graphically so the listener *sees* in his mind the idea you are presenting. You can sell yourself in an application interview; you can get the job you want, win recognition and promotion, be given more responsibility, earn more money — if you use the right words.

Practice makes perfect. You will find many opportunities to work on building a better vocabulary. Say you have a letter to write. If you have trouble expressing your thoughts, ask yourself the question, "What am I trying to say?" Answer your question aloud. You might say, "I'm trying to tell Mr. Jones I can't accept his offer of a job because I've already started working for Mr. Smith." This is what you want to say. Now you must find the best way to say it. Try several different approaches. After a bit of fumbling, your ideas will begin to assume greater clarity. With each repetition you may be able to improve your courtesy, clear up ambiguous phrases, discard words that clutter up your meaning. You may substitute words, place adjectives, phrases, and clauses nearer the words they modify, perhaps transpose the subject and predicate. Finally you will have a more effective sentence.

Another aid to effective written English is to write as you talk. It is distinctly old fashioned to use trite expressions like "at an early date" and "your letter has been received and contents noted." Yet such expressions do creep into millions of letters every year. When you are writing a letter, try to visualize the reader. How old is he? What kind of education has he had? Is he an informal or formal type of person? When you have a complete mental picture of the reader of your letter, talk to him. Write only such sentences as you would use if you were talking face to face. This device will eliminate many trite expressions you would otherwise be tempted to use.

It is actually easier to write effective English than it is to speak it effectively. In writing you have the opportunity to review and correct what you have written. You may feel less self-conscious about using new words if you use them first in written communication. Some of the larger words, however, are not as effective as the simpler ones. Just be sure the word you use is the best for the meaning you have in mind. There are many suggestions that might be made to improve your written communication. Space limitations make it impossible to go into this problem deeply, but the following should be helpful:

1. Be specific. Speak and write specifically rather than in broad generalities. Say *the Rotary Club* instead of *a well-known service organization.*
2. Use action verbs. Say, "John threw the book on the table," not, "The book was thrown on the table."
3. Keep your verbs parallel. If you start out with one verb form, all others in that sentence should be that form. For example, don't say, "Her duties were taking dictation and she typed and filed," but, "Her duties were taking dictation, typing, and filing."
4. Avoid negative words if you can. If you must use them, try to place the negative words in a dependent clause: "Although No. B 238-968 is out of stock, we are shipping No. B 290-300." In other words, stress what you can do rather than what you cannot do.
5. When you must say something unpleasant, start with a positive statement. This helps get your reader in step with you and will make what you have to say more palatable.

Learn the vocabulary of your job. The first thing you must do (either before or immediately after being employed) is learn the trade terms of your business. An excellent source of such terms is one of the business or economic dictionaries. These books list most of the business terms that might be new to you but which are part of the general vocabulary of most firms. Such a book is also helpful in looking up terms that come up in your work and for which you have only a vague understanding. Further knowledge of terms is necessary if you are employed in a doctor's office, a law office, or an engineering firm. There are textbooks containing such vocabularies (some also include shorthand outlines), and these should be studied until you become proficient.

Dare to be different. Study grammar and learn to apply your knowledge in speaking and writing. Learn that adjectives add quality, that verbs create action. Use adjectives to adorn, as you use accessories to brighten a dull garment. Use verbs to bring life and motion to your thoughts. Adjectives add color, and colorful words create definite pictures. You do not attempt selling a customer a "blue dress" — it is a "robin's egg blue," an "Alice blue," a "morning glory blue." "That *schoolgirl* complexion," "the *Savage* automatic," "the *Safety* tire" are slogans that have selling value because of the adjectives used. The richness or the paucity of your thinking is revealed in your ability to put color in your words. Take a look at a few advertisements in a current issue of a magazine:

"They're frying eggs on the sidewalk" sells a fan.

"Sh-h-h — they're sleeping soundly" sells an airplane ride.

Note that the words that give strength to these lines of copy are verbs.

Your vocabulary reveals your personality, and as your vocabulary grows, your personality will reflect wider horizons, deeper insights, stronger sympathies. Careless or slovenly speech habits rate you as the possessor of traits not acceptable in business life. If your speech indicates that your thinking is vague, the conclusion drawn is that you do not possess sufficient knowledge to meet the situation. If you have not grown in spite of your years of schooling, you are not material in which business would invest time and money while waiting for you to make good.

If your writing vocabulary is to grow with your speaking vocabulary, it is important that you know how to spell correctly. If your speaking vocabulary is to grow with your reading vocabulary, it is necessary that you know the correct pronunciation of the words you use. Clear enunciation, correct pronunciation, and good diction, which means the ability to use English speech acceptable to educated English-speaking people, are specific requirements in business life. Acquiring a working vocabulary from which you may draw specific words as the situation demands is a goal worthy of your best endeavors.

How do you pronounce it? Mispronunciations of frequently recurring words are objectionable to many people. Whenever you are in doubt regarding the pronunciation of a word, you should consult a dictionary and then practice the correct pronunciation of the word until you have thoroughly mastered it. As a first step toward more careful speech, ascertain the correct pronunciation of the italicized words and then read the sentences aloud:

1. This *quiet, quaint restaurant* is in an *unfrequented* part of the city, but you may recognize the *address*.
2. The *protestations* that you *address* to me are *indisputable* but *irrelevant*.
3. The *statistician prefaced* his remarks with *prosaic data*.
4. The *metallurgist, physicist,* and *mathematician* contemplated the *effect* of the *variables* on their experiment.
5. You can *attain* an idea from the pages of *history* about the effects of *municipal mismanagement*.
6. A few minutes after *takeoff,* the *altimeter* on the jet showed that it had reached *cruising altitude*.
7. How *often* have you answered *inquiries* about the form of address on *envelopes*?

8. That *pronunciation* is *disputable* and should not be stated *absolutely* and *positively*.

9. Only a stupid, *awkward bungler* would so handle the *apparatus* in the *university laboratory*.

10. An *aqua cashmere cardigan* and a *suede* jacket with a *milium* lining were two of her purchases in Europe.

11. If you *acclimate* yourself to *weather* conditions, you may develop an *immunity* toward *respiratory* diseases.

12. He was *indicted* on an *embezzlement* charge, but most of the evidence proved *circumstantial*.

13. "*Aye*," answered the *swarthy brigand*, "the *route* is open to you."

14. The *seventh siren* in the film *contributed* an *integral* part to the *drama*.

15. The *comptroller* of a company is one who checks *expenditures* and *disbursements*.

16. The *aviator* startled his *colleagues* with some photographs taken during a *reconnaissance mission*.

17. While in the *infirmary*, he was given *penicillin* shots to *combat* bronchial *pneumonia*.

18. Don't you enjoy the *amateur vaudeville* performances that indicate *inimitable initiative*?

19. Because he is *senile*, his *version* of the *alleged demise* was disregarded.

20. Five *decades* ago "*chauffeur*" was a new word in the English *language*.

21. *Adult education* is a service being provided through *governmental* agencies.

22. The *stationery* used by the firm was a *genuine advertisement*.

23. The picture has *intrinsic* value as an *authentic etching* of the last century.

24. How *adept* is the *actor* in his *incomparable* version of the title *role*!

25. Take an *inventory*, *preferably* after the *Tuesday* sale.

Does Your Voice Attract?

A man cannot speak but he judges himself. With his will, or against his will, he draws his portrait to the eye of his companions by every word. Every opinion reacts on him who utters it ... Emerson

Speech is not only a social necessity; it is an emotional necessity as well. There can be communication without speech, but how much more satisfying it is to be able to *talk* with someone who is important to you. It is also important that you be able to listen. In fact, one of the best ways of learning to speak well is through the medium of listening well.

Is your voice pleasing to others? If you would like to know how your voice sounds, just make this easy test. Cup your ears forward and then speak in your normal way. This is the way your voice sounds to others; you will be amazed how different it sounds to you! You may also find that your voice needs to be improved in one or more of the following ways:

Pitch. A low voice is more pleasing than one that is too high. A high, strident pitch may be caused by tenseness. To correct this fault you should relax and open your throat. The easiest way to do this is to yawn; try it. Do you feel the difference? When you yawn, your throat is open as it should be all the time. A relaxed throat, correct breathing from the diaphragm — these are the bases upon which you should build the placement of your speaking voice. Practice reading aloud with your throat relaxed. Once you become familiar with the way your voice sounds when it is pitched properly, you will be better able to control it.

Rate. If you speak too rapidly, too slowly, or at a monotonous rate, you will defeat your speech personality. Rapid speech is usually a result of nervous tension. Again, the cure is relaxation. Take a deep breath; let your shoulders drop a bit; then go on at an easier pace. A rate that is slow, on the other hand, may be the result of hesitation. If you are hesitant, you are probably insecure. Don't think about yourself or of what others think of you. Think about the listener and about what you are saying.

Volume. There is a proper volume for your speech, depending on whether you are speaking to one person or to a group. If the latter, you should project your voice by speaking to the person who is farthest away. The old bit of advice to speak to the last row in the room or hall is still good. If you are speaking to one person, the volume will usually take care of itself. You should speak just loud enough to be heard and understood.

Quality. The quality of your voice can be improved. Go to a record shop and make a record of your voice as you speak or read. Take the record home and listen to it critically. Pretend the voice you are hearing belongs to someone else. In any case, it will sound like the voice of a stranger at first. You may find that variety of inflection is needed or that more color on important words would be helpful. When you know what is lacking, you can begin to work for improvement. Go to the public library and find a book on improving your speech. Read aloud from the exercises that are suggested. In a short time you should find a big difference in the quality of your voice.

Remember, your voice should express *you* at your best. If you feel friendly toward your listener, your voice will sound friendly. If you feel assured, your voice will mirror this assurance. You can see from this that voice improvement involves the emotions as well as the vocal chords. Nervousness is a common problem and should be attacked at once. A good cure for nervousness is to make a list of all the reasons why you are nervous. The action of making the list takes away some of the power these causes have over you. The known is much less frightening than the unknown.

Part of your campaign to improve your voice depends on practice. Welcome every opportunity to speak to others, whether one or a large audience. Stand up and talk whenever you have the opportunity. You will find that with practice your confidence will grow, and that is all you need. If you think **you** can speak well, you will be able to speak well.

Improving Your Feeling Tone

It isn't what you say; it is the *way* you say it that sometimes makes the difference. If you are to improve *tone*, or the way you say it, you must develop the traits of sympathy and tact. You may think there is no place in the business world for sympathy, but this is not true. What you will find is too little time for the expression of sympathy. In any case, you should be concerned with being sympathetic yourself, not with having others sympathize with you. Your employer is working under a much greater strain than you are. You should be sympathetic to his problems and understanding of his impatience and irritability.

Sympathy. You will have many opportunities to show understanding and sympathy. If you are sensitive to the feelings of others, you will try to make them feel at ease. This ability to make others feel at ease is an important factor in getting along with others. If you are relaxed and natural yourself, it is because you are able to think of others instead of yourself.

In addition to putting others at ease, you will be careful to treat others as you would like to be treated. Nothing has ever made the Golden Rule obsolete. You will speak in a friendly manner to new employees; you will take the trouble to be kind to those who are in trouble; you will be sensitive to moods and not infringe on another's desire for privacy. The human touch is not absent from business entirely. Flowers are sent to those on sick leave; visits are paid to old, retired employees; donations are made for wedding gifts and anniversaries.

But, in the matter of sympathy, it is better to give than to ask. You must not exploit sympathy. You should not ask that exceptions be made for you because of bad luck. You should not be so noble that you become a martyr in order to get more sympathy from your co-workers. If you are ill and must ask for time off or decreased duties, do so. If you injure your health in attempting to carry too much work and cope with trouble at the same time, your problem will be aggravated.

Another way of exploiting sympathy is in expecting raises and promotions because you have responsibilities or heavy expenses. Promotions and raises are not based on need; they are based on what you can offer your employer. If you describe in an employment interview the many misfortunes you have experienced and the burdens you carry, you will place yourself in a dubious role. Your interviewer will hesitate to employ or promote you, fearing you will continue to ask for favors and exceptions because you are troubled. Business is interested in the happiness and comfort of employees, but wise employees will not take advantage of this interest by exploiting it.

Tact. Tact is a sixth sense that makes us aware of what would be fitting to do or say at a given moment. It puts us in the other fellow's shoes. If you are tactful, you will make life infinitely easier for yourself and those around you. Tact involves understanding the other person's needs and wishes. There is hardly a situation in business that cannot benefit from a tactful approach. The following list of such situations should be studied carefully. Describe how you would use tact in each of them.

1. Maintaining any business relationship on an impersonal basis.
2. Handling a telephone communication in order to facilitate the smooth operation of the business situation involved.
3. Dismissing unwanted callers.
4. Making visitors feel at ease if they are kept waiting.
5. Answering questions about the office that are asked by outsiders.
6. Avoiding being pumped by outsiders for information about the business.
7. Ascertaining a caller's business before disturbing your employer.

8. Giving a caller the impression that, no matter how trifling the interview may be, your employer will be glad to see him if possible.

9. Keeping annoying, disturbing, or trivial matters from your employer's office, especially if he is already irritated.

10. Reminding your employer of work still to be done.

11. Knowing when and how to enter your employer's office or to withdraw from it.

12. Making executives of the organization feel comfortable and secure in their own self-esteem.

13. Being the scapegoat for the employer's mistakes, if necessary, when outsiders are concerned.

14. Suggesting improvements to be made, equipment to be installed, and supplies to be furnished.

15. Asking for a promotion or a raise.

16. Finding ways of putting the dictation of the employer into good English without offending him.

17. Listening with interest to the jokes your employer wishes to try out on you.

18. Finishing work that the employer has left undone.

19. Accepting your employer's ideas on unimportant matters about which you may disagree.

20. Reminding the employer of an appointment.

21. Asking the employer for information when he is busy.

22. Suggesting a new method of doing work so that your employer will not think you are trying to run his office.

23. Suggesting to your employer that you keep his desk tidy.

24. Making your employer think that your suggestions are his ideas.

25. Responding pleasantly and courteously when you have been spoken to in a rude manner.

26. Putting people at ease.

27. Taking care of an unpleasant situation so that those involved will be spared embarrassment.

28. Making necessary criticisms of other people in such a way that you will not hurt their feelings unduly.

29. Being considerate of subordinates.

30. Complimenting a fellow worker on a job well done.

31. Dealing with adverse criticism. Thank the critic and show an eagerness to improve.
32. Settling a difference of opinion among fellow employees.
33. Disagreeing with another without being offensive.
34. Remembering the names of people for whom and with whom you work.
35. Taking the initiative.
36. Sending a salesman away satisfied with the interview, though he has made no sale.
37. Dealing with an angry customer.
38. Collecting an account.
39. Explaining to a customer, without losing her trade, why she cannot return an article.
40. Explaining to a dissatisfied customer why her order was not sent on time.
41. Arranging an appointment with an important customer when the employer is not in the office.
42. Appealing subtly to the hobbies of the people with whom you come into contact.
43. Replying with enthusiasm to a tiresome, oft-repeated question.
44. Accepting casually the idiosyncrasies or the physical defects of others.

FOLLOW-UP ACTIVITIES

1. List five trite expressions that you use habitually. Substitute other words for variety.
2. List ten specific words used in the automobile industry; in the insurance business; in banking; in the legal profession. Add other industries belonging to your community, and list words under these headings.
3. Distinguish between the following words by using them in sentences.

mistake	error	blunder		
answer	reply	response	rejoinder	
dark	obscure	dim	mysterious	
surprise	amaze	astonish	astound	appall

4. Listen to the radio or television speech of any of the well-known announcers and bring to class a list of his colorful words, of his specific words, or of the words he pronounces differently from the way you are accustomed to hearing them.

5. Locate an article in a current newspaper or magazine bearing on a current problem, and underline the words that give the article color and life.

6. Substitute more colorful expressions for these trite ones:

pale as a ghost   busy as a bee
green as grass   sweet as sugar
pure as snow   white as a sheet

7. Describe a business office that you have visited. Be specific in giving details of arrangement and equipment.

8. List five adjectives to describe each of the following:

a house for sale
a calculating machine
a new typewriter
a bookkeeper

9. Refer to the dictionary to get the exact meanings of the following overworked words; then use them in sentences:

nice   fine   pretty   grand   perfect
beautiful   wonderful   gorgeous   magnificent

10. Make a list of the slogans of ten of the large advertisers. What specific, colorful, pungent words are used?

CASE PROBLEMS

1. When To Interrupt the Dictator

Alice Curtis took dictation from Mr. Grayson, the head of the advertising department. Mr. Grayson was a rapid speaker and occasionally slurred words to the point that Alice could not understand them. One day during dictation, Mr. Grayson used the word *hybrid*, but Alice heard the word as *high-bred*. Not getting the idea, Alice interrupted, "Do you mean high-bred?" Mr. Grayson was annoyed at losing his train of thought. "Use better judgment," he said, "and don't interrupt."

1. Assuming that Alice had been working at this position for more than six months, is there some way she could have avoided this situation?
2. How should Alice have reacted to this reprimand?
3. What clues should she have had from the context to help her in deciding which word was intended?
4. Is there a grammatical rule that might have helped her in this case?
5. Some dictators prefer to be interrupted during dictation. What personality clues would help you in deciding when to ask and when not to ask a question during dictation?

2. Use of Initiative

George Andrews has just completed a report that must be sent out in the afternoon mail. His employer intends to send a letter with the report, but he is called out of the office just before closing time and without having been able to dictate the letter. He says nothing to George before leaving. George knows, however, that the letter will be similar to the one sent the previous month. He decides to type the letter and sign it with his employer's name and his own initials.

1. What would you have done in George's position?
2. Which would be more serious, sending the letter without being told or sending the report without a covering letter?
3. If you were George's employer, how would you react to having an employee act in this way without instructions?

3. Better Than Good

The Home Insurance Company employs two girls as switchboard operators. This position has always been an initial job for girls who, if they show a degree of proficiency, are transferred to more advanced positions. Judy Graham and Lois Fenton are the two operators. Judy has a slight seniority in time of employment. A position in the clerical force in one of the offices will be open soon, and Judy expects the promotion. It is given to Lois, however. Judy knows that her work at the switchboard has been good. She has always displayed courtesy, has a good voice and clear enunciation, has the essential telephone techniques, and is efficient in her work. Lois has all the ability that Judy displays in the performance of duties at the switchboard. In addition, Lois has taken every opportunity to learn facts connected with the organization, has taken on work occasionally to help some other employee, and, by judiciously allotting some of her spare time to study, has shown that she is promotional material. Judy feels that she has been unjustly treated and decides to quit her position.

1. In what ways is Judy lacking in promotional possibilities?
2. How can this lack be changed? What would you recommend that Judy do first?
3. If you were the personnel manager, what would you say to Judy to convince her that she should remain with the company?

4. A Place for Sensitivity

Ann Madison is a secretary in a large plastic surgery clinic. Her task is to fill out routine records concerning patients for the files. The data are of a factual nature and contain no medical information. When talking with a middle-aged man, she observed that he was embarrassed by having to supply such information as his name, age, address, and business. When she had recorded these answers, Ann said to the patient, "And now will you tell me why you have come here?"

"Look, young lady," he answered, "is it the practice for a patient to have to give you that kind of information?"

Ann answered, "I'm sorry, sir. I'm only doing my job. My instructions from Dr. Reynolds are that I must get this information."

1. Do you feel that Ann was sensitive to the needs of others?
2. About what types of needs or feelings are some people very sensitive?
3. Should Ann have insisted that the man answer her question? How would you have handled this situation? Why?

Chapter 8

Your Telephone Personality

You may have spent countless hours talking on the telephone to your friends, but do you have a good telephone personality for business? Not all beginners in business do, and their lack becomes a big worry to them as they become aware of how much their business success depends on the telephone. There is hardly a phase of business that does not necessitate the use of the telephone: interviews are arranged or canceled, orders are placed, information is given, mistakes are corrected, and buying and selling go on in large or small amounts according to the size and type of business. As a time-saver, the telephone has no equal in the perfection of organization and routine. Communication by telephone is a necessity in business life.

No telephone conversation in business can be considered trivial. Whether you are answering a call that requests the middle name of the second vice-president or one that involves taking an order for goods, your response is important because you are the representative of the entire business concern. The information you give must be accurate; the policy that you express is that of the business itself.

TELEPHONE TECHNIQUES

How is your telephone personality evaluated? The only medium available to the caller is your voice. By your voice the customer or client will form his opinion and be influenced in his future dealings with the firm. You have heard the expression "The voice with a smile." This slogan should guide you in using the telephone in your work. Confidence can be established and friendliness can be maintained if your

111

Personality shows in your voice, too.

voice carries enthusiastic interest in the affairs of your business as well as personal attention to the affairs of the customer or client.

The telephone directory should be studied; it contains information with which you should be familiar. For example, you should not guess about a number. If there is any doubt in your mind, refer to the directory for accurate information. When calling long distance, know when to dial direct and when to call person-to-person. Know what the charges are before you begin to speak. Know when and how to reverse the charges and how to make collect calls. Learn to use coin telephones and telephones connected through private branch exchanges. There are definite techniques you should master both in answering the telephone and in placing calls.

Answering the Telephone

The most important factor in answering the telephone is promptness. Always answer the telephone on the first ring if you can. The customer or client who places the call is always critical about a delay. Your firm may have an approved form of greeting that you must use, but you can make that greeting a cheerful one. The approved greeting may be, "Good morning," followed by your identification. This is important. Always identify yourself immediately; that is, give the name of the business or the department, or your title or name. Circumstances will indicate which of the following means of identification you should use.

Name of the company. You will identify the name of the company when you answer the outside line, as in a small office. In a small real estate firm, for example, you would give some such identification as the following: "Becker and Forest Company. Good morning." The caller would then talk to you or ask to speak to someone else in the firm.

Name of the department. You will identify the name of the department if the company has a private branch exchange (PBX) and you are one of a number of workers in that department without a particular title. If you were a clerk in the accounting department, for example, your caller would reach you by telling the switchboard operator he wanted to talk to someone in the accounting department. Giving him this information, therefore, would enable him to go on from there, either by speaking to you or by asking for someone by name or title. In answering the phone in this situation, you would say, "Accounting Department," because the name of the company and the "Good morning" would already have been given by the PBX operator.

Your name or title. You would identify yourself by your name or title if you were the assistant to an executive. Your choice would depend on the circumstances. In a small town or city you would probably give your name, as you would if you worked in a school office. If you are well known by name, you should give your name. If your firm is located in a large city, on the other hand, it would usually be more helpful to your caller if you were to give your title. In this instance, you would say, "Mr. Henry's secretary speaking."

You should always keep a pad and pencil near the telephone so you will have something to write on and something to write with when messages need to be taken down. Never trust to memory about numbers, addresses, or the time for appointments. A pad of telephone message blanks (similar to the model shown below) will make it easy to report messages that are taken for others in their absence.

Your enunciation is important when telephoning. In face-to-face conversation, facial expression helps to make your message clear. Over the telephone there is nothing to help you but the way you speak. Always speak clearly, slowly, courteously, and directly into the mouthpiece of the telephone. Be sincere; then your voice will sound sincere. Develop a listening ear along with your sincere voice. Concentrate on what is being told you or asked of you. Some voices over the telephone are hard to understand; some use gutteral tones, some speak with accents, some use whispers, some crack against the eardrums. Concentrating on what is being said with your listening ear will help you to understand the speaker.

Be courteous, too, in your choice of expressions. For example, it is more courteous to ask rather than demand, as "Will you wait just a moment, please?" It is also more courteous to use the person's name, as

G-201 3/56	N. Y. TEL. CO.
MEMO OF CALL	

To M r. _Keller_
M r. _Robertson_
Tel. No. _TR 9-9970_   Ext. _267_
of _Baker, Weeks Corp._

☐ Telephoned   ☑ Will call you later
☐ Please call   ☐ Called to see you
☐ In response to your call   ☐ Wishes to see you

Call Operator _____ at _____
    and ask for _____
Message: _____
_____
_____
_____
_____

Rec'd by: _RE_   Date: _6/3_   Time: _3:20 p.m._

"Yes, Mr. Jones." Slang expressions are taboo in business telephoning; be sure to avoid them. If you do not understand the speaker and must ask to have something repeated, be sure to assume the blame yourself. If you say, "I can't understand you," the caller will take it as criticism of his enunciation. But if you say, "Would you mind repeating that name? There is quite a bit of noise in this office," the caller will be free of any blame and will probably be glad to help you.

Placing a Call

You must learn how to place a telephone call for your employer. Men of importance have prerogatives that should be respected. It is a matter of business etiquette to know which person is to be kept waiting, if only for a few seconds. For example, you should get an outside man of lesser rank on the line before you call your employer, but you should get your employer on the telephone before a man of equal or greater rank is called to the telephone at his end of the line. Never place a call for your employer until you make sure he is available to take the call when it comes through.

Direct dialing. Since the advent of direct cross-country dialing, telephone numbers have changed from prefix letters and numbers to all numbers. The local telephone number will consist of three digits, then a hyphen, followed by four more digits. When dialing direct, you must first dial 1 for long distance. This is followed by the area code, such as 204. After this, you dial the seven digits of the number desired. You use direct dialing as you would party-to-party long distance calls. That is, you dial direct when you are willing to speak to anyone in the department or firm that you are calling.

Local dialing. When dialing a number in an office having a PBX, you may call out by first dialing 9. You then listen for the dial tone (a steady humming sound on the line).

The telephone number is then dialed, whether all numbers or prefix letters and numbers. If you should get a busy signal (a rapid "buzz-buzz-buzz" sound), hang up and dial again later. If you interrupt someone else's dialing on a party line, say you are sorry and hang up. If someone else interrupts your dialing on a party line, tell that party about the matter in a pleasant tone.

Telephone Judgment

You must use judgment in telephone matters. One tried-and-true statement, for example, is being dropped by many executives. So many secretaries and clerks have used the sentence, "Mr. Blank is in conference," to get rid of an unwanted caller, that the response is now suspect. Now, rather than using this sentence, you should say, "Mr. Blank is in a meeting. May he call you after 3:30?" when he is in a meeting. If your employer is away, you should give this information; but you should make the statement neutral as far as giving additional information goes. That is, you do not say, "Mr. Blank has gone to San Francisco," as this may be information that a competitor can use to his advantage. Merely say, "Mr. Blank is out of the office until next week," or some equally non-informative statement.

It is good telephone judgment to follow disappointing answers with an offer to help. If someone asks for your employer and he is away, you might say, "Mr. Blank is out of the office this week. May I connect you with Mr. Clarke? He is handling Mr. Blank's accounts until his return." If there is no other person in charge of your employer's work during his absence, you should ask if you can help.

In answering telephone calls, it is good judgment to attend to as many details as you can without calling anyone else to the telephone. Try to become conversant with as many details and policies as possible, as you will need to answer many questions. If you work in the office of a retail store, for example, you may be called upon to know at what time the last delivery leaves the store, what the sales specials of the day are, or at what time the store post office closes. The more diversified the duties of your job, the wider is the field from which you are expected to draw your information.

Remember that at your end of the line you are the agent representing the business; that your voice and manner reveal desirable or undesirable traits and attitudes; that, invisible though you may be to the person at the other end of the line, and unimportant though you may be in the organization as a whole, you are a powerful influence in business affairs when you use the telephone.

COURTESY

Courtesy is based on respect. If you respect a person, you will show this respect by treating him as you would like to be treated. You will do nothing to make his work more difficult; you will do nothing to offend his dignity or to make him lose face. Although you may not respect all people in your work, you must treat them as though you do.

You should learn the language of dignity and respect. In such language you do not use slang, profanity, angry words, or verbal attacks, even though others may occasionally use these methods in speaking to you. Do not criticize religious faiths, political parties, or personal tastes.

Always call your employer by his last name and Mr., Doctor, or some other title of respect, even though he may call you by your first name or even a nickname. The use of a last name shows respect for his position, an important factor in business. Other important factors are knowing the names of customers, clients, or callers, and receiving callers pleasantly, and determining the importance of their calls. A sense of courtesy helps you to know how to congratulate others on honors they have received, how to avoid unnecessary noises that disturb others, how to dispatch desired information when it is needed.

Simple courtesy is involved in the habit of saying, "Thank you," and "Please," "Good morning," and "Good night," to your office associates. The same habit of courtesy will help you to refrain from excessive borrowing from others, from laughing at their mistakes, from being curt or ungracious to business inferiors. A lack of courtesy is shown in slamming doors, banging the receiver of a telephone, interrupting office routine or business conversations unnecessarily, and tactlessly correcting another's mistakes. Behavior like this will soon win hearty disapproval for you, because it indicates that you lack a feeling of consideration for others.

PUNCTUALITY

Punctuality is another trait that you should cultivate, for in business, time is money. Both management and labor are paid, not only for their skill and their intellectual contributions, but also for their time. Because of this, a great deal of emphasis is placed on wise and efficient utilization of time. Such efficiency is shown by promptness as well as by industry.

If the work of only one person is delayed because you are late, the firm must consider the cost and mark it against you. Sometimes, of course, you may have a good reason for being late. When a high value is placed on time, however, you should do everything in your power to be prompt. Be on time for the day's work, be prompt in attending committee meetings or conferences, in keeping appointments, in answering the call of your superior, in answering the telephone, and in replying to letters.

If you are prompt, you will not waste time in getting settled at work when you arrive or after you have been interrupted. Neither will you take more than the allotted time for lunch or coffee breaks. You will take no more than the necessary time for smoking or caring for personal needs.

You will also avoid prolonging telephone conversations and talks with co-workers.

Where time is money, it will pay you to learn to be brief and concise in conveying ideas to others. You will learn to ask questions directly, without a preliminary introduction. If these suggestions present difficulties to you, it would be wise to consult a business communications textbook. In both written and oral communication, it will pay you to be brief and clear in what you say.

FOLLOW-UP ACTIVITIES

Dramatize the following situations. Make use of the suggestions given on the preceding pages. If it is possible to have three telephones connected on a battery, two to be used by students and the third by the teacher or another student who listens in for the purpose of offering criticism, these practice exercises will be most interesting.

Some of the following exercises require the addition of the telephone conversation of the person at the other end of the line. As such exercises will require time and careful consideration, the missing conversation should be provided in home preparation. In school you will dramatize the situations and discuss the techniques employed.

Answering Telephone Calls

The telephone rings. One student, who represents a salesman of the Brown Drug Company, answers the call. The customer is Mrs. Jones, a part played by another student.

SALESMAN. "Brown Drug Company. Mr. Walters speaking."

MRS. JONES. "This is Mrs. Jones of 202 Broad Street."

"Good morning, Mrs. Jones."

"Is Blossom soap on sale today?"

"Yes, our sale price on Blossom soap is 12 cents a bar, one dozen to a customer."

"What about Luster soap? Is it on sale?"

"No, there is no sale price on Luster soap."

"I think I'll come down to the store to decide."

"We also have other standard articles on sale. You may be interested in them."

"I'll wait until later. Thanks."

"You are welcome. Call again. Good-bye."

"Good-bye."

. . . .

The telephone rings. One student, the cashier of the Orpheum Theater, answers the call. The conversation of the inquirer is to be supplied by a second student.

CASHIER. "Good morning. Orpheum Theater."

INQUIRER. "_____."

"The feature picture is on at 3:15."

"_____."

"You're welcome. Good-bye."

"_____."

. . . .

Placing a Call on a Manual Telephone

One student is Robert Jones of the Jones & Co. Restaurant. The conversation of the person at the other end of the line is to be supplied by another student.

MR. JONES. "Seven-two-one — five-four — nine-nine."

MR. HOLMES. "_____."

"Good morning, Mr. Holmes. This is Jones of Jones & Co. Restaurant. I am calling with regard to the extra bread we ordered to be delivered at 10:00 o'clock this morning. It has not been delivered, and it is now 11:00."

"_____."

"You say it left an hour ago and should be here by now? Will you check the route, please?"

"_____."

"Thanks. We expect a rush at noon today, and we don't want to be short. Good-bye."

Placing a Long-Distance Person-to-Person Call

One student is John Evans, the bookkeeper of the Emerson Wholesale Grocery. The answering conversation of the long-distance operator is to be supplied by another student.

MR. EVANS. "Long distance, please."

LONG-DISTANCE OPERATOR.   "_____"

"I want to place a call to Mr. William Brown, cashier of the Mississippi Mercantile Company, Longview, Mississippi. I do not know the telephone number."

"_____"

"Call me at 631-7700, and charge the call to the same number.   This is the Emerson Wholesale Grocery, John Evans, bookkeeper, speaking."

"_____"

"Thank you."

(Mr. Evans should have at hand all invoices, letters, or the like that may be needed in his later conversation with Mr. Brown.)

Taking an Order over the Telephone

One student, who represents a clerk of the Home Grocery Company, answers a telephone call.   A second student, as Mrs. Williams, places an order.

CLERK.   "Good morning.   Home Grocery Company."

MRS. WILLIAMS.   "_____"

"Yes, Mrs. Williams?"

"_____"

"Peaches are a dollar a dozen.   They are very fine and large for the early crop."

"_____"

"One dozen?   Anything else?"

"_____"

"Best creamery butter is 80 cents a pound."

"_____"

"Two pounds? How about some fresh cottage cheese? We have just received today's order, and it looks very appetizing."

"_____."

"Thanks, Mrs. Williams. Your order will be delivered this morning. Call again. Good-bye."

Taking a Call for Your Employer

One student, as the stenographer, answers a telephone call. A second student is the client calling.

STENOGRAPHER. "Shore and Silver's office. Miss Whitney speaking."

CLIENT. "_____."

"Mr. Silver is very busy. Perhaps there is something that I can do?"

"_____."

"An appointment for Friday? I can arrange an appointment for Friday afternoon at 3:00 P.M."

"_____."

"Thank you very much. Good-bye."

"_____."

In case arrangements that satisfy the client cannot be made, any one of the following conversations may result:

"I am very sorry, but Mr. Silver is out for lunch now. Would you like to leave a message?"

"_____."

"Shall I call you when he returns?"

"_____."

or

"I'm sorry, but Mr. Silver is out of town for the week. This is his secretary speaking. Perhaps I can help you."

"_____."

"In that case may I call you when Mr. Silver returns to town?"

"_____."

"I am very sorry. Good-bye."

or

"I'll connect you with Mr. Silver." (To Mr. Silver the following announcement is made.) "Mr. ——— is on the telephone, Mr. Silver, and wishes to speak with you."

Answering the Telephone When the Wrong Number Has Been Called

You are a busy clerk, one of whose duties is to answer the ring of the telephone.

"You have the wrong number. This is 871-7100."

Notice that you give politely what information you can, even though you are busy.

Answering the Telephone When the Call Is for Someone in Another Office

"Miss Dobbs is not in this office, but you can reach her at 541-4348."

In a courteous manner give what information you can.

Reporting Telephone Trouble

Time must be taken to have the telephone trouble corrected. The whole matter is annoying, perhaps, but the requirements for being courteous are ever present.

"Service department, please."

"_____."

"This is 922-9100. We are having trouble hearing distinctly over this telephone. Will you please check the matter?"

"_____."

"Thank you. Goodbye."

Obtaining the Telephone Number of Someone Not Listed in the Directory

"Information, please."

"_____."

"Please give me the number of Mr. Robert L. Anderson. His address is 2516 West Main."

"_____."

"441-1977?"

"_____."

"Thank you."

Notice that the information received is checked.

Receiving a Telegraph Message Over the Telephone

"Dr. Walker's office."

"_____."

"Dr. Walker is not in, but I am his secretary and will take the message."

"_____."

"Let me read the message back to you to see if I have taken it correctly."

By giving her position, the secretary indicates her right to receive such messages as this. The accuracy of the message should be checked to avoid an error.

Making Use of the Telephone Directory

Make a list of the telephone numbers you might need in your home. Include the number of a grocery, a drugstore, a doctor, and a dentist, as well as the numbers of other businesses and persons near your home.

How do you report a fire by means of the telephone?

In case of trouble how do you notify the police by means of the telephone?

Choose a particular business, and make a list of telephone numbers that you might need if employed as a bookkeeper or clerical worker.

CASE PROBLEMS

1. The Seamy Side

Louise Ryan is the secretary to a small-town welfare association. Her work is to keep the unemployed individuals satisfied as far as possible and to try to create a feeling of goodwill between the association and those on relief. One day, when she answered the telephone, a man's voice demanded to talk to the head of the association. Louise replied that he was not in the office and asked if she could help. The man answered in a loud voice, using abusive language. Louise had never heard language like this and she put the receiver down with a bang. The telephone rang for some time, but she refused to listen again to such talk.

1. What is the correct attitude toward difficult individuals in social work situations?
2. Was Louise behaving in an objective manner?
3. Why do you think Louise acted as she did?
4. What might Louise have done that would have served the association in a better way?

2. The Customer is Always Right

Louis Johnson works in the office of the sales department of a coffee company. He keeps the records of the men who are on the city routes. His books show the supplies the salesmen take out of stock and their returns in cash and merchandise. Louis is exceptionally efficient. If there is a mistake in the record of a route man, Louis always catches it; if there is an argument about reports, Louis can offer the needed facts to eliminate further talk. Louis does have one fault; he has not developed a courteous telephone technique. The manager has had a number of complaints from customers who are annoyed at the way Louis handles situations over the telephone. Typical of Louis' conversations:

> An irate customer says, "But I told the salesman I wanted a light roast and he left a package of dark roast." Louis answers, "Why don't you give the dark roast a try? It's one of our best sellers."
>
> A dissatisfied customer says, "I just received my bill and you have charged me $10.16 for Saturday, November 18. I did not place or receive an order on that date." Louis says, "You must be mistaken. The bills are checked most carefully before we send them out."
>
> An angry customer says, "I asked that my orders be delivered on Saturday morning, and this is the third time it has been sent out on Monday." Louis says, "This is the first time I have heard about it. Are you sure you told the deliveryman?"

When the office manager speaks to Louis about the complaints he has received, Louis defends himself vigorously. He knows he is right; he says he is positive the customers are mistaken. The next time the office manager has to come to the rescue to keep a battle from developing he resolves to tell Louis what he should have said in each of the above cases. Assuming that you are the office manager, how would you have answered each of the three customers?

1. Why does Louis talk as he does? Do you think he may be covering up a lack of confidence?
2. What personal techniques should Louis develop in addition to keeping records?

3. No Personal Calls

Ruth McDonald is busy with her work when she receives a personal telephone call from her friend, Harriet. Harriet wants to find out about a weekend trip that is being planned. Harriet is working at her first job; Ruth knows she does not realize that the office is no place for personal calls. Ruth doesn't want to hurt Harriet's feelings, so she tries to be tactful. Finally, she says, "Harriet, I must go now. Mr. Maxwell is buzzing me. See you Friday."

1. Do you think Harriet was made aware that she should not call Ruth during office hours?
2. Should Ruth have been more honest with Harriet so she would understand how to behave in the future?
3. Can you think of a tactful way that Ruth could have informed Harriet of the general rule regarding personal telephone calls during business hours?

Chapter 9

Conversation: The Game of Talking With Others

If you were to survey 1,000 people to find out what they considered their greatest social difficulty, you would find most of them expressing a fear of conversation. Why is this such a problem? Most of us have no trouble talking with close friends or with members of our family. The difficulty arises when we must talk with those we know slightly, or perhaps not at all. You may be fearful, ill at ease, afraid you will be judged by what you say. How can we overcome fear of conversation?

Actually, the secret of success in conversation is one that has been mentioned before — just being yourself. Part of the strain that causes feelings of uneasiness stems from trying to impress others with a false personality. But if we pretend to be what we are not, we must be constantly on guard. The other person can feel this guardedness. To him, however, it is a defense against him. He judges our attitude as an attack against some weakness in himself of which he is aware. He may defend himself with similar pretenses. This vicious circle can produce nothing but disaster.

WHY WE NEED CONVERSATIONAL SKILL

You have already learned that the human element is the most important one in business. If you can get along successfully with others, you will have many of the qualities you need for success. Most of "getting along with others" involves conversation. You must ask others to do things for you; you must express appreciation for a kindness; you must persuade a sales prospect; you must put your customer or caller at ease. All of this involves conversation. The importance of the ability to establish friendly relations with others cannot be overemphasized. Much of your success and happiness will depend on it. Some of the specific areas in your business life where conversational skill will help you are discussed in this chapter.

Improving Personal Relations

You will improve your relations with others if you improve your conversational skills. The secret lies in making your listener feel important. If you talk about yourself and your own accomplishments, you will be considered a bore and a braggart. If you talk sincerely about the accomplishments of your listener, you will have a fascinated audience. Everyone is interested in himself; no one feels he is properly appreciated. For example, the story is told of a man who picked ten names at random from the telephone directory and sent them telegrams with a one-word message, "Congratulations." He signed his name and address to the wire and awaited results. Nine of the ten individuals wrote him warm letters of thanks. All of them stated they had not been aware that anyone knew of their recent accomplishments. Only one person wrote to ask, "Congratulations for what?"

Getting and Giving Information

Another way conversational skill can aid you is in giving and getting information. The teacher, the supervisor, the foreman, and the head clerk must have the ability to talk conversationally to those whom they wish to instruct. Getting information is involved here, too; it is a two-way process. If you can ask pertinent questions, if you can show with a nod or a smile that you understand, you will be using your conversational gifts to advantage. Knowledge can be pursued in several ways, you see. Some get their knowledge from books; some go on to higher and higher levels of education; but one of the most effective ways to learn is by listening to those who know. Intelligent conversation can bring you the twin rewards of interest and information.

Getting Things Done

Conversation is also an aid to getting work done. If you can write conversationally, you will be able to persuade through letters. If you can lecture conversationally, you will be able to get large groups to do your bidding. If you can talk to your staff conversationally, they will be more likely to follow your suggestions. A good conversationalist has a friendly interest in others. This interest is contagious. If you can express it, you will be more likely to receive it in return.

"TEN EASY LESSONS" IN CONVERSATION

It is all very well to say you should be able to converse with others with ease. But such a statement is certain to bring the question "How?" The following paragraphs will tell you how; after that, you need only practice.

1. You Must Like People

If you don't like people in general, this will be your first task. It is helpful if you realize that *everyone* is insecure to some degree. So if you feel insecure about liking others, you are not the only one who feels as you do. One of the best ways of starting on your "people-liking" campaign is to act "as if" you did. You will be surprised at the reaction of others. You may even begin to like them!

2. Don't Talk Too Fast

Good conversation should be relaxing, so if you talk too fast, you will find your feeling of tenseness spreading to your listeners. A good way to slow your speaking tempo down is by frequent pauses. Don't be afraid of silence. Constant chatter can be extremely wearing, and an occasional pause will point up what is said afterward. Clear enunciation is important. If you speak with a relaxed manner and with clear enunciation, you will find others listening to you. Your words will take on a new importance from your method of delivery.

3. Learn To Listen

One of the hardest lessons to learn is that of listening, but it is one of the most important. If you will think of your conversational group as a basketball team, for example, it may help you see the necessity of giving each player a chance at the basket. Throw the conversational ball to others; listen with concentration; show your interest in your face. Learning this one lesson well can make others think you are a gifted conversationalist. You won't need to say much yourself if you can make the conversation of others seem more important. A good listener must keep out all feelings of criticism, too. If you think, "This fellow is stupid," you may show it in your manner and thus defeat all you have been trying to accomplish.

4. Avoid Flat Negatives

If you want to become extremely unpopular, all you need to do is speak out flatly for the viewpoint opposite to that expressed. When you contradict the speaker, you are guilty of being rude. Even more unpleasant, however, you will usually stop the conversation dead. A mild response is much more effective, even if the speaker has made a foolish remark. "Do you really think so?" may sound spineless to you in such circumstances, but it is better conversational tactics than a flat contradiction. You should eliminate all feelings of competitiveness in conversation. There is no winner or loser; there should be, instead, a feeling of friendliness in a group who are talking together.

5. Don't Be Backward

If you are excessively shy, you may worry about yourself; yet you may never have considered the effect of your shyness on others. For the "backward" conversationalist makes the others feel too forward. By fading into the background, you create an unnatural atmosphere that makes normal talkativeness seem excessive. Another difficulty with being overly shy is the tendency to appear cold and unfeeling to others. This makes people uncomfortable in your presence. You can see that shyness, which may appear to you to be based on feelings of inferiority, will impress others as being based on selfcenteredness. It is much better for you, and for the group in which you find yourself, to make an effort to be interested in others. If you start with showing interest in what others say, it won't be long before you will be able to say something now and then.

6. Don't Hold Center Stage Too Long

If you tell a story, make it short. If you explain the way you think about something, hit the highlights only, leaving out the details. You must do this in order to leave space for others to talk, too. If you monopolize the conversation more than a moment or two, you will seem to be seeking the spotlight. This should be avoided, especially by the beginner in the game of conversation.

7. Watch Your Eye Contact

A very important part of talking in a group is looking at all of the members of the group. This makes them feel included; again, it builds up the other person. If you look at just one person as you speak, the others will feel excluded. It is hard to tear your eyes away from someone who seems to be responding to you; but if you are to converse well, you must make the effort to do so. Try looking first to your left, then to your right, and then straight ahead. As you look in each direction, focus your eyes on some feature of one of the persons in that area. It *is* hard to look listeners directly in the eye; but you can fake this look, and no one will be any the wiser, so long as you look at the person's face.

8. Keep Your Statements Positive

When you first start playing the game of conversation, you should avoid unpleasant topics, criticism of others, sarcasm, and pessimism. In fact, it would be a good idea to avoid them entirely. It is especially important, however, for the beginner to refrain from derogatory remarks. In the first place, few people admire the person who makes them. In the second place, they destroy the spirit of comradeship that is built up by good conversation.

9. Make Yourself Talk

The conversational beginner may have some trouble getting started. It is a good idea, therefore, to have some plan ready before you begin. You may decide to compliment one of the speakers; this is always a good approach. Just saying, "How interesting. I had never thought of that," is really praise of the other person's remarks. Or you can say, "Do you really think this will happen?" This is complimentary to the person speaking because it shows you are thinking about what he has said. Another opener for the beginner is a question. The speaker is always glad to have a question because this gives him a chance to talk to a definite point. If someone has been talking about his painting hobby, for example, you might ask, "How long did it take you to learn the technique of oil painting?" A question is another sincere form of flattery. It is an easy way, too, to get started.

10. Avoid Laying Down the Law

A good conversationalist keeps a tolerant attitude. If you preach, if you hand down judgments, you will not be listened to with pleasure. The secret is to keep an open mind. A conversation should be a free exchange of ideas. No one person should try to dominate it. Avoid, then, giving the final word on any subject. This will permit another person in the group to add what he thinks. This is one way of keeping the conversational ball rolling.

WHAT TO SAY WHEN

Many of us have no difficulty carrying on a conversation after it has been started, but we do have trouble starting it. Is there any rule to help get that first minute of conversation under way? Think for a moment of the most common subject of casual conversation: the weather. Why do strangers who must say something to each other resort to, "Is it hot enough for you?" The reason is that, banal though such a remark may be, the other person is certain to have something to say on the subject. When starting a conversation, then, it is best to begin with something about which everyone has an opinion.

When you use a question as a conversation starter, be careful to choose one that cannot be answered by a flat *yes* or *no*. Instead of the question asked in the previous paragraph, which would be almost sure to be answered, "Yes," you might say, "How long has it been since we had a good rainstorm?" This is no more sparkling than the previous question, but it does require some thought and a more or less complete sentence in reply. Asking a question that requires a statement in answer will keep the conversation going for a time, at least.

Some questions should be avoided. These include personal questions, particularly those involving health and money. If you are in doubt as to whether a question is too personal, put yourself in the other person's shoes. Would you like someone to ask you why you are limping? Would you like someone to ask how much you paid for the suit you are wearing, or how much your car cost? It is also wise, when starting a conversation, to avoid emotionally tinged subjects, such as religion and politics.

Talking With Your Superiors

One skill you must develop is the ability to talk with your superiors. This need not be difficult, once you have learned the art of general conversation; but there are specific suggestions that apply when the conversation is between the employer and the employee.

First of all, you should be respectful. This does not mean that you should be completely self-effacing. You should keep your own self respect, too. You should try to be relaxed because your superior does not want his staff to be tense when he is speaking to them. Your replies to questions, however, should be prompt and to the point; and you should keep to the topic under discussion. In most cases, it is better to let the superior lead the conversation; and you should listen more than you talk. In fact, being attentive is of great importance in conversations you have with your superiors.

Talking With Your Workers

When you become the person in charge, such as the foreman, the supervisor, or the chief clerk, your role is reversed. Now it is important that you put your staff member at ease. Putting others at their ease must not break down the barriers between you, however. There is a fine line between being domineering and being too familiar. This is the line you must walk. You should be courteous but dignified. One rule that is always helpful is to praise your workers when they have done good work, but you should never let your workers overstep the bounds of good taste.

Creative Listening

If you are an attentive listener, you will contribute a great deal to the conversation. In business it is particularly important that you develop the skill of creative listening. First of all, you should watch the person who is talking; there is much to be learned from his expression. If you mentally put yourself in the place of the speaker, you will gain even more because you will know how he feels.

The second part of creative listening is to organize in your mind what the speaker is saying. If you are being told something that you are to do, it is better if you can take notes. If this is impossible at the moment, however, you can gain considerably from mentally putting the important statements made by the speaker in logical order.

The third factor is interest. You should show that you are interested in what is being told you. An alert expression will follow suit if you *are* alert. This expression will tell your speaker more than words could tell him. If you are interested, however, you will also want to say something to further the statements that are being made. Such responses as, "I see," "That's a good suggestion," and "I'll get right at it," will help the speaker and also help you. In all aspects of conversation, whether of speaking or listening, success depends on cooperation.

FOLLOW-UP ACTIVITIES

1. Conversation can be changed by associating what has been said. Suppose you were in a conversation with several co-workers at a coffee break. Someone has just said he can't stand Mr. McFarland, the supervisor. Realizing this is not the kind of talk that should continue, you decide to change the conversation. What would you say? How would you include the previous speaker so he would not be offended?

2. You have been asked to show a new clerk around the office. As you start back to your floor, you have an opportunity for conversation. You know the new worker is keenly interested in bowling. How would you start a conversation on this subject?

3. You have a friend who is extremely interested in current politics. In order to converse with him, go over one of the news magazines for this week. Choose five topics that might interest your friend and learn something about each topic.

4. Humorous stories, particularly if they are brief, add interest and emphasize certain points of view in conversation. Go through some of the latest magazines and collect five stories that you could use in ordinary business conversation.

5. The next time you are talking with a friend, try this experiment: See if you can remain silent exactly half the time. When your friend is talking, you may need to spur him on with such remarks as, "And then what happened?" See if you are talking too much or too little as a general rule.

6. The way to avoid arguments is to *relax* and wait for the whole story. The next time you are tempted to argue with someone say nothing. Just wait and listen. Write down the result of your experience. Did you accomplish anything? Do you feel this is a helpful solution for you?

7. Choose someone in your place of business who seems aloof and with whom you do not ordinarily talk. Then deliberately start a conversation with him or her. What opening remark did you use? How did the conversation go? If your opening statement was not successful, can you see why? What other statements do you think might have been better?

8. Bring a quiet person into the conversation at your first opportunity. What method will you use? What sort of thing must you avoid?

9. Assume that someone is especially argumentative with you. Resolve to avoid argument by saying one of the following: "Oh?" ... "Is that so?" (Be sure to sound interested.) Put this plan to the test and report your experience. Were you able to escape an argument?

10. Make a list of three men and three women whom you like very much. After each name, write five traits they possess that make them likeable individuals. Does this give you any ideas about your own trait development?

CASE PROBLEMS

1. Shyness is Selfcenteredness

Edmund Holmes, a young bookkeeper from a small midwestern town, has found no friends in the office in the city where he is employed. He has been away from home for three years, but he is still homesick. He is very lonely and does not know whether to stay in the city or go back to his hometown. It seems to him that everyone in the office shuns him; they have never asked him to join in any group activities.

1. Is it possible that Edmund is to blame for the attitude of the others toward him?
2. Assume that Edmund has talked to you about his problem. What would you advise him to do in order to break out of his shell? Be as specific as you can.

2. Keeping Distance

Irene Mears has worked for the ABC Company for five years and has just been promoted to office manager. Jane Harrison has been working in the same office for just two weeks. Her job is in the stenographic pool. Jane and Irene were in high school together. At noon on the first day after Irene had accepted her new job, Jane asked Irene to go to lunch as her guest to celebrate the promotion.

1. If you were Irene, what would you say to Jane?
2. What would be the best attitude for Jane to assume toward Irene in the future?
3. What would be the effect on the office force if Irene were to accept the invitation?
4. What attitude should Irene have toward all her former co-workers — and Jane?

3. A Spoil Sport

The salesgirls in a small store decide to have a party on Friday night. One of the girls says that she cannot attend because she is a Seventh Day Adventist and her beliefs do not sanction a party on a Friday night. One of the others says, "Oh, for heaven's sake, what difference will it make? Don't be a spoil sport." Another says, "It isn't really necessary that we have it on Friday, is it? Why can't we have the party on Thursday just as well?" Most of the girls agree, but the first speaker says she thinks it is absurd to have to change their plans.

1. What rules of conversation have been broken in the above exchange?
2. If one person has strong convictions and the others do not, what should be the attitude of the group?
3. What would you do in a similar situation? Would you stand up for your principles or go the way of the majority?
4. What attitude would you take if you were one of the majority in this situation?

PART 4 PSYCHOLOGY AND BUSINESS BEHAVIOR

Chapter 10

Business Psychology in Selling

Why do people behave as they do? In other words, why do people act like people? Many laymen believe they know. They have watched television shows; they have read popular articles; they can tell you all about inferiority complexes, overcompensation, and so on. Most psychologists, however, believe they are still learning about people. They dislike giving the impression that human nature is an open book. Still, research continues at an ever-increasing rate, and more and more of the complexities of people are being understood. We do know some of the factors causing behavior. Some of them are conditioning, or building up habitual responses to certain words, rules, and other stimuli; illnesses, particularly those affecting the nervous system; conflicts, both conscious and unconscious; and the pressures exerted by the different groups that are active in a person's life.

Such knowledge of psychology is helpful in understanding ourselves and others. A beginner in business is making a wise choice when he enrolls in courses in psychology. Although a discussion of general psychology is beyond the scope of this book, some psychological principles and traits that are particularly useful in business will be mentioned.

PRINCIPLES AND TECHNIQUES

A psychological principle is a generalized statement that is reached through research and reflective thinking. One such principle states that people are motivated, or persuaded by themselves or others, to a greater extent when they have a positive feeling toward the action in question. In other words, we do the things we like to do or for the person we like more frequently than when we dislike the activity or the person. A technique is a small part of an activity; it may be in line with a certain principle. If we wish to succeed in business, we will develop good psychological techniques.

Techniques in Selling

You have been using techniques in your work and in your play all through your life. You have learned that some techniques are effective and that some are not. At the age of three or four, you may have tried the technique of lying on the floor and screaming to get your own way. You may have discovered, too, that this didn't work too well at nine or ten. In this same way, you may have tried and discarded many techniques of behavior. If you should decide to try for a career in selling, you should sharpen up some techniques you now use and perhaps become familiar with some entirely new ones.

Develop a friendly attitude. A friendly personality is an asset anywhere, but in sales work a friendly attitude is essential. If you were born with a liking for people, you should do well in selling. If strangers make you hide in your shell, don't give up. Some of the greatest salesmen of all time achieved their status through long, hard hours of working and improving. The technique of courtesy is a good place to begin working on creating a friendly personality. Sometimes it is easier to learn a form, a technique of manners, than it is to *feel* friendly. Memorizing rules like standing when a woman enters a room (applying to men) or when an older woman enters (applying to both men and women) is not difficult. After you have followed the rules for awhile, you will actually *feel* more friendly.

The following illustrates how a friendly attitude pays. One afternoon when the weather was dark and gloomy and business was bad, a drab little woman, modestly dressed, came into a furniture store. One of the older salesmen said, "Don't spend any time with her. She'll look and look and

The successful salesman
is friendly.

Ewing Galloway

never buy anything." But one of the younger salesmen stepped forward with a friendly greeting. He showed the woman furniture for the rest of the afternoon. Then, as the older salesman had predicted, she left without buying anything. A few weeks later, however, the young man was pleased and surprised when he was asked to help decorate the new mansion of the Andrew Carnegies. The woman whom the salesman had helped so patiently was Mrs. Andrew Carnegie.

Know your merchandise. The young man in the foregoing story had a second valuable technique. He knew his merchandise and could show it intelligently. If you are to persuade, you must be able to inspire confidence. You will inspire confidence in others if you have confidence in yourself. To develop self-confidence you must build it on a solid foundation of knowledge. Learn everything you can about the merchandise you sell. If you are working in a dress department, you can build assurance by studying the fashion magazines. If you are selling sporting goods, how much more effective you will be if you read the sports news and sports magazines.

Be enthusiastic about your merchandise. Enthusiasm is contagious. Know the "talking points" of everything you sell. The ability to answer objections, to supply necessary details, to give information — and all with the point of view of the customer's needs — is a skill required by those who would succeed in the career of selling.

Help your customer feel important. An important technique in selling is learning how to play second fiddle. This may seem an odd way to make a sale, yet it is an effective one. Your customer is the one who must be built up. His self-esteem should grow during the selling conversation. If you watch successful salespeople, you will notice their easy, relaxed manner. This manner sets the stage; it provides the kind of atmosphere needed in selling. If this atmosphere is friendly, if the customer feels important, and if the salesman can explain the product and answer questions intelligently and courteously, the customer will feel free to choose but will be more likely to choose in favor of the salesman. If the atmosphere is friendly, the salesperson will present facts in a non-argumentative style; yet he will still be able to meet objections accurately and honestly.

The biggest reason for making the customer feel important is the help it will give you when you deal with the "difficult" customer. Most customers, of course, will be pleasant and courteous; but many, in the frenzied rush that accompanies shopping, show dispositions that require the use of tact to insure smooth going. It takes practice to serve those who are irritable, inconsiderate, talkative, or snobbish. It requires skill to satisfy the suspicious type of buyer or the close buyer. It calls for patience to deal with the "smart-aleck" customer. It may take pressure to close a sale for a timid buyer. Yet all these tasks will be easier if you have given the customer a feeling of importance and worth.

Study the art of selling. How can you best learn the art of judging people? Formulas may be learned, but their success in your case will depend on you — on your own personality — and on the effect of your personality on the customer. If you have the native qualities this work demands, a friendly spirit, an innate enthusiasm, a charm of manner, an attractive appearance, a quick intelligence, you should by all means take courses that will prepare you for selling.

No matter how much you learn in school, however, you will find that selling requires that you learn from experience. In your grandfather's day they called it learning from the "school of hard knocks." But, whatever you call it, experience will help you learn what to do and what not to do by trial and error. Eventually, you will discover the traits and attitudes that are so vital in dealing with the public.

TRAIT TRAINING

Some of the traits you will need in dealing with others are adaptability, cooperation, generosity, initiative, and honesty. If you were to analyze these traits, you would find they all have a common denominator: other-centeredness, or the tendency to be more interested in others than in yourself.

Adaptability

You are adaptable when you are able to adjust, to alter, to fit into or respond to changing conditions. Any kind of work in business requires this trait, but it is particularly needed in selling. Your first adaptation must be to your firm. You may have worn sports clothes most of your life, yet you must change willingly to tailored suits and even hats if your firm wishes it. You will adapt yourself, too, to your merchandise and develop an enthusiastic appreciation for what you have to sell.

Second, you will adapt yourself to your customer. You may be quick and alert in everything you do or say; yet you must talk slowly and adjust to long pauses if you wish to sell to someone who thinks, speaks, and reacts slowly. You will be tolerant of mistaken ideas, and you will refrain from criticism. One adjustment you will be sure to find necessary is that of talking and dealing with people much older than you. If you treat older customers with courtesy and respect, you will be successful.

A third adjustment must be made to changes in the business world. You will serve your firm best if you are constantly alert to changing routines, to changing conditions of the times, to the growth and progress of your business. Even the moods of your customers and the weather conditions may require that you demonstrate your ability to adjust. If you are set in your ways, if you cling obstinately to procedures and methods of the past, you will have failed to develop and practice adaptability. Furthermore, you will be less effective in serving your firm.

Cooperation

In this age of competition the ability to cooperate, or work smoothly with others, is in danger of becoming a lost art. But cooperation is like a bank account. It is an investment that may not pay immediate dividends. Yet, if deposits are made, the dividends will eventually become both frequent and of a high rate. Like a bank account, too, cooperation may demand the sacrifice of immediate conveniences for later reward.

You must earn the reputation for cooperation. You will earn it by thinking, not of your immediate comfort, but of the ultimate welfare of your firm and your customer. Cooperation is actually an expression of self-interest and unselfishness. It demands that you adjust your immediate pleasure to the best interests of others. Yet the reward for immediate sacrifices is a reputation for cooperation which will contribute to your success.

Cooperation may be a simple little act of sharing your materials or equipment with a co-worker. It may mean covering the territory of another salesman who is unable to do it himself. It may mean willingness to go out of your way to help a customer or co-worker. It may mean holding your tongue when you want to disagree, being a good sport when you have lost a sale, or showing tolerance in listening to the ideas of others when your own ideas seem superior.

If you are cooperative, you can still express your ideas; you should still make suggestions when you feel they should be made. You must use your good judgment in deciding when you should speak and when you should keep silent. In some cases you should protest, but you should also listen to the ideas of your superiors and your customers. If a decision is made and your ideas have been overruled, you must abide by the decision in a cheerful manner. There are times when a frank discussion may be required, but there are also times for cooperative submission to your firm or your customer.

Sometimes you may have to ask a subordinate employee to assume some of your responsibilities, but you should never take advantage of another or shirk your own work. When you do ask for help, you should speak well of the person who helps you. If you are cooperative, you will not place another worker at a disadvantage by calling attention to his faults or errors unless you are his superior and your work requires you to be critical. Even if such criticism is part of your work, you will show more cooperation if you point out inefficiencies in an impersonal way.

Teamwork in a business is founded on cooperation. Unless every member of the force practices it, there is a lack of unity of purpose; and the final results are likely to be ruinous. As a beginning worker, you will first cooperate by being loyal to the business that employs you. You will demonstrate your loyalty by following the suggestions and directions of your supervisor willingly and enthusiastically. You will abide by their decisions because they are made with the welfare of the entire organization in mind.

In every minute of your business life you will find an occasion when you are expected to cooperate. These occasions include keeping your office and belongings neat and tidy, assuming additional duties and assignments without complaint, and so forth. They include working overtime when there is a need and offering your services even when you are not obligated to do so. You will surrender your own ideas if they do not fit in with the policy of the organization. You will tell others of devices that may help them, showing unselfishness of action whenever you can. You will pass on your ideas and the results of your own experiences; you will listen when another tries to help you by giving his ideas and the results of his experiences. You will work harmoniously with others to advance the interests of the organization.

Another way of cooperating is by being on time for appointments. This shows your customer that you respect his time and his interests. You should also observe cheerfully all of the rules of the firm and work cheerfully with the fellow employee who has been promoted. You will go out of your way to help those who have not yet adjusted to their work. Keeping your reports up to date and turning them in on time is one way of cooperating greatly appreciated by sales managers.

Cooperate in maintaining good human relations. Do not criticize the business that employs you, your superiors, or your co-workers. If you possess business information that should be kept secret, you will not divulge it. You will never pass the buck when things go wrong, nor will you try to "get by" when heavy assignments are made. You will show consideration for others by feeling no resentment when you are called on to do extra work caused by the error of another worker. But you will try not to create extra work because of your own errors. You can see that the trait of cooperation covers a lot of territory.

Generosity

Generosity is defined as liberality in spirit or act. It is as necessary a trait in the business world as it is in life generally.   Business is not mechanized to the extent of excluding the personal element. On the contrary, business affairs are directed and influenced by the individual personalities of workers and superiors. As with the trait of cooperation, you will find many opportunities for showing a generous, unselfish spirit. When you acknowledge the ability of others, when you help other workers, when you help a new employee, when you lend your personal possessions to aid the work of another, or when you share office equipment, you will be demonstrating the trait of generosity.

Generosity is shown when you contribute willingly to worthy organizations endorsed by your business. You will add your mite to a joint office gift, not just for conformity's sake, but because of your unselfish desire to give. You will give a customer all the time and the attention he requires. You will give other employees the gift of being pleasant, one of the most welcome you have in your power to give.

Generosity is best shown by overlooking the shortcomings of others and by praising others when praise is merited. Do not begrudge the time you give to your job; you are investing with the hope of future returns, but this thought should not be uppermost in your mind. You will show the trait of generosity when you refuse to listen to ridicule or gossip regarding your employer or your fellow workers. In the first place, this is a dangerous pastime. Repeated gossip (and it is sure to be repeated) will react most unfavorably against you. In the second place, gossip is unkind, ungenerous, and unworthy of the *best you.*

Initiative

Initiative means the energy or aptitude displayed in the action that tends to develop new fields; self-reliance; originality; enterprise; resourcefulness. You can hardly read such a definition without thinking of the selling field. The successful salesperson *must* have initiative. He must think of new methods of reaching his customers; he must sometimes seek out new customers; he must stress the new features of his merchandise. Initiative is a central trait in selling, but it is useful in all business jobs. When you are a beginner in an office, you do not find many important situations calling for the use of initiative. The first job calls for following orders implicitly, doing what you are told to do without question. In time, though, you will grow through experience and practice. You will then be given larger responsibilities and demands that call for independent thinking and action.

When to use initiative, as well as how much to use, calls for the use of your own good judgment. Again, put yourself in your employer's place. If you were he, how would you like your employee to proceed? The new salesman should not rearrange displays so they will look more attractive. This is showing too much initiative. On the other hand, failure to act in a crisis when there appears to be no precedent may be even worse. For instance, if a customer is upset because he received different merchandise than he ordered, the salesman or other employee should certainly show he is concerned. He should say that something will be done about the situation whether he had been previously instructed to do so or not.

You will be showing initiative by learning all you can about the business and your place in it. Initiative is also shown when you find additional tasks to do when your assigned work is finished, by taking courses to prepare yourself for promotion, and by going ahead with work that must be done even though it has not been definitely assigned to you. Initiative is displayed also by learning how to think and act swiftly in emergencies, by doing more than you are told to do. If new and unusual situations arise, aside from your regular routine, you should handle them.

You will show initiative if you are able to take another employee's place without detailed instruction. You should be able to apply information received in one situation to a similar situation. You will plan and carry out new duties with a minimum of help from others.   You will attempt constructive creative work.

Learn to handle all telephone calls adeptly and to arrange conferences to the satisfaction of both or all persons concerned.   Experience will enable you to determine whether your employer should be called at his home or at his club if an important customer appears unexpectedly.

If you are alert, original, and determined to see opportunity and to make the most of it, you will learn to take advantage of situations by a display of initiative.   The person who is enthusiastic about putting new ideas into effect does not say, "It can't be done."   Nor does he bother superior officers with trifling matters or wait to be told what to do.   Nor will he need to have work laid out for him or to be told repeatedly how to perform a task.   Do not let new and unfamiliar situations upset you.   Through the use of initiative, let them be stepping-stones to greater efficiency.

Honesty

Honesty means straightforwardness and fairness of conduct and speech; it means integrity and truthfulness. Honesty is a trait you must have if you are to succeed in business.   In selling, for example, you must be trustworthy; your total selling situation demands that you be believed. Business and personal friends will usually give you a second chance if you fail in most qualities; they are most unwilling to do this after you have proved to be dishonest.

Business men and women are expected to keep their word. When you make a promise, it must be fulfilled.   If you make an error, you must accept the responsibility.   Because you are honest, you will never shift the blame for your errors on an innocent person; neither will you accept credit or praise for something you have not done.   Instead, you will indicate the person who should receive the credit.

When you are called upon to state your opinions, you should do so frankly and honestly.   You need not go out of your way to be tactless, to give opinions you know are painful to your listener, especially on controversial subjects like politics or religion. If you are asked, reply correctly and honestly, but apologize quietly if another's statement is being contradicted. If you should be questioned about another's dishonesty, you must give honest testimony. In the matter of expense accounts, handling money, and keeping records, show by your honesty that you are worthy of responsibility. You must work an honest day for a day's pay. Your working hours do not belong to you. Give your best to your job, not just your share.

It is disturbing to have to speak against someone, but when questions of fact are referred to you, do not try to deceive by understatement, by exaggeration, or by omission. You should never lie to avoid an unpleasant situation; neither should you try to smooth things over with half truths. Do not misappropriate funds by direct theft, by petty trickery, or with the intention of paying the money back. Honesty means you will never steal time, money, office materials, or another's ideas.

FOLLOW-UP ACTIVITIES

1. If you are selling shirts, you suggest the purchase of matching ties to your customer. If you are selling shoes, you suggest hosiery. What suggestions would you offer to customers who purchased:

   gloves   a toothbrush   a bar of soap   a sweater

2. How would you spend your time while waiting for customers:

   in a dress shop   in a bookstore   in a drugstore

3. In order to get along with all sorts of customers, you will need intelligence and tact. What would you say:

   (a) To an angry customer who says, "I thought you said this material was silk. It's marked synthetic blend." (You had made a careless mistake in stating facts.)

(b) To a trying customer to whom you have shown the entire stock. She finally says, "I want to see the model on display in size 42." (It has an accordion pleated skirt and would be most unbecoming on the short, stout lady.)

(c) To a customer who runs a large account who says, "I've worn these gloves only once, and look at the seams!" (You know that it took more than one wearing to get the gloves that color!)

4. What will determine your selection when the customer says, "I want to see a hat"?

5. What qualifications do you possess that you think will be needed in a selling position?

6. What disagreeable personality traits may cause a salesperson's discharge? Have you ever shown any evidences of possessing any of these traits?

PRACTICE EXERCISES

Dramatize situations that provide opportunity to develop habits and traits that are acceptable in the sales field.

A Good Approach (With a Smile)

"Is there anything I may show you?"

"You are interested in the latest models?"

"Are you interested in shoes today?"

"Good morning, Mr. Jones. May I serve you?"

"Would you like to look at these purses?"

If the customer is looking at the purses, you might say, "Black suede is being used this fall."

Many stores suggest phrases that the employees use for greetings. Do you know examples of such phrases?

Some stores permit the customers to look over what stock is in sight and then to make the first move in asking to be served. If the customer speaks first and asks for a certain article, your task is simple. Willingly and immediately, you show your desire to serve. "Certainly," you say, "I'll get it from the stock room (or wherever else the article is kept) immediately."

If you should be employed as a salesperson, find out what custom is in effect in the store in which you are employed.

To a Waiting Customer When You Are Busy with Another Customer

"There will be a salesman here to wait on you in a moment."

If the Article Is Not in Stock

"We do not carry that article, but let me show you what we have."

Making Positive Suggestions to the Customer

"Isn't this a practical style for general utility?"

"Isn't the quality excellent?"

"Prints are new this spring."

"These are the shoes shown in *Fashion* this month."

"This fabric holds a press very well."

Closing a Sale

"As we have only this one model left, you should not hesitate."

"The style is becoming; the quality is excellent; the value is good. You should buy this coat."

Following Up a Sale

"I hope you will like your new dress. Come in next week. The new fall coats will be in then."

To a wealthy customer: "I hope you enjoy your gown."

To a practical customer: "I'm sure you will find this coat satisfactory. The material wears well."

The pleasant way to close a sale is to say simply, "Thank you."

If No Sale Can Be Made

"If you will wait until next Tuesday, we are expecting a new shipment of fall coats at the beginning of the week."

"I am sorry. We are out of your size. If you wish, I shall order it for you."

If Merchandise Is Returned

"I'm sorry the robe did not fit. We received some new styles this morning. Would you like to see them?"

"I'm sorry you received a defective pair of shoes. I'll call the manager. He will approve your exchange."

Handling the Disagreeable Customer

After you have shown such a customer all the stock of a particular article, she may say, "Haven't you anything else, something better than what you've shown me?"

You reply, "I've really shown you the best we have. If you don't succeed in finding what you want elsewhere, won't you consider this very excellent style and come back?"

Filling In a Sales Slip

Get sample sales slips from local merchants, and fill them in correctly with such information as the date, the quantities, the descriptions of the articles, the prices and amounts, the amount received, the department number or name, and your designation.

If the sale is a charge sale, fill in the name and the address of the purchaser. Ask "Miss or Mrs?" if you do not know which title to use.

Plan definitely through some association of ideas — name and face or name and related incident — to remember the names of regular customers. Good salesmen remember facts of importance. You can train yourself to remember such facts, too.

CASE PROBLEMS

1. Job vs. Career

Betty Lawrence is a salesclerk in a dress department. All the sales force in the store is paid a weekly salary. No bonus is paid for the amount of goods sold.

Betty is very industrious and is usually the first to greet a customer. After serving her customers, Betty returns the dresses to their racks. She then keeps busy arranging merchandise or studying dresses that have been recently put in stock. She is always pleasant and courteous.

Ann Clinton, who works with her, tells Betty she is foolish to work so hard when she receives no extra pay. Betty knows that Ann's attitude is characteristic of the feeling of many of the members of the sales force.

1. Is it profitable for Betty to work as she does?
2. Do you feel that Betty may be rewarded for her work attitudes?
3. If Betty does not receive a promotion, can you think of any advantages her attitude would have?
4. Why do you think the other clerks feel as they do about their work?
5. If you were in charge of Betty's department, how would you handle this situation of indifference on the part of some of the sales personnel?

2. Is the Customer Always Right?

An irate customer enters a shop with a dress that she has purchased from a salesgirl who said the dress would not fade or shrink when washed. The customer has the dress and it is badly faded. The customer proceeds to vent all her anger on Irene Carpenter, who is taking the other girl's place that day.

1. Is this situation a common happening?
2. If you were Irene, what would you say to the customer? Would you try to handle the situation yourself? Why or why not?
3. Was the customer justified in her complaint?
4. If you had been the customer, how would you have handled this situation?

3. Hard, Not Heartless

Doris Cunningham is feeling low. She has been at work only a week, and today Mr. Johnson, the floorwalker, spoke to her sharply because she spent half an hour showing dresses to a fussy customer who walked out without making a purchase. Doris is hanging the dresses back on the racks and trying very hard not to show how dark her world has grown because she knows the store is no place for the display of emotions. Mrs. Walton, looking across the store, notices Doris and remembers how she felt the first time she had been reprimanded. She decides to say something to Doris to help her to feel better.

1. How might Mrs. Walton help Doris over this episode?
2. Why does Mr. Johnson speak to his sales personnel as he does?
3. Should Mrs. Walton tell Doris not to worry about Mr. Johnson's reprimands?
4. What constructive suggestions could Mrs. Walton make?

4. Beginning at the Top

John Richfield has obtained a subordinate position in an advertising firm. In high school John capably handled all the advertising copy for the various school publications. He feels, therefore, that his experience fits him for doing creative work, and he is not interested in the tasks assigned to him. He considers them to be prosaic, routine duties. The manager knows that because John cannot do the type of work he wants to do, he often neglects to do well the work he has to do. John's negligence also causes more work for others in the office. They, in turn, complain to the manager. When John is called to the manager for questioning, he explains that he does not like his present tasks and tells of his ambition. The manager does not seem to be impressed with his reasoning.

1. What is your opinion of John's attitude toward his work?
2. If you were the manager, what would you say to John?
3. Why did John's ambition fail to impress the manager?
4. Have you observed this attitude toward starting at the bottom in other lines of work? Explain.
5. Why was John's attitude not fair to the other employees?

5. Set in the Groove

Miss Palmer, who has been transferred from the central office to one of its branches, finds it difficult to adjust herself to the new methods. She is continually referring to her old position: "Mr. Brown told me to fill out this form in this way," or, "Mr. Brown wanted letters written in this style." Some of Miss Palmer's ideas are good, and in time she may be able to contribute to the efficiency of office routine. At present, however, she annoys everyone else in the office. Unless Miss Palmer adjusts to the new situation, she is in danger of losing her position.

1. What should Miss Palmer's attitude be toward her job?
2. Why is it best for a newcomer to refrain from making suggestions about changes?
3. If Miss Palmer's ideas are good, how and when may she present them for consideration?
4. Is there a similarity with this situation and the common practice of saying, "This is the way my teacher in school told us to do this"?

6. Expense Accounts

Sam Little and Harry Dahl are salesmen for the Marshall Company. Their territories are adjoining, and sometimes it is possible for them to spend Sundays together in a middle-sized city. To have this meeting, it is necessary for Harry to go twenty miles out of his way. He reasons that the inconvenience caused him is compensated for by his not having to remain in a small town over the weekend. He feels, however, that the extra traveling expenses should be borne by himself. Sam tells him that he is a fool, that the company should pay all of his traveling expenses.

1. If you were Harry, would you charge such trips to your expense account? Why or why not?
2. What are the rules for charging expenses to the company?
3. What regulations have recently been made by the federal government in the matter of expense accounts?

Chapter 11

Business Psychology in the Office

The office worker *must* understand why people behave as they do. Facts and figures may be supplied by machines, but people still make the office go — or break down. One person in a large office can create enough friction to make it break down, too. You must make sure that *you* are not a behavior problem, but you must also learn to understand others when they are.

The successful office worker, first of all, uses his head. He follows the motto THINK. He does not let his feelings, his emotions, tell him what to do. But even the best of us cannot hope to be 100 percent objective — even part of the time. There is a good possibility that we do things, and say things, for an unconscious reason. The thing we must do is be on our guard for this possibility. If we are promoted to a new and difficult job, for example, we may find ourselves in a state of panic. If you should find yourself in this position, don't look for sensible reasons for your fears. They may be caused by an excessive desire to be perfect. Thus, you may be afraid of failure and not afraid of the job. The cure for your panic may lie in telling yourself that mistakes will almost surely occur at first. The expected, you see, is not so frightening as the unexpected, and you may find your fears disappearing.

An understanding of the possible reasons for behavior will keep you from hasty judgments of others. If the girl at the next desk to yours takes offense at everything you say to her, don't stop speaking altogether. It may be that your co-worker is extremely insecure. She may want to succeed just as much as you do, but she may feel inferior to the other workers. She may have no idea how to seek help for her real or imagined inadequacies. Try reassuring her now and then.

Sometimes unattractive personality traits cover up a tendency that is their exact opposite. Thus, the braggart may be doubtful of his worth; the girl who laughs too much may actually be shy; the excessively sweet girl may be covering up a real dislike of people.

You have read in Part 1 of this volume about the basic needs that are common to all of us. It will help you to understand your co-workers and your supervisors if you review what you have read. Everyone has these same needs. Your employer may seem to be the ultimate in success, yet he may feel completely unappreciated. In fact, the higher you climb the ladder of success, the more lonely you may become. It will help you and your firm if you take the initiative in the friendly greeting, the approving word. No one gets enough appreciation. If you are able to show your appreciation of others, you can make a good start in building a better psychological climate around you.

If you are committed to a greater understanding of others, of their quirks and foibles, the next step is to keep from being a behavior problem yourself. It is better to be positive, to be cheerful. Perhaps you have made great strides in eliminating the negative side of your personality. You have learned about clothes, about grooming, about speaking. Now, let's talk about *working*. Work in an office is made up of two factors: service with a smile and good work habits.

Service With a Smile

The office is the service hub of the company wheel. Everything that is done in the office is of service to some other department. Records are kept, papers are filed, correspondence is carried on, plans are made, all to serve the company as a whole. Any worker in an office, then, must be service conscious. He must be willing to do all in his power to make the company run smoothly. To fit into an office, you must be willing to serve. The office is no place for the temperamental person.

To recognize the importance of service in an office, imagine that you are a member of a "bucket brigade" engaged in putting out a fire. A long line of people pass the buckets along the line from the stream at one end to the fire at the other. Suppose you drop the bucket when it gets to you? What will happen to the group effort? This is how important each member of the office group can be. To carry your share of the office work, you must: (1) be willing to work, (2) be able to communicate, (3) know how to organize, and (4) be respectful.

Be willing to work. It may seem redundant to explain that an office worker must be willing to work. But many office workers seem to spend their time in other ways. There are a number of clues to tell your supervisor or employer how willing a worker you are. You willingly perform the task that is assigned to you. After the assignment has been made, you arrange your duties so that the work is completed on time. Because mistakes can be as serious as dropping the bucket when you are putting out a fire, you take great pains to be accurate. You proofread *every word* you type; you verify every number that comes your way; you look up needed information in the files or in reference books. You take pride in your craftsmanship; the finished product has a careful, painstaking look.

Be able to communicate. Because office work is almost synonymous with paper work, the office worker must be precise in all written communication. This may mean a brushup on grammar and punctuation. Your use of these tools will "peg" you, as far as education goes. There are many inexpensive paperbacks to help you. If you have a little trouble with verbs and adverbs, for example, do some studying on your own. You communicate with arithmetic, too, so be sure that yours can be trusted. Always double check discounts and extensions, even when using calculators and adding machines. A reputation for accuracy in English and arithmetic is worth working for.

Know how to organize. Offices are being run more and more scientifically, and you must get in step with the trend. One way is by reading up on job analysis and motion analysis in expediting work. You will find that planning saves time, energy, and supplies. A necessary part of planning and organizing is the ability to write instructions, memos, and reports in a concise form. Those who read them must be able to follow your thoughts with understanding. This ability can hardly be overstressed. Learn to break instructions down into steps; number the steps; and be sure you cut out all ambiguous words. Be sure your handwriting is legible; that your spelling is perfect; that your figures can be read accurately.

Be respectful. Service is without value unless it is joined with respect. You will show respect through a knowledge of business etiquette gained, if necessary, through reading and observing. Respect the flow of authority in the firm and particularly in the office in which you work. This means that you will "go through channels." You will take your questions and problems to your immediate superior; he takes them to his boss, and this boss takes his problems to *his* boss. If you should "go over the head" of your superior, you not only fail to show respect for his position, but you put him in a bad light. You should study the organization chart of the firm, which lists the officers of the company, the heads of departments, supervisors, and so on. You will then know how the whole organization works; you will also have a clearer picture of your position. You will know the path downward and upward of directions, information, suggestions, and grievances. It will also show you where your work ultimately goes, a knowledge that adds to your feeling of worth.

Respect means that you will become familiar with the flow of business papers utilized by your firm. You will know the purpose and the processing routine of these papers. It means you will become acquainted with your firm's policies and regulations. These can usually be found in office manuals or printed brochures about the company. Because you have respect for your firm, you know what information is to be discussed and where and with whom to discuss it. You will keep confidential information inviolate and share facts only with those employees who share responsibility for them.

Good Work Habits

If you have never worked or if you have never put in a full day's work for a day's pay, you will have little conception of what this means. Any job contains a certain amount of routine work, and most of this work is concentrated in the beginning levels. The way to emerge the victor over drudgery is to make your habits work for you. Work habits, like other habits, are built up day by day. It will pay you to form good work habits from the very beginning of your first job. For convenience, the work habits you should form are grouped according to time, neatness, efficiency, and integrity.

Time. When you work, you are paid for your time and the way you spend it. In business, of course, time is money; many of the good work habits you will need involve the proper use of time. For example, you will arrive at work on time — or even a few minutes early — every day. This habit cannot be overstressed. It is important because it shows others that you value your job, but the greatest value in arriving on time is its effect on you. This is best illustrated by what happens when you are late for work. Everything you do becomes shaded by the fact that you were late. You are behind with your work, so you hurry to catch up; because you hurry, you make mistakes; making mistakes causes you to become flustered, so you hurry faster. This circle of hurry and errors goes on all day. On the other hand, if you come to work early you are relaxed when you start your first task. Relaxation helps you work rapidly and accurately. Working in this way brings you a feeling of satisfaction, and this feeling helps you with the next task at hand. The result is a circle of excellence that works for you all day.

Leaving early should be avoided. Clock watchers seldom get promoted, you know; and the person who starts to clear his desk *before* the closing hour is advertising his clock-watching habits. Time that belongs to the company is involved if you leave early for or return late from lunch and coffee breaks, or if you spend extra time talking in the washroom. Time is involved in the rules that govern smoking in your office. Whatever the rule may be, whether smoking is permitted at the desks or only in the lounges, you must abide by and not exploit the rule.

Neatness. You can build neat work habits without too much effort. One of your first mottoes should be the adage, "A place for everything and everything in its place." This means that, first of all, your desk is arranged neatly. Study examples of neat, efficient layouts for desks. Notice how supplies should be arranged for quick and easy handling. A neatly arranged desk will make *you* more *efficient*. You will be ready to plan and organize materials, supplies, and the work itself so that tasks can be completed as rapidly and as accurately as possible.

Efficiency. Efficiency involves discovering the work standards in your office and working hard to meet them. One difference between actual office work and school assignments will soon become apparent: Perfection is always desirable, but sometimes must give way to practicality. For instance, if a letter is not centered, you might have to mail it anyway, because time and supplies might be more important than perfection. In other cases, such as a letter to an important client, you will need to rewrite a letter that is improperly placed on the page. Being efficient involves judging the relative values of tasks when measured in terms of time, energy, and supplies. These judgments will vary, of course, according to the needs of your particular firm.

Integrity. Honesty has been discussed in a previous chapter as an important personality trait. But it is not enough to *feel* honest, to have good intentions. If you are to build all the work habits you will need in your job, you must make a *habit* of honesty and integrity. Integrity means, for example, that you will give your complete attention to the task before you. Daydreaming on the job is out! Habits of integrity involve working just as carefully and quickly when the supervisor is away from the office as you do when he is watching you. It means that when you need help or directions, you ask for them at once.

Absenteeism is a big problem in business these days. Habits of integrity include being absent from work only when you have a good cause. You should also report the cause of absence honestly. There is another kind of absenteeism, even though you may be seated at your desk. This absenteeism takes place every time you make or receive a personal telephone call on company time. No matter what the rules in your office may be, it is better to use a pay telephone during your *free time* for your own calls. When a friend calls you at the office, it is best to say courteously that you will call back after working hours. This is usually sufficient to warn your friend that he or she should not call you during business hours.

"Don't's" for the Office

Do you irritate your co-workers? If you have any of the following negative habits, you probably do. Just as there are habits and techniques you should cultivate for success in office work, so there are habits that you should avoid. Unfortunately, most of these unwelcome habits never slip into our awareness. We notice them in others, but we fail to recognize that we may be guilty, too. Most of the following objectionable habits come under the heading of bad manners. We can hardly be blamed if we fail to realize our faults, but certainly we should make an effort to correct any faults once they have been called to our attention. Ask a close friend to check you against the following list — and you do the same for your friend. Then make a sincere effort to eliminate any that you do — even occasionally.

Drumming or tapping with fingers, toes, or a pencil
Humming or whistling under your breath
Sniffling or snorting
Breathing noisily
Blowing your nose noisily
Clearing your throat with a rasp
Sucking your teeth
Coughing or sneezing without turning your face and cover-
    ing your mouth with a handkerchief
Coughing loudly
Fussing with your hair
Playing with rings, beads, or other jewelry
Adjusting your collar, cuffs, belt, or the like unnecessarily
Scratching your hair or picking at your face
Chewing gum
Yawning
Back slapping
Whispering
Drawing designs in your notebook as you wait for dictation
Wrinkling your brows
Slamming doors
Banging telephone receivers
Dashing in and out of rooms

Before beginning this improvement campaign, resolve to be objective about the whole thing, and do not feel hurt when your friend checks an item that is surprising to you. Remember, we are seldom aware of these habits. When you know which of the objectionable habits are to be eliminated from your habit structure, start on the first. When it is eliminated, go on to the second. To eliminate an undesirable habit: (1) be conscious that you possess it, (2) honestly de-

sire to get rid of it, and (3) stop it *now* and permit no re-
currence.

TRAIT TRAINING

In addition to the traits that have already been discussed,
there are others that will help you in office work (as well as
in other business jobs). There is, of course, no hard-and-fast
rule that says one trait is needed for selling and another is
needed for office work. You will find, instead, that all positive traits will help you, no matter what kind of work you
do. The traits discussed in this chapter, however, will
stand you in good stead in the office. They are judgment,
morality, and responsibility.

Judgment

When a prospective employer talks about a potential
employee, he may say that he wants someone who can use
his head, or someone who has common sense, or someone
with judgment. These are all names for the same trait —
and one that is missing in at least two out of three beginning
workers. One reason for its scarcity lies in the word *beginning*.
If you have had no experience in a certain field, you will have
few tools at your command for making wise judgments.
Perhaps the following situations will show you the kind of
judgment that is needed.

It takes judgment, for example, to determine the importance of a caller's business and his need for seeing your
employer personally. In placing a telephone call for your
employer, it takes good judgment to decide who will be
called to the telephone first. You need judgment to know
when to take a message yourself and when to interrupt
your employer. You must have judgment if you are to
recognize the relative importance of clients or customers
when they call at the same time.

If you are able to evaluate the situation, you will use
discretion in dealing with an angry customer, receive com-

plaints graciously (regardless of their number), learn when to keep your eyes and ears open and your mouth closed, and how to discriminate in giving information of a confidential nature to those who ask for it. You will reserve judgment of one who seems to have committed an error against you. If you measure yourself by the same critical standards that you apply to others, you will become more liberal, less critical, and better able to evaluate justly.

Judgment implies that you will not discriminate between fellow workers because of personal like or dislike, but that you will learn to keep business relationships on an impersonal basis during business hours. Judgment also implies that you will not interrupt a conference unless it is absolutely necessary, nor will you refer questions asked over the telephone to your employer unless you cannot find the answer elsewhere. Good judgment must function as an outstanding trait in your business life.

Morality

Morality means conformity to the standards of what is right. Some adults are concerned with the moral standards of young people. Many people are concerned by a lack of ethics and morality in business. Moral standards in business are certainly dispensed with by some firms. Because business is concerned with profits, because it is competitive, and because success is based on rivalry, the contention is sometimes made that business cannot be moral.

An ambitious businessman or woman, however, must look beyond the surface evidence and study the long-range results of morality in business. This scrutiny will reveal that companies that have become firmly established through years of service are more interested in protecting their good reputation than in making a single sale or in making transitory profits. Young firms, too, who want to establish lasting goodwill are more interested in their integrity than in the profit of the moment. In testing the effect of morality, it is well to examine the businesses that have stood the test of time with success.

The businessman (or woman) should guard his record of morality because it is a valuable possession. He should guard it because he is ethical, has faith, and because he has a sense of fair play and a social conscience. He should guard it for selfish reasons, also, because it is as valuable to him in business as capital or education. All businessmen and women should exhibit this type of selfishness.

Successful businessmen and women should also be interested, not in transitory praise or a moment of glory and success, but in long-range esteem and respect. Seldom are there any secrets in business. Even long after an incident of immorality, someone will remember. Facts can come to light in other ways, too, for there are many types of records. That a person did not make a sale, that a task was poorly completed, that an employee was promoted will be forgotten. But immorality will become a part of the record. If this record is not in writing, it will be whispered.

On many details of morality people do not agree, but some basic precepts are common to the consciences of all people. Other basic precepts in addition to those of all society are recognized by business people. The game is to be played fairly. All people have a sense of sportsmanship and justice. Nothing should be done outside of the office that would embarrass the firm. Feelings of others should be respected. In short, in business as elsewhere in life, "...as ye would that men should do to you, do ye also to them likewise."

The following should be considered rules of business; they should not be violated.

Do not take office supplies for personal use.
Do not show a too friendly emotion toward your employer.
Do not make unfair demands of subordinates.
Do not take expensive gifts from customers or salesmen.
Do not appear in public under the effects of alcohol.

Do not repeat gossip about the private lives of your co-workers or superiors.

Your personal morality requires that you abide by ethical standards that you prize. You should not be unduly critical, however, of those whose standards are not the same as yours. This is an important point. Not only will the moral codes of other people differ from your own in some respects, but sometimes through thoughtlessness, stress, or grief some of your fellow employees or even your employers may violate their own moral codes. Whenever possible, be charitable toward these shortcomings. In similar crises, you may also err.

Responsibility

Responsibility means the ability to respond or answer for one's own conduct or obligations; trustworthiness; dependability. Employers are crying for employees who can take responsibility. To develop this trait, you must learn to be dependable. When you say you will do something, force yourself to do it — no matter what circumstances arise to make it difficult.

When you have been given the responsibility for some task, the responsibility is yours, not someone else's. If you ask others to help you, *you* must check what they do. If you have been given the responsibility for getting certain checks in today's mail, you must do just that, even though it means working overtime. Responsibility also means that you will handle money matters entrusted to you with the utmost care. When you develop the trait of responsibility, you add to your own maturity.

ILLUSTRATIVE CASE

An Imperfect Secretary

Judy Stevens is employed by Mr. Goodman, an attorney, as a general clerk. She takes his dictation, attends to the files, answers the telephone, and receives his clients. Mr. Goodman's practice is growing and Judy's days are full keeping up with his increasing duties. She has learned that she must keep occupied every moment if she is to have the day's work completed at closing time. With the pressure of new business, Judy's patience sometimes grows short.

Mr. Goodman is in conference with an important client and has told Judy he is not to be disturbed. There is a lengthy brief which Judy is to have typed before the day is over and she hopes that the conference will give her a period of undisturbed time. She settles down to work and the telephone rings. "Sorry," says Judy abruptly to an inquirer for Mr. Goodman, "but he is busy and cannot be disturbed." She puts the receiver down hastily and organizes her work again. Mrs. Werner, whose legal affairs are in Mr. Goodman's keeping, enters the office. She is a friendly soul inclined to chatter. "Mr. Goodman is in conference," says Judy barely lifting her eyes from her typewriter, "and cannot see you today." Mrs. Werner hesitates in her explanation for her visit and leaves the office feeling abused. A third caller enters, but he is a newcomer to the office. Judy does not know his name and dismisses him with a barely civil, "Mr. Goodman is busy and cannot be disturbed." The man leaves without giving an explanation for his call. Eventually Judy completes the typing of the brief, Mr. Goodman emerges from his conference, and the day goes on.

If Judy were conscious of her shortcomings, she would know that three errors could be chalked against her in her dealings with the three callers. The telephone inquirer would have been pleased had Judy said, "I've had strict orders not to disturb Mr. Goodman, but is there any information I may give you?...You must speak to Mr. Goodman?...Please give me your name and telephone number and the moment Mr. Goodman is free, I shall have him call you." Mrs. Werner would have understood had Judy said, "I wish I could chat with you, but Mr. Goodman must have this brief this afternoon, and I dare not lose a moment. That chair by the window is comfortable, and here is the new issue of *Fashion.* Would you like to glance through it while you wait for Mr. Goodman?" The unknown caller was the cause of Judy's gravest blunder. Here was a prospective client whose business would have meant money — the owner of large tracts of oil lands with questions of leases to be settled. But how was Judy to know? "I'm sorry Mr. Goodman gave me such strict orders," Judy might have said, "I don't dare disturb him. But would you like to take a chance on waiting for him? He may not be much longer...No?...There's nothing I can do for you?...How about an appointment for this afternoon? I have Mr. Goodman's engagement book and he will be free at 2 o'clock. Is that agreeable to you? Let me have your name and telephone number so that I may get in touch with you if there will be any need to change this plan. I'll give you a ring to confirm the 2 o'clock appointment as soon as Mr. Goodman is free."

What did Judy lack? Interest in the larger affairs of her employer and interest in the affairs of the clients of her employer. Maybe, too, Judy lacked the surplus power needed in handling rush jobs with ease. If Judy stays in business, she will learn to mend her ways...but she is doomed to learn "the hard way."

FOLLOW-UP ACTIVITIES

1. Get samples of business letters and check them for accuracy of detail — spelling, punctuation, grammar, etc. Exhibit in class those whose appearance and content are superior in quality.
2. Since remembering names plays such an important part in office and store routine, the following suggestions made by Dick Carlson[1] are quoted with the hope that you will put them into practice:

---

[1]Dick Carlson, *How To Develop Personal Power* (New York: Harper and Brothers, 1937).

a. When a person is being introduced, be sure that you not only hear the name but know how it is spelled. If there is doubt in your mind about the spelling, ask him to spell it; never ask the man who introduced you.

b. When you have the name, turn your attention to the face. Look at him and in some way associate the name with the face.

c. File this association away in your memory, *knowing* that you will remember him next time you meet him.

d. Whenever you meet him, make it a point to address him by name at the beginning of your conversation.

PRACTICE EXERCISES

Dramatize the following situations, which may be met in the course of a day's work in an office. In some of the scenes the conversation of the other person is not provided. The missing conversation should be provided in home preparation, and the various situations should then be dramatized in class and criticized from the various angles presented in the preceding discussion of techniques.

Greeting Your Employer

YOU. (With a smile.) "Good morning, Mr. Young."

MR. YOUNG. "_____."

YOU. "Yes, it looks as though it might rain all day. You have an appointment with Mr. Canter in an hour."

. . . .

YOU. (After the usual greeting.) "When would you like to sign the form letters we are to send out today?"

MR. YOUNG. "_____."

YOU. "Very well, I shall bring them in."

. . . .

YOU. "Good morning, Mr. Young. You will find on your desk a report that I thought you might like to see immediately."

. . . .

Note that the day's work begins immediately after the greeting.

Greeting Callers

YOU. "Good morning, Mr. Baker. Won't you sit down? Mr. Young hasn't arrived, but he will be in at nine o'clock. He wants your advice about the installation of the heating plant."

. . . .

YOU. "Good morning, Mrs. Logan. You haven't been in for some time. What can I do for you?"

. . . .

YOU. "Won't you sit down, sir? Mr. Young is in conference now, but he will be through in a few minutes."

. . . .

YOU. "Good afternoon, sir. I'm sorry Mr. Young is out for the rest of the afternoon."

CLIENT. "_____."

YOU. "Yes, I can arrange an appointment for you at ten in the morning. Would that be convenient?"

CLIENT. "_____."

. . . .

YOU. "Good morning, Mr. Hansen. Mr. Young is expecting you. Come this way, please." (To Mr. Young.) "Mr. Young, Mr. Hansen is here to see you."

. . . .

YOU. "Good morning, Mr. Hansen. Mr. Young will be glad to see you. He just stepped out of the office for a moment but will be back soon. Will you wait for him?"

MR. HANSEN. "_____."

YOU. "Good! Be seated until he returns."

Turning Away a Caller

YOU. "Good morning, Mrs. Thomas."

MRS. THOMAS. "_____."

YOU. "No, I'm sorry. Mr. Young will be out of the office until noon. If you will tell me the nature of your call, I may be able to help."

MRS. THOMAS. "_____."

YOU. "I am sure Mr. Young can help you. I shall tell him that you called and shall let you know when he can see you. We have your telephone number in our records — 631-7084, is it not?"

. . . .

YOU. "Good morning, Mr. Moore."

MR. MOORE. "_____."

YOU. "I'm sorry, but Mr. Young isn't interested in your stock of goods just now. At some other time, perhaps. Thank you for calling. Good-bye."

. . . .

YOU. "Good morning. Whom do you wish to see?"

MR. BARTON. "Mr. Young, please."

YOU. "What is your name, please?"

MR. BARTON. "Joseph N. Barton."

YOU. "What company do you represent, Mr. Barton?"

MR. BARTON. "A. T. Smith & Co., Publishers."

YOU. "About what do you wish to see Mr. Young?"

MR. BARTON. "I think he will be interested in our new issue of the *Digest.*"

YOU. "He's very busy now. This would be an unfavorable time to interrupt him. Suppose you come in later."

MR. BARTON. "Very well. Good-bye."

Mr. Barton may not accept your suggestion. In that case how would the conversation be concluded?

Reminding the Employer

Notice the tactful ways in which an employer may be reminded.

"Mr. Young, you have an appointment at 10:30 with Mr. Jones in his office."

or

"Mr. Jones will be in to see you at 10:30 this morning."

or

"I know you haven't forgotten that Mr. Jones will be here at 10:30."

. . . .

"Mr. Young, I must send out the bills this afternoon, and I shall not be able to work today on the report that you need for the Friday meeting."

. . . .

"Mr. Young, would you object to my coming back this evening to finish the report for Friday's meeting? If you will check it this afternoon, I shall be glad to come back to complete it."

. . . .

"Mr. Young, if you will give me the dictation now, I can be getting the letters out while you are in conference this afternoon."

. . . .

"Mr. Young (he is on his way to the golf course, or a ball game, or whatever will keep him out all afternoon), you have not forgotten to confirm the report that must be mailed today?"

Giving Orders to Subordinates

"Miss Miller, will you help me get these pamphlets out to the customers on this list? You made such a neat job of the last mimeographed work that was assigned to you."

. . . .

"Carl, will you deliver this package to the post office? It must go out this afternoon. You probably would like some exercise anyway, wouldn't you?"

Taking Criticism

"Thank you for calling this error to my attention. If you had not discovered it in time, it would have been a costly blunder. I shall be more careful in the future."

Helping Dismiss a Customer Who Has Remained Too Long

"Pardon me, Mr. Young. This telegram just arrived. [He glances through it.] Shall I follow this with a letter of confirmation?"

or

"Did you wish a rush clause in the order to Johnson and Johnson?"

Supply whatever conversation may follow. Emphasize the need for Mr. Young's immediate attention to the matter at hand.

On Being Fair

MR. WILSON. "This is a very nice-looking report, Miss Roberts."

MISS ROBERTS. "Yes, isn't it? Miss Anderson typed it."

Taking Dictation

The stenographer's call bell rings. Miss Roberts reaches for her notebook and sharpened pencils, which are near at hand. She enters the private office quietly, takes her place at the side of Mr. Young's desk, opens her notebook, and looks at him inquiringly.

"Take this letter, Miss Roberts," says Mr. Young and begins to dictate.

She writes quickly and accurately. When he pauses, she sits still; she does not fidget, tap her pencil, yawn, or look out of the window. When the letter has been dictated, she looks through her notes and asks, "Is *Carl* spelled with a *C* or a *K*? Did you say Portland, Maine, or Portland, Oregon?"

Mr. Young gives the information and says, "Please get the letter to Smith & Williams into the next mail."

"Yes, sir," says Miss Roberts quietly, not mentioning the many duties that are awaiting her attention. She then goes to her typewriter to follow instructions.

Efficiency Plus

MR. YOUNG. (He has to attend an important meeting of the board of directors.) "Miss Roberts, are those reports ready? Where are the data sheets I gave you to type? Where did I put those statements? Did you call Mr. Olsen?"

MISS ROBERTS. "Yes, Mr. Young. Everything has been taken care of. Here are the data sheets and reports. I'll get the statements from the files. Mr. Olsen will see you in his office at five o'clock after the meeting."

Later in the busy day the following scene takes place. Mr. Young is in a bad humor. He rings the buzzer. Miss Roberts enters.

MR. YOUNG. "Where in thunder did you put that letter from Washington? I had it yesterday. Can't I put a letter down for two minutes without someone running off with it?"

MISS ROBERTS. (Crosses to the files, gets the letter that he had instructed her to place there, and puts it on his desk.) "Will that be all, Mr. Young?" (She is calmly impersonal, takes no offense at his ill humor, and does not assume an air of "Don't blame it on me!" or "Am I efficient!")

Still later in the busy day, Mr. Young is in conference and has told Miss Roberts that he is not to be disturbed. An important client comes in on urgent business. Miss Roberts recognizes him and his connection with the firm. She enters the conference room and waits for Mr. Young to recognize her presence.

MISS ROBERTS. "I'm sorry to disturb you, Mr. Young, but Mr. Burke is here to see you about the bridge contract. He says it is very urgent. Would you like to see him?"

. . . .

Is it any wonder that Miss Roberts is given more and more responsibility? And so *the stenographer becomes the secretary!*

CASE PROBLEMS

1. Delegating Responsibility

Jane Heiman was instructed by Kay Bishop to obtain some information for the latter to use in making out a report of customers who had overdue accounts. By error Jane added the name of a good customer who had never been in arrears. When the customer was approached by the credit collection bureau, he became highly indignant, called the general manager of Kay's company, and threatened to take his business elsewhere. The general manager called Kay into his office and reprimanded her. Kay insisted it was not her fault, that Jane had made the error. The general manager said nothing to Jane, but persisted in blaming Kay.

1. Do you agree or disagree with the general manager?
2. What was Kay's responsibility in the matter?
3. If you delegate some of your responsibility to another, what must you be sure to do?
4. If you are capable of assuming responsibility, what would your reaction be to the reprimand from the general manager?

2. Keeping the Record Straight

Jack Greene and Henry Pearce are bookkeepers for the same firm. Jack has been threatened with discharge because he sent a valued customer a bill for an account that had been paid. Henry realizes the fault is his because, through some error, he failed to record the payment in the books. As Henry has just been promised a promotion as a reward for his good work, an admission of his error might jeopardize his standing.

1. What should Henry do in this situation? Why?
2. If you were Henry, what would you say? Is there any way you can explain this error and still keep in your employer's good graces?
3. If you were Henry's employer, what would be your decision? Why?

3. Time for Decision

Russ Palmer has been working in the duplicating department of White and Charters, Inc., since he graduated from junior college a year ago. Since the time he began working with the firm he has received no raises in salary. The work of the duplicating department, however, has increased to the extent that two new employees have been hired to help him.

This involves some supervisory work on his part. In checking the salaries paid by other firms for similar work, Russ finds that he is not earning as much as most other companies pay. As Russ is debating what to do, a friend who is office manager of Hanson and Hanson Company offers him the same type of job at 15 percent higher salary. Russ likes the people in his department, as well as the other personnel of White and Charters. Hanson and Hanson do not provide the fringe benefits he is receiving.

1. What would you do if you were Russ?
2. If you decide to ask for a raise, would you tell your employer about the other offer?
3. Write down the "case" you would present to your employer in asking for the raise.
4. In accepting a position, what factors in addition to salary should be considered?

4. Petty Larceny

Alice Yates and Sue Jenson are stenographers in the office of Mr. Hawks. Alice has been using stamped envelopes and letterheads belonging to the office to write to her boyfriend each day. She has also helped herself to special delivery stamps when she needed them. Mr. Hawks notices that the supply of stamps is nearly exhausted. He calls Alice and Sue to his office and tells them they must not take the supplies for personal use and that, if this practice is continued, both girls will be discharged. Alice does not care whether she is discharged or not, as she is going to be married in two months. She therefore continues to use the office supplies. Sue likes her job and wants to keep it.

1. If you were Sue, would you have said anything to Mr. Hawks at the time of his ultimatum? If so, what would you have said? If not, why not?
2. If your answer to question No. 1 was no, what would be your decision now? Would you say anything to Mr. Hawks or not?

3. In a case of two conflicting standards (telling on others and keeping your own good name), what should motivate your decision?

5. Taking Responsibility

Mr. Limmer, a division manager of a business that distributes its products nationally, has been out of the office for a week. He is in the hospital recovering from an operation and cannot be disturbed with business affairs. The operation was an emergency, and nothing was said about who should make the decisions. John Shafer has just received a large rush order over the telephone from a new local customer whose credit rating has not yet been established. It is the policy of the business that all orders from new customers must have Mr. Limmer's O.K. before being delivered.

John takes it upon himself to investigate the credit standing of this new company. He finds it to be excellent. John has three alternatives from which he can choose. He can (1) refuse the order, (2) call and ask if the company can wait for two weeks (when Mr. Limmer will be well enough to discuss business matters), or (3) approve the order in Mr. Limmer's name and have the goods delivered.

1. What is John's responsibility in this matter?
2. What is John's authority?
3. Which decision should John make? Why?

6. Should You Sleep on It?

Mr. Graham, Miss Ross' employer, was infuriated because of a serious mistake in an order sent in by Mr. Yeoman, a salesman on the road. Mr. Graham immediately called in his secretary and dictated a letter discharging Mr. Yeoman. Because Mr. Graham had to leave at once for a meeting, he asked Miss Ross to sign and mail the letter. Miss Ross was aware that her employer was having an off day. Mr. Yeoman was a personal friend of hers, and she knew that up to this time he had been very efficient and well liked, both by his customers and Mr. Graham. Instead of transcribing and mailing the letter, she held it until the next day.

1. What do you think of Miss Ross' action?
2. Should personal friendship enter a business situation of this kind?
3. What chance was Miss Ross taking?
4. Do you think Miss Ross might have been motivated by feelings other than friendship for Mr. Yeoman? If so, what were they?
5. In case Mr. Graham is of the same feeling the next day, what should Miss Ross do?
6. Suppose Mr. Graham comes in the next morning and tells Miss Ross he has changed his mind and that he is going to call Mr. Yeoman to see if he can talk him into staying with the company?
7. Can you think of a more straightforward way by which Miss Ross could have accomplished the same result?

Chapter 12

Psychology — His and Hers

When women first invaded the office back in the 1880's, everyone expected the heavens to fall. Ministers preached from the pulpit about destruction that was lying in wait for these young girls. Doctors predicted early death from working in poorly heated and ventilated offices. Now the whole picture has changed. About forty percent of all the people who work are now engaged in some form of business activity. It is expected that by 1970, one out of every three workers will be a woman. Most of these women will be working in offices.

Are there any psychological techniques to aid us in this coeducational "rat race," the modern business office? There seem to be some, but all of them do not apply in all cases. There are techniques for male executives, for male workers, for unmarried girls, and for married women with families to look after. Suggestions will be made for each of these four groups, but they will be classified into two main divisions — his and hers.

Isn't That Just Like a Man?

The male executive in today's office may find that his troubles are mostly feminine! Whether feminine peculiarities are innate or learned, no one knows; but they seem to be there. For example, marketing research has shown that a woman's senses are sharper. Because of this, perhaps, they react to harshness (whether of voice, word, or surroundings) to a much greater extent than men do. Some psychologists even say that women are fifty percent more sensitive than men — or at least that many more of them are too sensitive for their own good.

If you are a male executive, then, you will need to treat your women workers with politeness. Gruffness, brusqueness, snapping remarks are all resented more deeply by women than are long hours and low pay. In fact, better work would certainly be better motivated if the supervisor or manager would just compliment good work now and then. This is another area where women workers are different. They are more deeply motivated by words.

As words are powerful in dealing with women, it is only sensible to use considerate ones whenever possible in dealing with women. If a mistake has been made, it must be pointed out — but not necessarily with hammer and tongs! In fact, any boss will get fewer errors in the work of women employees if he compliments the work that is errorless. Almost any woman will work her fingers to the bone for a word of praise. And 99 women out of 100 will think, "What's the use," and not even try if the typical reaction by the boss is fault-finding.

An admirable quality in male executives is a sense of fairness. When a man becomes an executive, he may be called upon to work overtime more and more. If it is necessary to have a secretary or clerk work overtime as well, the executive should not attempt to make the occasion a social one. An executive, too, receives a higher salary to compensate for longer working hours. The clerical worker, however, usually does not receive this kind of remuneration. It is only fair that such work be either infrequent or that it be remunerated with "supper money" or overtime pay.

If a man should find that he must work late or on Saturday, he should notify in advance the employees who must help him. Girls may have dates, and they cannot always cancel these plans on short notice. The girl may not mind, but if her escort has purchased tickets to the theatre or for a sports event, he may hesitate to ask her again. Fairness on the part of the executive would make it optional for girls to remain after hours. Such questions as, "Would it upset any of your plans this evening, Miss Taylor, if you stayed until about 7:30 to finish this report?" leave it up to the girl. Also, in fairness, the employer should not be upset if Miss Taylor replies, "I'm sorry, but I do have a date. Would it be all right if I asked Marilyn if she is free?"

If late work seems to be required habitually, the boss and the staff should get together to discuss the matter and devise a plan that will be fair to all. It may not be possible to please everyone concerned, but at least everyone will have had a hand in making the arrangements. Under these circumstances, too, some kind of overtime pay should be given to those who work late. When such arrangements are made (such as time and a half for overtime), many employees welcome the extra work.

The unmarried co-worker of women in an office who wishes to ask one of them for a date should invite her for some social occasion. He should then call for her at her home. Social engagements are strictly for after hours, however. At the office, friends should treat each other with the same businesslike courtesy they show other co-workers.

If a young man should meet one of the girls from the office in a restaurant, he should be under no obligation to pay the check. Each one pays for his or her own lunch or snack. There are other social customs, too, that are not observed in the office. For example, a young man does not rise from his desk to carry a heavy ledger, nor does he open and close doors for her. This is because an office does not represent a social situation. Women in business should not expect special favors of men co-workers. They should accept the same conditions that men face. The rules of the game allow no exceptions. Women neither expect nor desire the chivalry that men accord them in the social world.

Isn't That Just Like a Woman?

The Cinderella story of modern times is usually set in an office, so many girls may look upon office jobs as the Royal

Road to Romance. Of course, an intelligent, perceptive girl will know this idea is pure fiction. To her, the impersonal nature of business relationships is obvious. She will know that most businessmen are far too engrossed in their work to have time for flirtation. The perceptive girl will also be too interested in her job and in growing in her own capabilities to be interested in shallow relationships. Strangely enough, a girl is more attractive when she is deeply interested in something other than herself and her personal affairs.

Girls and marriage. Most girls have one or both of two goals. They want a successful career, and/or they want a happy marriage. A generation ago these goals presented more of a conflict than they do now. Still, many girls consider the business world merely as a stopgap until they get married. This attitude, however, is one that may spoil their chances in reaching either goal. Every girl should have some goal in mind, of course, and she should analyze the threat of "marking time" in an office to her own success.

You will improve your chances of career success if your attitude is entirely businesslike during the working day. Naturally, you will be flattered if you notice that someone in the office is attracted to you. The important point, however, is this: You should have or develop enough self-confidence so that you will not need this kind of flattery. A girl who is cool and businesslike is more attractive than one who obviously tries to interest the men in the office. No girl should show how she feels before the man does. Sometimes it helps to act a role. If you can't feel calm and cool, perhaps you can act as if you were.

The girl who is beginning her business career will do well to keep her former friends, and to go out of her way to keep these relationships intact. The fact that you do have other friends seems to make itself felt. Others will be attracted to you because you don't need them. The psychology of not being too eager in any kind of relationship would make a fascinating study, but it is beyond our scope.

If you should become interested in one of the single men in your firm, your best procedure is to follow the rules of acceptable behavior. So many men are frightened of marriage responsibilities that, again, the light touch is much the best one. Don't be too interested. Let the man make the first move. If he is interested, he will invite you to dinner, to a movie, or to some other entertainment. And here we come to an important point. If a man asks you for a date, you are his guest; you do not offer to "go Dutch." One of the undermining influences at work is the assault on a man's ego when his girl makes as much or more money than he does. This assault is aggravated by any aggressive display of money. It is much better to take a walk with a man than offer to buy theatre tickets and meals at restaurants. The one exception is when tickets are given to you. Be careful even in this instance, though. Don't go too far in taking the initiative. The rare occasion when you have been given tickets should be handled as follows: The man should call for you at your home; you should hand him the tickets; and from then on the evening is up to him.

Following the conventional ways is best. If you should decide to return the hospitality (and then only after a man has invited you several times), the best plan is to invite him to a small party at your home or apartment. When others are invited, too, it looks like what it is, merely a wish to be friendly and appreciative.

Girls and emotions. One criticism commonly leveled at businesswomen is that they are too emotional. This criticism is actually based on fact. Women's emotions seem to be closer to the surface — whether by heredity or training. The best thing to do in business, however, is try to control them. A display of unpleasant attitudes or uncontrollable emotions is immature and definitely not one of the traits desirable in a businesswoman. Emotional outbursts do not belong in the office — whether they be tears, angry words, or hurt feelings. Count to ten — or a hundred. Realize that your boss is under greater pressure than you are. Go bowling after work. But don't indulge in your emotions during working hours.

Sex should also be kept out of your thoughts. You should get rid of those wishful thoughts that some day you will marry the boss — or the boss's son. One help in this will be to interpret what your boss says to you as having a business meaning and nothing more. Your boss is interested primarily in his business. Don't let your imagination create situations that do not exist.

What about invitations from your employer? The best rule here is to use your common sense. If the invitation to have dinner when you are working late is made casually, if the situation can be kept on a business basis, then you may accept. If the invitation has overtones of something more, however, you should make some excuse. This may be similar to walking a high wire in a circus. You must keep your relationship on a businesslike level, yet you must not offend your employer. The best excuse, again made casually, is that you are sorry but that you have a date. You do not want to become a target for gossip, and you do not want to make your office relationship difficult.

The best cure for possible or present emotional entanglements in the office is to keep a wholesome interest in affairs outside the office, in a circle of congenial friends. If you fill your days with work and your evenings and weekends with play and self-improvement, you will not look for a leading, romantic role during working hours. You will keep such situations from developing if you dress becomingly but appropriately, if your manners are serious and self-reliant, and if your work is done skillfully and competently.

Career vs. marriage. A social revolution of the greatest magnitude has been going on for two decades. To the accompaniment of cries of anguish from some people, married women have been entering the labor force in ever-increasing numbers. The U.S. Department of Labor predicts that by 1970 at least two out of every five women will be working outside the home. These are the facts. Is there any way to make them more palatable to husbands, employers, and one's children?

There are a number of ways: Regardless of how career-minded a woman may be, her first duty is to her family. This being true, the married worker must see that the *quality* of the time spent with her family is as high as she can make it. A mother who spends eighteen hours with her children can snap at them now and then, but a working mother who is with her children from four to six hours a day cannot. The working wife will be more successful if she pampers her husband. Of course this kind of self-discipline is not easy, but the rewards are great.

It takes discipline, also, to keep the two lives of a working wife separate. At work, she must concentrate on *work*. At home, she should put all thoughts of work out of her mind. If her children are small, the wise woman will forego the lure of the "top jobs" because these require too much night work at the office, too much work taken home on weekends, too much "away-from-the-office thinking" about one's job. She should leave the big opportunities until after the children are grown up. In these days of early marriage, there will still be thirty years left in which she can be ambitious!

The next disciplinary task a working wife must take up is organizing her life. Every day must be planned, and the best time to plan it is the night before. The working wife should write down a short list of the items that must be done the next day. At the top of the list goes the important duty that must be done no matter what happens. And this *is* done, regardless of the other crises that come up. The other duties are done if possible. The ones at the bottom of the list that never get done are treated nonchalantly. No one can work eight hours a day away from home and hope to be a perfect housekeeper.

Housekeeping helpers will have to be organized. If a part-time cleaning woman can be found, this will be a great help. In addition to outside help, however, the children must be pressed into service. And it is excellent training for them. No working mother should feel guilty about sons who iron their own shirts or daughters who have to do the marketing and the cooking one week out of four. Some of the personal chores the children should do for themselves — picking up clothes, keeping their rooms in order, washing socks, hose, and so on, their own ironing and pressing, making their own appointments, and taking their clothes to the cleaner and their shoes to the repairman. If the working mother is in there taking care of her duties, too, there will be no resentment.

Financial icebergs may appear in a family with two incomes. The wife should consider these possible troubles before she takes her first job. There are many ways of handling the two-salary home, and the procedure chosen should fit the circumstances of the parties concerned. One method that has proved successful is the following:

1. Both paychecks go into the bank.
2. The better financier gets the job of paying the bills. If possible, the wife should encourage her husband to be the financier.
3. A certain percentage goes into savings — first.
4. A fixed amount is given each for a "none of your business" allowance — with no questions asked.
5. Under no circumstances should the wife consider the check she brings home as "her money." This is a partnership; she should not be an embezzler.

There are many advantages to working outside the home after the children are grown and gone. Unfortunately, if a woman waits until then to think about a career, it will be too late to find a rewarding job. One of the best plans for working out the problem is (1) to get as good an education as possible before marriage, (2) to keep working after marriage until the first child arrives, (3) to stay home and take care of them until they go to school, but to keep reading in her field, (4) to get a part-time job at first, and then gradually increase her involvement in her work until she is a career woman by the time her children are grown.

Grooming is just as essential to a working wife and mother as it is to the unmarried girl. Again, the time to plan the next day's wardrobe is the night before. Pressing, brushing, mending, washing, all should be done before your working morning. A working wife should not try to compete with the single girls in the matter of money spent on clothes. A few suits, skirts, and blouses can keep you dressed attractively. This should be your only goal.

You should never telephone the office to say you are sick so that you can catch up with your home duties. An employer will be sympathetic toward an occasional emergency, but you should not try the limits of his patience. Household help, reliable nurseries, or adequate child care will simplify your problems. Whatever you do, don't bewail your lot. You have many advantages. A happy home life makes a happy person. A cheerful person is a desirable co-worker. You can have a maturity and mastery of living that single girls rarely possess.

INTRODUCTIONS IN BUSINESS

In social circles introductions are performed as follows:

A man is presented to a woman: "Mrs. Porter, may I present Mr. Stockton?"

A young woman is presented to an older man or woman: "Mr. Graham [or Mrs. Graham], may I present my sister, Alice?"

One of lesser rank is presented to a celebrity: "Judge North, may I present Mr. Green?"

An unmarried woman is presented to a married woman: "Mrs. Davis, may I present Miss Randall?"

In business, performing the introduction tests a person's knowledge of business and social etiquette. Social standing outside the office does not hold precedence over business standing. In business introductions it is business standing that determines the importance of the persons being introduced.

"Mr. Charles [the head of the business], may I present Judge Woods?"

If Judge Woods were an important customer instead of a visitor on an inspection tour, the reverse order of presentation would be better business form.

An office or a store worker does not expect to be introduced to a caller unless the latter is going to work in the office or the store.

A salesman is presented to the employer unless he is much older than the employer.

"Mr. Charles [the head of the business], Mr. Taylor, our new salesman for the southern territory."

"Mr. Nichols [he has been with the company many years], Mr. Jackson, the new member of the board of directors."

A woman is presented to a man in a higher position.

"Mr. Charles [the head of the business], this is our new bookkeeper, Miss Cooper."

A woman caller is presented to the employer unless she is much older.

"Mr. Charles [the head of the business], this is Miss Daniels from the Children's Bureau."

An employer is not expected to introduce his secretary to visitors.

A man usually introduces his wife to his secretary. The secretary says, "How do you do?" and leaves the office during the duration of the wife's visit. Or she may smile and say, "How do you do?" and then turn quickly back to her work.

It is better to assume that the customer is more important than the employer and therefore to present the employer to him.

"Mr. Johnson [the customer], may I present Mr. Charles, our general manager?"

Make introductions as simple as possible. "Mr. Jones, Mr. Smith." "Mr. Henry, this is Miss Holmes." "Mr. Brown, may I present Mrs. Holmes?"

A few words to identify the person being presented are helpful. "Mr. Charles, this is Mr. Johnson. His window display this week is attracting much attention."

Cultivate a self-confident bearing and maintain poise of manner. In introducing people, speak the names clearly.

The correct response on being introduced is "How do you do, Mr. _____?" or simply, "How do you do?"

Listen carefully to catch the name. Repeating it in your acknowledgment gives the other person a good impression of you at the start. If you do not understand a name, say, "I beg your pardon, but I failed to get your name."

Double introductions, such as the following, are in poor taste: "Mr. Brown, Mr. Smith; Mr. Smith, Mr. Brown."

In an introduction a man waits for a woman to offer her hand. This she may or may not do as she pleases. Women in business, however, offer their hand in greeting when the business contact seems to require it, which it does more frequently than do the usual social situations. The customs in business are established by men, and women in business are expected to conform. If a handshake from a man's point of view seems to be in order, the woman extends her hand. Displaying feminine mannerisms in the business world is in poor taste. Overemphasizing the feminine role may cause ridicule.

If a man offers his hand first, the woman, to save him embarrassment, should extend hers.

If a woman is an executive, it would not be unusual for her to rise and shake hands with the president or with another official from a distant office.

A man removes his glove before shaking hands with a woman. A woman is not obliged to remove hers. A heavy driving glove, however, out of which her hand slips easily, should be removed.

There may be times when, in refusing to shake hands, you show thoughtfulness. You may say, "My hands are soiled. I've been running the mimeograph [or changing the ribbon in my typewriter, or looking through some old records]."

If you have a cold, show consideration by not presenting your hand. Do not offer an explanation. It is in poor taste to say, "I have a cold and should not shake hands."

The grip of a fraternal organization is not to be used in a business relationship because such a handshake would indicate an attempt to take an unfair advantage.

Shaking Hands

Handshaking under normal circumstances carries with it an index to the sincerity of the individuals who are meeting. Practice needs to be given so that an effective and desirable habit may be formed. When meeting people for the first time, you may not be at ease. The grip of your hand may be cold and lifeless; it may give the feel of "a cold hot-water bottle." Such an introduction may give the person meeting you the impression that you are a colorless individual; but actually, because of your earnest desire to make good, your hand may have suddenly become cold and lifeless. Practice of the performance until the right habit is formed will give you a sense of assurance that will permit your true personality to reveal itself. All the dread and the uncertainty of the unfamiliar person and contact will be lost in the knowledge that you know how and when to perform this social rite.

Practice shaking hands in class, one student with another, using the clinic method, until each one has had the opportunity of judging whether he has mastered an acceptable handshake, firm, decisive, sincere, cordial, and coordinated.

TRAIT TRAINING

The battle of the sexes may come closer to being resolved successfully if you pay attention to certain personality traits. Again, these traits are useful in all of the roles you play; but in smoothing relationships in the office they are invaluable. Following is a discussion of these traits: appreciation, gratitude, and happiness.

Appreciation

If you have cultivated the trait of appreciation, you have the ability to understand and to recognize the worth of people, humor, and things. It may surprise you to learn that almost all of us are starving for appreciation; for all of us are troubled by doubts of our worth. How welcome is the person, man or woman, who can express appreciation — and how rare!

Before you can express appreciation, however, you must learn to evaluate the individual differences, the attractive qualities, and the abilities of people around you. The results others are getting in the office, the attempts of employees to progress or to better their conditions, calls for your consideration. If you are fair, you will not be envious of favors granted others because of good work, or of promotions given others more efficient than you. Even if you have never before been able to congratulate a co-worker for some success or honor, force yourself to do so. Practice by yourself until you can bring it off casually, but keep your wording simple. If you say, "I see where your suggestion took first prize last month, John. Congratulations," in a casual way, John will be pleased (but not embarrassed); and you will find the next occasion for expressing appreciation easier to bring off.

Sometimes it is even harder to accept appreciative remarks than it is to give them. Again, keep it simple. Don't say, "Oh, it wasn't anything," as this tells the person who complimented you that he doesn't have good judgment. It is *not* a sign of modesty to answer in this fashion. It is a sign of conceit! Unconsciously or consciously you are telling the other person he should make his compliment even stronger. "Fishing" for compliments in this way is resented by anyone who has been sincere in expressing appreciation. The best response is a simple, "Thank you."

There are many opportunities to be appreciative without saying anything. For example, you should appreciate the trouble your employers have taken to provide you with modern equipment, attractive working conditions, and fringe benefits. Do not take the cynical attitude that these extras are mere "bait" to induce workers to stay with the company. Executives are interested in the happiness and well-being of their workers. If you are appreciative, they will feel repaid.

Situations arise every day which will give you an opportunity to be appreciative. Your wife or husband may help you more than you realize; take the time to be appreciative. Your supervisor may say, "Not bad," when you bring a finished piece of work for his approval. Don't bristle because of the faint praise, but say, "Thank you," casually. This kind of behavior shows discernment and appreciation for the point of view of business; it labels you a person of judgment. Experience in business is needed before you can discover where the emphasis is placed, before you learn what to appreciate and how to express your appreciation. The beginner should keep the importance of appreciation in mind and strive, gradually, to learn how to show it.

Gratitude

Gratitude means thankfulness, and it is very close to appreciation. The slight difference in meaning is that gratitude is in response to a kindness or favor received. People do not always perform acts of kindness for others because they expect a favor in return; however, most people like to feel that kindnesses are appreciated. They have a feeling of reward when they think their thoughtfulness and efforts are recognized by those people who benefit from them. These kindnesses deserve expressions of appreciation, and anyone worthy of success and capable of representing a business should know when and how to express gratitude.

Gratitude may be expressed in words. Simple courtesy demands that you thank the one who does a favor for you.

You may also express gratitude in deeds. For example, if an experienced worker helps you get started in a difficult job, you could, in turn, help another beginner get started. Another means of showing gratitude is by way of a "thank you" note. Write notes of thanks for gifts received, for congratulations received through the mail, for honors, for special attention. You will be surprised at the good feeling such notes cause, even in the most successful people.

Business occasions where you should express gratitude in words follow: When you receive permission to be absent from work when urgent business or personal duty demands that you be elsewhere; when you receive a salary increase; when someone helps you with heavy or difficult work; and when someone calls to your attention a fault which may impair your opportunity for promotion.

Examples of occasions in which gratitude should be expressed both in words and in actions are the following: Through the efforts of a former employer you obtain a good position; your appreciation should be expressed to him directly (perhaps in a note) but also indirectly through a genuine attempt to do a good job for your new employer. If you receive an increase in salary, your gratitude can be expressed through words (a simple word of thanks) but also through renewed efforts to improve the quality and quantity of your work. When better equipment or working conditions are provided for you, you should thank the person who made it possible; you should also take special pains with the equipment and with your work. If another employee assumes your duties during your absence, you are naturally grateful and express thanks; but you also try to serve others as kindly as you have been served. Form a pattern of always expressing gratitude when favors have been shown you.

Happiness

We all know what happiness is; we daydream about it even if we don't experience it. But many psychologists believe that happiness depends, not so much upon what happens to a person, but upon his emotional habits. That is, some people form the habit of cheerfulness and an optimistic viewpoint toward life, while others form habits of worry and depression. There are two ways you can be happy: You can get what you want, or you can want what you get.

All people are worried or sad part of the time, and all people are happy part of the time. Most people also have long periods during which they are neither happy nor depressed. Periods of sadness or some anxiety are natural; but if you are habitually upset or dejected, you should do something about it. It may be that realization that you are tense and unhappy for long periods will be enough to start you on a determination to change the situation.

Although some anxious and some gloomy people do succeed, it is in spite of, not because of, such tendencies. A cheerful, relaxed person has a big advantage both in business and in social and personal situations. Emotions are contagious, and an anxious person will make others anxious; a depressed person will spread gloom; and a cheerful person will cheer others.

Only to a limited degree is a person "master of his fate," but he can react in the best possible manner. Watch the expressions of the people you see on the street. You will observe that possessions may or may not make people happy, that sickness and need may or may not master their victims. Happiness does appear to be a habit that is not entirely dependent upon good fortune.

Both for your own welfare and for the effect on your associates in business, you should form habits of happiness. Just how this is to be done is the subject of some psychological research. Still, all of you know some ways that you can develop particular moods. By thinking pleasant thoughts, you can usually develop a good mood. By thinking of anxieties, you can develop fears. By dwelling on the tragic, you can become depressed. You may need to plan a campaign to banish fears and gloom and thus seek to substitute pleasant thoughts.

The companionship of cheerful people is helpful. Clubs, church groups, sports, and activity courses are ideal for associating with people who are *doing* and hence probably not in the grip of bad moods. Hobbies of all kinds can help you to create a cheerful mood. Dwelling on misfortune can make it an affliction. Detachment can make misfortune a problem to which one can adjust. One technique may help you: Think for a moment. Visualize the scene where you were the happiest you can remember. Is it a lake in the mountains, a white beach on the ocean, a field of wild flowers? Whatever this scene is, visualize it in detail and in technicolor. Then, whenever you feel a gloomy mood coming on, snap this picture into your consciousness. Think about it intently. As long as this picture is in your mind, those dark, dismal feelings cannot enter.

Happiness is greatly to be desired because it helps banish fear; happiness also has a pleasant effect on others. But there is another advantage: Happiness enables you to bring greater attention and concentration to your work. The worried person may be so preoccupied with his problems that he cannot give his full attention and ability to his tasks. The depressed person may lack the enthusiasm and purpose so essential to any work involving mental activity. You may be able to perform your assignment in a routine way if you are habitually depressed or anxious, but you cannot offer that plus quality required for success.

FOLLOW-UP ACTIVITIES

1. For one day, list the irritating things done in business or at school by one member of the opposite sex.
2. For one day, list the irritating things done in business or at school by a member of the same sex.
3. Compare the two lists. Which sex tends to irritate you the most? Do you think you may be doing something to

bring out the worst in some people? What are some of the things you do that might irritate women? that might irritate men?

4. For one day, casually express appreciation for everything that is done for you. If anyone opens a door, helps you carry anything, passes you the sugar, or is of assistance in any other way, say, "Thank you," and smile. Report to the class whether it made your day any more pleasant.

5. Have you ever lost your temper or in any other way lost control of your emotions in a working situation? If so, what was the result? Do you see any other way you could have handled the situation? Explain.

6. If you are working, make up a budget for one month. Include all your expenses of any kind. (If you are not employed, find out what beginning salaries are in your area and use this figure.) Take the amount you have listed for entertainment and divide it by 4. Spend exactly this amount for entertainment this weekend. Are you living within your entertainment budget at present?

7. This week, every time a person says anything to you of a complimentary nature, say, "Thank you." Force yourself to do this.

8. This week, casually compliment five of your co-workers or classmates. Keep your words and tone casual — but not sarcastic.

9. Write a short "thank you" note for some favor that has been done you in the past year. Keep the note short, sincere, and conversational. (If you are unable to think of any favors done you, write a "thank you" note to a member of your family.) *And mail the note.*

10. For one week, keep a record of your moods. Each night before you retire, write down which of the following phrases best described your prevailing mood that day:

Very happy	Somewhat depressed
Moderately happy	Very depressed
Neither happy nor depressed	

At the end of the week, see if you need to work on your emotional habit patterns.

11. A good customer has goods to be exchanged, and you, the clerk, send for the department manager. How will you introduce these persons?

12. A new girl comes to work. She is a stenographer and a friend of yours. You want her to meet the other workers in the department and also your chief, the head of the accounting department. How do you introduce her?

13. Your mother comes to the office to meet your employer. How do you introduce her?

14. When two young men meet, what is the form of greeting? Practice it.

15. When a young woman and a young man meet, what is the form of greeting? Practice it.

16. Practice removing your glove before shaking hands.

17. A young man offers his hand to another whose hands are soiled from cleaning a mimeograph. The latter says, "My hands are soiled from cleaning the mimeograph." Dramatize this situation.

PRACTICE EXERCISES

Dramatize the following scenes, which should give practice in meeting certain types of situations:

An invitation to dinner

Mr. Adams, a junior clerk, invites you, a stenographer for the same business, to have dinner with him.

"Will you have dinner with me tomorrow, Miss Turpie?"

"Yes, thank you, Mr. Adams. I shall be pleased to do so."

"May I call for you at 6:30?"

"I'll be ready on time. You know the address? 813 Fourth Street."

. . . .

If the work of the day has not been completed, your employer may say, "Perhaps we had better go to the Blank Cafeteria and have dinner before we finish the report."

With all propriety you may reply, "Thank you, Mr. Wilson. I'm hungry and I believe we could work much faster if we took time to eat."

Remember, however, that —

You do not make a social function of the meal.

You do not linger over the meal.

You do not consider it an opening wedge to greater intimacy.

You think of the meal as a fitting completion of the day's work.

A "Dutch treat"

Pay your way if you lunch with a fellow employee.

"Here, Jim. You pay for mine," you say as you hand him the amount spent.

or

"I'll pay you for my lunch later, Jim." (And remember to do it!)

Presenting an employer to a customer

"Mr. Brown, may I introduce the manager of our department, Mr. Gray? Mr. Brown has placed a large order."

or

"Mr. Brown, this is Mr. Gray, the manager." And you may add, "Mr. Gray, Mr. Brown is considering air-conditioning his home," or whatever else of importance and interest shows the relationship of Mr. Brown to your business.

Presentations to a manager

A young woman:

Mr. Gray is the general manager. Miss Haver, just out of school, is applying for an office job. The employment manager is impressed with her manner and wishes Mr. Gray to meet her. You make the introduction as follows: "Mr. Gray, this is Miss Haver."

A young woman has an appointment with Mr. Gray. You make the introduction as follows: "Mr. Gray, this is Miss Stance with whom you have an appointment."

An older woman:

"Mrs. James, this is Mr. Gray, our manager, with whom your appointment was made."

A personal friend:

"Mr. Gray, may I present my friend, Hazel Blair, who has come to see about the vacancy?"

A man caller:

"Mr. Gray, Mr. Stein."

or

"Mr. Gray, this is Mr. Stein of Browning & Company."

or if Mr. Stein is much older

"Mr. Stein, this is our manager, Mr. Gray."

Introduction of a secretary by her employer

(If there is a business reason for the introduction)
"Mr. Jones, this is my secretary, Miss Frey."

CASE PROBLEMS

1. When Business Interferes

Marian Carden, the secretary to a busy executive, has been looking forward to a dinner-dance with John Haimes for two weeks, and tonight is the night. At four o'clock her employer brings in a sheaf of papers and tells Marian to return after dinner to type a report. He must have the report completed this evening, as he is leaving on an early morning plane for a distant city. As a result of this trip he hopes to complete a transaction that will mean good business for the firm. He has seldom asked Marian to return to the office in the evening, and when he has done so, he has always notified her in advance if possible.

1. Is Marian justified in refusing her employer's request?
2. Is it possible that some other arrangement can be worked out with another typist? If so, who should make the request?
3. If the work demands Marian's particular skill and knowledge, what is her responsibility in the matter if another typist does the report?
4. Is willingness to meet periods of crisis one of the indications of promotional material?
5. Should Marian take into consideration the fact that her employer has been thoughtful and considerate in the past?
6. If Marian is frequently required to work overtime, what should she say when she accepts dates?

2. The Business Code

Helen Herbert is a stenographer in the office of a department store. The sales manager has shown a friendly interest in her; and one day while she is in his office he says, "How about a drink?" There is a rule against drinking and smoking in the office, but they have a drink and a cigarette. Helen goes back to her desk, and the personnel manager, in speaking to her, notices that she has been drinking. When asked about the matter, Helen admits that she has had a drink with the sales manager. She is then discharged.

1. Was the personnel manager justified in discharging Helen?
2. Should rules of the firm be kept, even though an executive suggests breaking them?
3. Why do you think the rule against drinking and smoking was made?
4. If the personnel manager had given Helen a warning, do you think this would have had a bad effect on the morale of the other employees?
5. Do you think the personnel manager will say anything to the sales manager? Why or why not?

3. Is a Whistle a Compliment?

Lester MacDonald has a secretary who is a striking beauty. She wears extreme clothes that attract attention. The men in the office seldom think of her only as part of the office machinery. Responding to their interest, her manner is a little too warm and her smile a little too intimate. His colleagues tease Lester about his secretary. At first he tried to be a good sport. Now the ridicule is becoming embarrassing. After all, he wants to work in his office, he loves his wife, and he is tired of his colleagues' jokes. He asks an older woman in the office to speak to his secretary.

1. If you were given this task, how would you begin?
2. What would you suggest in the way of appearance?
3. What would you suggest in the way of behavior?
4. How could you soften the blow so the secretary would really want to follow your suggestions?

4. "Who's Afraid . . .?"

Mr. Kane left the office a little early in the afternoon. He told Jane Starr, his secretary, that he would not be back during the day. Soon after he had left, Mr. Dodson, an important customer, came in.

"Is Mr. Kane in?"

"I'm sorry, but he has gone for the day. May I make an appointment for you for tomorrow morning? Or how about my calling you as soon as he comes in?"

"No, I shall be in town for only a few hours. See if you can find him for me."

Jane knew that Mr. Kane liked to forget the office as soon as he left it and would be irritated if called at his home. She hesitated for a moment before answering, then said, "I'll see if I can reach him for you." Risking Mr. Kane's anger, Jane dialed the number of his home.

1. What would you have done in Jane's place?
2. If you decide you would not call Mr. Kane, what would you say to Mr. Dodson?
3. If you did as Jane did, what would you say when you get Mr. Kane on the telephone?
4. In case Mr. Kane is angry with you the next day, what would you say?

5. Say It With Flowers?

Mr. White, a lawyer, was very considerate and understanding in the case of Pamela Marshall, one of his assistants in the office. She had been absent because of the illness of her parents; but Mr. White, knowing of the financial difficulties and the sickness in the family, had not let this absence affect her salary. Pamela wished to show her appreciation to Mr. White for his kindness and asked her friends in the office what she should do. She decided that she would buy a plant for Mr. White's desk. One friend to whom she had talked felt that such action would not be in good taste. Another friend felt that it would be all right because plants are always welcome additions to the furnishings of an office.

1. What do you think about Pamela's decision?
2. What is the preferred way to express appreciation for kindness shown in business?
3. What would you do in Pamela's place?

6. Artistic Temperament?

Bill Gates is exceedingly temperamental. When things go right, he is exuberant and can outsell any of the other salesmen. When things annoy him, however, he is moody and sullen. Bob English is the steady type, always optimistic, trying to forget personal affairs while at work. He is not a brilliant salesman, but he has a good consistent record. Both Bob and Bill are eligible for promotion as manager of a retail store.

1. How much would Bill's temperamental disposition affect his work as the manager of a store?
2. What has Bob to offer in recommendation for the promotion?
3. Which man do you think should be selected for the promotion? Why?

PART 5 GETTING THE JOB YOU WANT

Chapter 13

Applying for the Job You Want

The aim of much of your education probably has been pointed toward earning your own living. There is important logic back of this goal, too, for you must be able to support yourself and, possibly, your dependents. Earning money also gives you confidence. You feel like you really are somebody when that first paycheck comes your way. Exciting as this prospect may be, however, there is another side of the picture.

When you work in business, you spend around eight hours a day, five days a week, and about eleven and a half months a year in a certain kind of work. This is a lot of time, particularly when you multiply it by the thirty to fifty years that you may be a member of the labor force. Naturally, you want to make this vast amount of time as enjoyable as you can. If you do enjoy your work, you will be a much more pleasant person; and your chances of living a happy life are increased. If you dislike your work, on the other hand, you can see the hours of misery that will be added one upon the other.

Finding enjoyable work is not a simple matter. Many young people have no particular inclination toward one certain job at first. They only discover their liking or disliking for their jobs after they have been working for months or even years. Any formula that will help you to choose wisely, therefore, is a valuable tool. Some of the parts of such a formula are your schooling, your skills, your hobbies, your personality traits, your energy, and your health. The list is actually endless. You can see, though, that you must understand yourself before you can find the job for which you are best suited.

YOUR PERSONAL INVENTORY

As you approach the end of your last year of school, you should start your job-finding campaign. This beginning will be an important part of the entire process, too, because it may mean the difference between happiness and unhappiness on the job. The first step in selling anything, you see, is to learn all you can about the product. Getting the job you want involves selling yourself; and before you can do this, you must know yourself. If you have never thought about yourself in this fashion before, it may help if you look upon this whole process with an impersonal eye. Pretend you are someone else; be as objective as you can.

Making Your Inventory List

The first step in learning about yourself involves making a personal inventory of everything you can think of that would have a bearing on your success. One good way of doing this is first to jot down items as they come to you. For example, you might make a list beginning with the following:

> Born March 15, 1943
> Enjoy sports, tennis and swimming
> Not married or engaged
> Father's occupation, grocer
> Father's education, high school
> Mother's education, business school
> Physical handicaps, none
> Height, 5' 11"
> High School, East High
> Courses taken, business
> College, Westfield Junior College, 1 year
> Courses taken, clerical
> Best grades, math and machines
> School activities, swimming team;
>   business manager, football team;
>   advertising manager, *Clarion*

This is not a complete list, of course, and these items have no relationship to each other. Organizing your information comes with the second step. Now you do nothing but write down items about yourself. Just to be certain you omit nothing important, keep in mind the following additional areas: (1) your skills (typewriting, shorthand, machines, musical instruments, foreign languages), (2) subjects you have studied in school, (3) your hobbies, (4) your liking for people. Some jobs require the ability to meet the public, to mix well with others; in other jobs you may work entirely by yourself. It is important to rate yourself in this area and also to see how any prospective job can be evaluated with respect to this quality.

There is one other part of your inventory demanding some attention. You may be a person with many talents, one who changes his career choice with every new class he takes. If this description fits you, there are two ways of getting down to your fundamental interests. The first one has to do with routine work. All jobs have some dull, routine sides to them. If you dream of becoming a great ballet dancer and have never studied this art, you may know nothing about the six hours a day of endless exercises that must go on for years and years before a young dancer is permitted to do any actual performing. Make a list of all the routine activities you can think of that you rather like to do. Perhaps you don't mind tinkering with cars (and this would be drudgery to some people); maybe you find proofreading something of a challenge; or you may enjoy checking figures. After you have made your list, choose the routine activity you would dislike the least. This may be a real indication of your interests.

The second way to cut through too many interests in order to find the real one is to go back to your early interests. What activity did you enjoy the most when you were in the elementary grades? If you can remember back to the first three grades, you will find your interests before they were changed by favorite teachers, pressures from parents, and so on. If you were always elected president of your class — even in the elementary grades—you may safely say you get along well with others, or at least you have that basic ability. Or you may have been the one who was chairman of committees when you were ten or eleven. If so, you may naturally lean toward a job involving some leadership. Were you the class poet in the second grade? This may mean you have abilities in writing. With the increasing importance of communication in business, such a talent is vitally needed.

Organizing Your Inventory List

When you have written down every item you can think of (and you should have at least thirty items), you must organize the items into separate classifications. Some of the headings you might consider are the following:

> Schooling
> Early interests and routine enjoyed
> Work experience
> Abilities or talents
> Skills
> Machines
> Physical details
> Liking for people
> Organization memberships
> Appearance

Now take a large sheet of paper and turn it the long way. Enter your headings across the top of the sheet. Below the headings, list the items from your inventory that belong in each category.

When each item has been placed in its proper place, see if you can rank the categories in the order of their importance to you. Which classification has the most important items? Mark this classification "I" and the next most important "II" and so on. After you have arranged your headings in this manner, write down the first three. Assume that your first three were the following:

> I. Skills (high speed typewriting and calculating machines)
> II. Interests (have always liked detail)
> III. High grades in math and accounting

You can see that these three items suggest work in an accounting firm, either as a junior accountant or a combination statistical typist and clerk. Whatever your three highest classifications may be, they will give you a similar lead into the type of work you will likely do best and find most satisfying. Keep this classification at hand; you will use it next in preparing your data sheet and application letter.

Sources of Possible Jobs

After you have analyzed the product (yourself), you must analyze the market (the jobs available). Look over your own qualifications again. What other possible lines of work do they suggest? After you have settled on two or three alternative lines of work, the next step is to look around for one or more specific jobs. There are a number of sources where you might inquire: school placement service, newspaper want ads, state and federal merit tests, public employment bureaus, private employment agencies, and dealer agencies.

School placement services. Larger schools now have formal offices concerned with placing their students. The placement officer will ask you to fill out an application blank or a data sheet; he will interview; and he will consult the references you give him. This is an excellent source for you to consider. The school may know more about your abilities than any of the other sources named could possibly know. Businessmen who have had good results with such offices are glad to use their services again. In this way, a knowledge of the available openings is assured. One caution should be given in connection with the use of references. Always ask the former teacher or former employer if you may use his name as a reference. This is a courtesy to your reference, but it is also good insurance for you. Teachers, particularly, have so many students in one year that they may be grateful for the opportunity to renew your acquaintance. This, in turn, will make it possible for them to give you a more detailed recommendation.

Small schools usually do not have placement services. This does not mean, however, that you should not keep in touch with your former school in such cases. Placing of graduates in small schools may be handled by the business teacher, the teacher in charge of the work experience program, the school counselor, or by the principal. Ask your former business teacher whom you should consult; then go to this person and leave your name and your qualifications and references.

Your responsibility does not end (in either the formal or informal placement situation) with the interview. You should cooperate with the placement officer by following his leads *at once*. If the placement officer receives word that a job is available at 9 a.m., it may be taken by 2 p.m. A second need for promptness lies in reporting the results of your job interview with the placement officer. If you are given the job, he should send no other applicants for it; if you were late in applying and the job was taken, you should give the placement officer this information. If you did not get the job and it is still open, the placement officer will want to send other applicants. In the latter case, too, he may be able to refer you to other positions.

Newspaper want ads. You should always take advantage of the help wanted ads in your daily newspapers. These are not only a source of openings; they also show a trend as to the type of openings most prevalent. If you are undecided between two possible areas of work, for example, a study of the available jobs listed in the help wanted section should tip the scales in favor of the one providing the best opportunities. A further help can be found in the want ads, namely, the level of competence desired. In the secretarial field, for example, the majority of the ads may specify 60 words a minute in typewriting and 100 words a minute in shorthand dictation. A clerical job may ask for skill on the calculating and adding machines. A receptionist ad may ask for experience on the switchboard.

There are certain dangers to be avoided when responding to a want ad. Some of them are disguised attempts to sell merchandise. Be wary, then, of those asking for a cash deposit, or those asking that you buy samples. If the job requires that you take a course for which you pay tuition, this, again, may merely be a device for attracting students rather than a *bona fide* job opportunity.

Assuming, however, that the ad is for an actual job, there are two ways of replying to it. If an address is given in the want ad, you must go in person for an interview. This topic is discussed in Chapter 14. If a box number is given, you must reply with a data sheet and an application letter. These topics are discussed on the following pages.

State and federal civil service tests.   Two excellent sources of jobs are the federal civil service and state civil service. If you are interested in either of these opportunities, you should inquire at the respective office building in each case. Federal civil service tests are given frequently throughout the year. The dates and places of these tests can be secured at your federal building or post office, either in person or by letter. State examinations are customarily given in the spring, and information concerning these tests can be obtained at your state capitol.

Public employment bureaus.   The United States Employment Service conducts tests, arranges interviews, and provides job leads without charge. This service was established in 1933. Agencies are located in the larger cities of all the states. The USES is an excellent employment agency and one that merits your acquaintance. Businesses using the USES turn the screening of applicants over to the agency. Two or three applicants considered best suited for a certain position are then sent to the firm requesting help. Beginners in business, especially, will do well to visit their public employment bureau to learn about the services offered.

Private employment agencies. In addition to the public employment services, there are many private agencies operating in most cities. These agencies do charge a fee for placement. In most cases the applicant is expected to pay this fee (which involves a certain percentage of the salary received in the first months of employment). The advantage of the private agency may rest on the fact that these agencies often specialize in certain types of jobs. One may specialize in placing executives, others may place clerical workers, and so on. With such specialization, of course, the agency should have a deeper knowledge of the field covered and may have the exact job for a certain applicant. Before registering at a private agency, it is a good idea for a beginner to inquire of his former teachers or employers as to the particular agency's suitability for him.

Dealer agencies. There is still another source available to beginning office workers. Some companies dealing in office machines and appliances are able to help young people who are skilled operators of their equipment to find openings. If you are a fast and accurate typist on a certain electric typewriter, for example, you could get in touch with the local sales office of the manufacturer of this typewriter and ask about any leads they might have. Because it is to their advantage to place skilled workers on their machines, they are usually glad to help you. If you should get a job through a dealer, be sure to call the person who helped you and thank him.

Preparation for Placement

The law of supply and demand has a great influence on both securing and keeping a job. If the supply of workers with a particular skill is large, the employer can be selective in employing and retaining personnel. If the supply of workers with specialized training is smaller than the demand, then the worker can be selective in choosing a position. The present market is, and has been for some time, an excellent one for office workers, and an increase in these opportunities is expected to continue through the next decade. Such factors as tax laws, Social Security regulations, and the increase of defense industries all combine to create more and more office positions.

There is one change, however, that has already begun to operate. This change is in the opportunities available to the unskilled office worker. There was a time when a beginner with no training could start as an office boy and learn the business on the job. This picture has changed completely. There is no place in business now for the person without education or skills. The higher both of these qualities are, the better the opportunity in business. As the job classifications go up, the number of jobs available also increases. There is no place in business for the high school dropout. Conversely, the more skill, knowledge, efficiency, and desirable personal traits you possess, the better you can compete for the job you want. This means that you will do well to obtain the best training you can afford. This training may be obtained in schools plus experience or in schools alone.

The wise businessman and woman will realize, too, that times of great opportunity will not always exist. If you are wise, therefore, you will get all the training you can. If possible, such training should precede employment; but if this cannot be arranged, additional training after you are hired should not be overlooked. In cities many private and public schools and colleges offer night courses or Saturday classes. If arrangements cannot be made to take these classes, you might consider home study courses. These courses have one distinct advantage for the working student: They may be completed at the rate you set for yourself. Information regarding home study courses may be obtained from the National Home Study Council, Washington, D.C. The Council publishes the *National Home Study Council Bluebook*, which lists thousands of excellent home study courses.

YOUR DATA SHEET

Perhaps the most important single job-finding aid is your data sheet. Whether you apply for a job on your own, without invitation, or whether you are asked by an executive of a firm to come in for an interview, your cause will be aided if you have a neatly typed data sheet to submit. One reason for the popularity of the data sheet is the ease with which it can be scanned by the interviewer. Whatever he may wish to look over, he can find in a moment. It is also helpful for the firm hiring you if they keep the data sheet in your personnel file. When opportunities for advancement arise, your data sheet will provide, in concise form, the information that will help them make a choice.

To be effective, your data sheet must "put your best foot forward." Go back, now, to your personal inventory list. See if you have checked off every item as you added it to your classified inventory. Then look over your classified inventory for "best feet" or plus factors. Your data sheet consists of an outline of these plus factors arranged attractively under centered headings. The headings covered in your data sheet should include the following:

College Training
    (or Education if you have not attended college)
Work Experience
    (or Experience with People if you have never worked)
Personal Details
References

You should use either the first or the second heading to start your data sheet. You must make the choice. If you have had little or no work experience, you will naturally begin with your education. If, on the other hand, you have a really impressive list of previous jobs, this might make a better beginning. Your decision will rest on which is the better selling point for you. In most instances, perhaps, the beginner will find his educational record to be the superior selling point.

College Training or Education

In listing your education, you list the last school you attended, with your major field of study and the date of your graduation. For example, if you finished four years of college work, this could be stated as follows:

Four years' study at the University of Houston (1958–1962); B. S. degree; major in accounting with B plus average.

If you graduated from a junior college, this could be shown as follows:

Two years' study at Monterey Peninsula Junior College (1960–1962); Associate in Business degree; major in office practice, B average.

If your education beyond high school was not completed for a degree, you could show this as follows:

One and one-half years' study at Clarke College (1961–1962); will complete work for certificate by correspondence; major in secretarial science, A minus average.

The listing of additional diplomas for high school and elementary school is not necessary, but if your final schooling was your high school years, this is shown in the same way, as follows:

Four years at East High School, graduating in 1963; major sequence in Business, B plus average.

Following the statement of school attended, degree received, and so on, it is wise to list the courses you have taken that are related to the job for which you are applying. This may be listed immediately following the first statement as to school attended.

Courses related to work as supervisor of machines section:

Accounting, elementary and intermediate	Human relations
	Economic theory
Data processing	Statistics
Office management	Survey of office machines

Work Experience

In listing your experience, it is best to be quite specific. Such statements as, "Worked in grocery store," do not give enough information. Dates, names of companies and employers, plus a description of the work, are needed. Another important point is to list the jobs you have held in reverse order (the last job first). Following is an example, assuming you have worked in two different jobs:

1962–	Typist for H. M. Wells, Contractor, Springfield, Illinois; typing specifications, contracts, and general correspondence afternoons while attending college.
1960–1962	Clerk and delivery boy, Arnold Grocery, Springfield; worked afternoons and Saturdays.

If you have held more than five different jobs, it is best to choose only the latest ones or the most important ones. The experience section of your data sheet is to show concisely that you are capable of doing satisfactory work, that you know what it means to do a day's work for a day's pay. The listing of additional positions adds nothing new and takes up valuable space that can be better used in other ways.

Experience with People

If you have never had a job, full time or part time, the second section of your data sheet is headed *Experience with People*. In this category you should list organizations you belong to, dormitory offices, church offices, and school activities. Of particular interest to employers are leadership activities in debating, campus newspapers and literary organizations, athletics, and class offices. It is believed that such activities denote a person who can communicate well and who has learned to work as a part of a team. These qualities are vitally needed in the business world.

Personal Details

Some data sheets begin with personal details or vital statistics, such as date and place of birth, height and weight, health, hobbies, marital status, and military status. You may list a minimum of organization memberships in this section. This information is not as interesting to an employer as your training and experience, however, and is thus more effectively placed after the more important sections. Furthermore, these details should not be given too much importance. The centered heading, *Personal Details*, should be underscored; other titles should be followed by a colon, as follows:

Personal Details

Birth date and place:	Organization Memberships:
Born in Pennsylvania	Phi Chi Theta (business
in 1944 of German	professional)
descent	Delta Zeta (social)
Physical status:	University Methodist
5 feet, 6 inches;	Church
130 pounds; no defects	Hobbies: Music (sing in
Health: Excellent	quartette), dramatics,
Marital Status: Single	tennis, swimming

References

The last section of your data sheet should contain the names, titles, and addresses of four or five individuals who can recommend your work, your scholarship, and/or your character. These should be arranged attractively:

References

Dr. Morton L. Smith	Mrs. Harriet Sholund
Professor of Economics	Office Manager
University of Denver	Tri-State Insurance Company
Denver, Colorado 80213	Minneapolis, Minn. 55428
Mr. Elliot Hendrie	Mr. H. L. Frank
Instructor in Accounting	916 Third Street
University of Denver	Kansas City, Missouri 64144
Denver, Colorado 80213	

Photograph

The wisest investment you can make when applying for a job is to have a number of photographs (2″ x 2½″) made in conservative business dress. This can be done quite inexpensively, and a photograph makes your data sheet much more personal and alive. When you are ready to start your job-finding campaign, you should arrange to have at least twelve of these pictures made. Then attach a photograph to each copy of your data sheet that you send out. The completed data sheet could be arranged as shown on pages 223 and 224.

As shown in the illustration, your data sheet will look better and command more attention if it is arranged with plenty of space around each section. This means it will probably extend over two pages. Do not crowd a data sheet in order to save paper. You should be willing to invest in your future to the extent of buying good quality bond paper for your data sheet.

YOUR APPLICATION LETTER

While a data sheet is often used in both personal applications and those carried on by mail, the application letter will not always be necessary. Ordinarily, you will send a letter in answer to a newspaper want ad or as an unsolicited application. You may write a fairly long letter and include the necessary details if you wish. The most effective method, however, is to write a short letter introducing yourself and to enclose a data sheet with picture.

The beginning of an application letter is the hardest part. What you should remember, though, are your selling techniques. Your application letter must interest your prospective employer in you. The first thing you must do, then, is get his attention. If you know someone who is a friend of your prospective employer, you might (with permission) begin your letter with this fact. The second good beginning is to show what *you can do* for your reader.

YOUR NAME

Your   Photograph   Your Telephone
Address   (If you desire)   Number

Education

--------------   --------------

------------   -----------------

----------------   -----------

Work Experience

Data Sheet Form

YOUR NAME   2

Personal Details

_____   _____

_____   _____

_____   _____

_____   _____

_____   _____

_____   _____

_____   _____

_____   _____

References

_____   _____

_____   _____

_____   _____

_____   _____

_____   _____

_____   _____

Data Sheet Form

For example, a young graduate of a four-year college wished to get a secretarial job with the State Department in a foreign country. She was an honor student, and she had had unusual experience in college activities. Yet a government official suggested that she begin her letter with an accomplishment that was sure to be in demand: her ability to type 80 words a minute. Look over your personal inventory. See what ability you have that would be of help to the reader of your letter.

The second paragraph should show that you know something about the work and the company and should give some information about your training. This may require that you do some research on each company before you send your letter. In this paragraph, as in the first, you will stress the reader's interest rather than your own.

In the third paragraph you should put in a personal touch, something that makes your letter different from all others that may be received. This touch will give your reader an idea about your personality. For example, one girl mentioned in her letter that she had spent the preceding summer making telephone appointments for an appliance sales firm and had learned the importance of a low, friendly voice and clear enunciation in all telephone conversations. This touch made her letter stand out from the others.

Your final paragraph is short. All it does is make it easy for your reader to get in touch with you. Just one sentence is enough: "Will you call me at 322-2410 and suggest a time when I may come in to talk with you?" This short sentence suggests action; it gives the reader your telephone number again; and it also shows courtesy. All of these factors will help you persuade your reader to give favorable attention to your application.

You can see that such a letter will follow the principles of successful selling. You will get attention, then create interest, next add a personal touch, and finally make it easy for the reader to act — by getting in touch with you. One final warning: Don't copy application letters verbatim from textbooks. In the first place, they will not represent you; in the second place, your reader may already have received dozens of that same letter. Just talk, conversationally and respectfully, to your reader as you follow the foregoing four steps. An illustration of a letter of application is given on page 227.

Now that you have composed your letter, to whom should you send it? Your first task now will be to find as many prospects as you can. This involves another principle of selling. Your campaign should be planned to cover several weeks and to involve from twenty to thirty companies. The beginner in business who tries for one or two jobs and then takes one that is not right for him may never find the right job. Before you send any letters, you should make a list of prospective jobs. This list should cover all available sources: want ads, leads given you by friends, leads given you by placement bureaus and employment agencies, and some companies to which you have not been referred but for whom you would like to work.

When your list is ready, you should decide on which companies you will make a personal call and to which you will send an application letter. For the latter group, you must type an original letter. You may decide to use the same letter for each company, with minor changes, but you *must* send each firm an original copy. Nothing will get your campaign off to a worse start than sending out mimeographed letters. *Never* send a carbon copy of an application letter. You should also enclose a data sheet (an original), complete with photograph.

Another important point is to address your letter to an officer of the company. This makes your letter more personal and may have a direct bearing on its reception. If the firm is in your city, all you need do is call the company and ask the person who answers if he will please give you the name of the person you want. This might be a department head or

278 Third Avenue
Madison, Wisconsin 53716
May 28, 19--

Mr. Robert L. White, Manager
Apex Enterprises, Inc.
5932 Wilson Avenue
San Bernardino, California 92402

Dear Mr. White

Have you ever wished you had an assistant who could turn out
your correspondence, contracts, and specifications quickly--
with that important touch of accuracy? I might be the one.

On June 16 I shall be graduated with honors from Cutler College
with the degree of Bachelor of Science in Business Administration. This course of study has covered two years of general
education, one year of business and economics courses, and one
year of intensive training in office procedures and management.
My favorite course in college was business writing; I like
writing both letters and reports.

Since last September I have been working part-time for General
Electronics, Inc. On this job I have gained the experience of
working under pressure. When my family decided to move to San
Bernardino, my counselor suggested that I write your firm for
an interview. Mr. Thomas A. Jennings, my present employer,
will be glad to write you about my qualifications. His address
is given on the enclosed data sheet.

I plan to be in California with my family the last week in
June. May I call you for an interview on July 1?

                        Sincerely yours

                        Ann Wilcox

                        Miss Ann Wilcox

Enclosure

Application Letter

227

a personnel manager. If the company is out of your city, you should inquire of your public or school library for an index giving this information.

When you have sent out your letters, take your time about making a decision, and don't get panicky when your favorite firm fails to answer. One or two answers for each ten letters is average; you should send out enough letters to assure yourself of three or four answers. The more letters you send out, naturally, the more responses you are likely to receive. Your letter will have a better chance, though, if it is mechanically perfect, if it is typed with clean type and a medium dark ribbon, if there are no erasures (or the erasures are invisible), and if it is attractively arranged on the page. Make certain of these details. If you are asked to come to one firm for an interview, you should consider your mail campaign to be a success. In Chapter 14, you will find a discussion of the interview.

TRAIT TRAINING

Three traits that are particularly important to consider in connection with job finding are foresight, thoroughness, and self-judgment.

Foresight

Perhaps the most important trait you can develop to help you succeed in your job-finding campaign is foresight. Foresight has been defined as the act of looking forward, of planning for the future. This trait is one that separates the leaders from the followers — in business as well as in other walks of life. Foresight consists, too, in anticipating life's difficulties before they arise. It means you will notice that supplies are getting low as well as prepare for the job ahead of you on the office ladder. If you have foresight, you will be able to think of many opportunities for exhibiting this trait. The following list is not exhaustive, but it may remind you of others.

English — both spoken and written — is needed in every business job; and the higher you go, the more important it will become to you. You will show foresight, then, if you constantly strive to improve your English through general reading and specific study.

You will be using foresight if you learn as much as you can about the latest trends in business and economics. Regular reading of the magazines and newspapers of business is one excellent way of keeping abreast of the rapid changes that are constantly taking place. You should also learn all you can about your specific industry or service.

When you are employed, you soon discover that certain questions, comments, and complaints tend to be repeated by customers or clients of your firm. You will show foresight if you prepare in advance an answer for the most commonly asked questions and if you know in advance to whom you should refer the usual complaints. Foresight means you must learn the names of the products or services provided by your firm.

When you apply for a job, you will show foresight if you look ahead to the years to come. Is there a possibility of advancement in your job? If there is such a possibility, accepting a lower starting salary might be wise. If you are employed and see no advancement in your present job, you should plan for another one.

An important aspect of foresight is intelligent listening. Through listening and asking intelligent questions you can learn much that is now unfamiliar to you. Be careful, however, that you review what has been told you so that you need not ask a question more than once.

Thoroughness

The second trait of great value to you both in getting and in keeping a job is thoroughness. If you are thorough, you finish what you start, you persevere, and you display exactness. It is difficult to impress most beginners with the im-

portance of thoroughness. Good intentions are not enough.
Every task entrusted to you in business must be performed
completely and accurately. Following through is as necessary in business as it is in tennis or golf.

One habit you should develop is that of thoroughly checking your work. You must be able to evaluate critically the
work you do. ⎧You must learn to check off details as they are
completed. Particularly at the close of the working day, you
must check to see that all details have been taken care of
before you leave the office. The rewards in business are
reserved for those who do all that is required of them and a
little bit more, for those who go the extra mile.

If you are selling, you must make out all sales slips completely, accurately, and legibly. If you do bookkeeping work,
you must see that each entry in your books is carefully and
correctly made. You must be sure that the statements you
send out are correct. You must be thorough in making out
all reports. You must check the correctness of all data in the
correspondence you transcribe and make sure that all questions have been answered. If you have *any* doubts about the
meaning or spelling of a word, look it up in the dictionary.
Proofread every word of every page you type, and check the
enclosures that accompany the correspondence.

One habit of thoroughness that pays big dividends is
learning the names and faces of important customers. If
you can remember a customer's name and business after
having heard it only once and use his name when speaking
to him, that customer will consider you a brilliant addition
to the firm.

Self-Judgment

The third trait that is needed when applying for a job is
self-judgment, which means self-analysis. You must have
the ability to evaluate your own skills, knowledge, training,
and personal traits if you are to succeed. And you must make
this evaluation objectively. This means you cannot let your-

self be sensitive, that you must not become emotional in your analysis. One good way is to think, "So what?" as you note your various good and bad points.

Believe it or not, you will make more improvement as a result of your self-analysis if you keep your emotions out of the picture. When your emotions become involved with your feelings about yourself, it is almost impossible to accept any kind of help from others. No matter what the criticism, you immediately rush to your own defense. A friend may tell you, with the kindest of intentions, that you have a tendency to complain a great deal. This is actually an easy habit to break. Yet, if you are emotional about criticism, you will only be hurt and angry at the person for criticizing you and make no effort to stop complaining. Saying "So what?" to yourself is a graphic way of expressing emotional detachment, and saying it will help you build detachment.

Too much introspection, or thinking about ourselves, is not good for us; so taking stock of our good and bad qualities should be done rarely. One time should be just before or after you get your first job. This is true because you may have had no need to do this before and thus have an unclear picture of yourself. The next time you will need to take stock is when you first become dissatisfied with your work. Small disappointments come to all workers, of course; these do not call for self-analysis. If you should have an extended period of disliking your work, however, you should take stock. Your feeling of dissatisfaction may be caused by a job that is actually unsatisfactory, or it may be caused by personal factors that are frequently unrecognized.

The best way to find out exactly how others are affected by your personality is to have some other person tell you. This is easier said than done, however. No one wants to make an enemy; you may take offense even if you ask another person to point out your faults. And this is true regardless of how much you assure the other person you will not be offended. If you have a good friend with whom you might trade suggestions, and if both of you take pains to be tactful in what you say, both parties should benefit.

Being tactful is extremely important. If your friend asks you to tell him frankly if you can understand why he was not promoted when he had expected to be, you must not say, "Because your work is always late." This may lose you your friend, and he may fail to profit by your suggestion in his anxiety to explain to you just why he was late. A better way is to start with his good points. You might mention his accuracy, his good judgment, his care in checking all details. Then you might say, "Perhaps that's it. You may be too conscientious. Your boss may prefer to have you submit some of your projects immediately, rather than take longer to check and recheck." If you can get your friend to make this suggestion himself . . . but then, you could be a counselor instead of a friend!

If you would rather not undertake a combined improvement campaign, you can follow this same suggestion yourself. Write down all of your good points on a sheet of paper; underline the ones you consider outstanding. Take the most outstanding virtue you have and look at its opposite. For example, the other side of generosity is selfishness. And every virtue, if carried to extremes, can become a vice. See, then, if you could possibly be going too far in that particular direction. Are you thrifty? Look at yourself again. Compare yourself with one of your more popular classmates or co-workers with respect to this trait. Just how thrifty are you? If you are much more thrifty than John, the man who was promoted instead of you, then it may be possible that you have gone too far with this virtue and become stingy!

Try the following plan with at least three of your predominant traits; the results may surprise you! When you have compared yourself with a successful friend and found that you need some improvement, it is really a simple matter to improve. Any negative trait can be eliminated. First, you attack one trait at a time. Second, you must plan in advance. If you are going to make yourself be more generous, for example, you must make a plan and carry it out. It is not enough to be more "giving" when the opportunity comes up. You must make your own opportunities. Ask one of your friends to have lunch with you, and get the check first. Keep working on one trait until your overdoing in that direction has been eliminated. Then go on to the next one.

FOLLOW-UP ACTIVITIES

1. Interview an experienced worker in a job that you would like to have. Ask this worker to tell you something about the qualities needed for the job, the personality traits that are aids to success, and something about the standards of work.

2. Interview an executive. Telephone for an appointment and ask if you may question him about the type of employee he seeks. Take notes on all that is told you.

3. One of the hurdles you must conquer in getting a job is talking with an interviewer. How do you rate when you talk with strangers? If you feel insecure in this respect, do some practicing. Talk with someone whom you do not know about employment matters. Possible sources are librarians, teachers in your school whom you do not know, the placement director in your school. Try to get over your fear before you go to an actual interview.

4. Practice interviewing a friend for a position you would like. Ask this friend such questions as the following:
   Why do you want to work for this company?
   How long do you plan to stay in one job?
   What machines can you operate? Do you consider yourself a competent worker on these machines?
   What make of typewriter do you prefer? Why?
   Are you married? engaged? What are your plans?
   These questions may be asked you in an interview. What attitude should you have toward semi-personal questions of this sort?

5. Office work is competitive. How will you compare with other applicants for the job you want? Rate yourself on the following qualities as follows: plus — very good; check — average; and minus — poor.

Reliability	Manners	Leadership
Good nature	Poise	Intelligence
Honesty	Concentration	Accuracy

Now rate three of your friends who are also ready to look for their first jobs. Be honest — and do not refer to your own scores — and then compare yourself with your friends. If you score higher, you are probably ready for employment. If you score lower, you have more work to do.

CASE PROBLEMS

1. Experience or a Change?

Bob Wilder was just graduated from high school. He has two job opportunities for the summer. One is a general office job in a large manufacturing company. The other, which pays more, is driving a truck. Bob likes to drive and enjoys being out of doors. He is planning to go to college in the fall to study business administration. If you were Bob, which job would you take?

1. What advantages would each job offer? What disadvantages?
2. How would you rate the following three factors in choosing a summer job? Salary, change of activity from school, experience in chosen career.
3. Are part-time jobs considered experience by businessmen?

2. Is Craftsmanship Important?

Barbara Vinson has a job in the office of a laundry. In the letters her employer dictates, he is very careless in his English usage. Such matters seem of little importance to him. Barbara believes that the English in outgoing letters should be of high quality.

1. What should Barbara do about the situation?
2. It has been said that policies and facts are the responsibility of the dictator, but that spelling, punctuation, and grammar are the responsibility of the secretary. If this is true, should Barbara say anything about the matter to her employer? Why or why not?
3. If Barbara decides to correct the mistakes in grammar, how far should she go in changing her employer's style or characteristic way of expressing his meaning?

3. Who is Responsible?

Claire Baker usually proofreads all letters after she transcribes them. Her employer dictated several letters at 4:15 p.m., and because Claire was in a hurry to leave, she mailed these letters without proofreading them. In one letter that asked for the payment of a past-due account of $50, she typed the amount as $40. A prompt reply was received with a check for $40 in full payment of the account. Claire's employer insisted that she make good the difference. Claire agreed, but she thought his demand was very unfair.

1. Who is responsible for errors of this type, the business or the employees who make them?
2. What is the rule when cashiers make mistakes in giving change?
3. Why does business insist on accurate records where amounts of money are involved?
4. What opinion would the customer who paid $40 have of the firm?

4. Be Specific

A wholesaler of carpenters' tools has a vacancy in the sales department. Mr. Peterson, Director of Sales Personnel, calls the local college and asks that interested young men submit letters of application and data sheets. When the letters arrive, he narrows them down to two, one from Charles Pittman and one from Joe Anderson. The letter from Charles Pittman contains the following as part of his third paragraph: "I am confident that I can sell tools because I am prepared to sell. I get along well with people. I believe that I can sell the tools because I have always been interested in selling. As I am going to be married soon, I am interested in a permanent job."

In the third paragraph of Joe Anderson's letter are these statements: "I like to make bookcases and do odd jobs around our house. When you have a hobby like carpentering, you appreciate the value of Camp's forged steel tools. Although I have not sold tools, I have been a clerk in a drugstore, where I learned the techniques of selling firsthand."

1. Which young man do you think Mr. Peterson will employ? Why?
2. Why is it better to speak of specific facts than to make general statements when applying for a job?
3. What specific statement could Charles Pittman have written as evidence that he gets along well with people?
4. Is approaching matrimony a good selling point? Why or why not?

5. Will Your Best Friend Tell You?

Ed Wright has the annoying habit of drumming his fingers on the desk whenever he is engrossed in work that requires concentration. Bill Cope, who is himself immune to such distractions, tells Ed that he had better try to break himself of the habit. Ed resents the criticism of this mannerism. Bill, however, has seen their employer look with exasperation at Ed whenever Ed drummed with his fingers. He is certain that it will be only a matter of time before the employer says something to Ed about the matter.

1. Such mannerisms as drumming with the fingers are said to be largely unconscious. If this is so, how can Ed break this habit?
2. What motives do you think prompted Bill to criticize Ed?
3. Put yourself in Bill's place. Try to word this criticism in a tactful manner. What would you say to Ed?
4. Put yourself in Ed's place. Even though you, too, would probably feel resentment at this criticism, force yourself to respond positively. What would you say?

Chapter 14

The Interview for the Job You Want

There is a secret ingredient to help you through your first interview for a job. Going to an interview is rather frightening, mainly because it is a new experience for you. If you worry about the result of your interview, however, you will only add to the hazards already present. The secret ingredient, then, is to concentrate on the means and not on the end of your interview. Don't let your mind worry about the success or lack of success in this particular interview. Instead, consider your interview to be a pleasant conversation in which you will do your best to answer all questions promptly and correctly. Also, be ready to ask questions of your own when the opportunity arises and try to appear at ease.

Why is it important to refrain from looking ahead to the probable results of your interview? The answer is contained in one word, tenseness. If you are concerned with the results of what you are saying, of the success or failure of the impression you are making, you will become tense. Tenseness causes all kinds of unfortunate reactions. Your memory fails you; you hesitate in answering the simplest questions, thus appearing to be unsure of your answers; your expression, your voice, your posture, all advertise that you are frightened. All of this can be eliminated if you concentrate on the *now* rather than on the future. Chalk this interview up to experience. Resolve to do your best, but possibly just for practice. Decide before you begin that the first two or three interviews will be for the sole purpose of learning how to conduct yourself, how to "put your best foot forward."

If you can eliminate tenseness by being relaxed, you will be able to show the real you to your interviewer — something you will not be able to do if you are tense. After all, your interviewer will appreciate your relaxed attitude. It is not pleasant to inspire fear in people you talk to, and your interviewer does not enjoy this any more than you do. Your interview will be much more successful if you are relaxed and if you are prepared. Successful preparation involves your appearance, proof of what you can do, and perseverance.

DRESSING THE PART

In the chapters on dress and grooming, proper business dress was discussed in detail. The statements made in these chapters, however, are even more important when you apply for a job. If someone knows you, he will judge you or excuse you on the basis of your personal qualities, your ability, your past accomplishments. When you go for an interview, however, none of this information is available. The only basis on which you can be judged, on which your efficiency can be estimated, is the way you look. Because of this, you must take special pains to look your best for the interview.

First of all, your dress must be appropriate. If you have one suit or dress that is dark colored, tailored, and in fashion though not extreme, this is the one to wear. It must be immaculately clean. If there are any white touches (blouse or shirt, collars, etc.), they must be spotlessly white. Shoes must be polished, and both men and women should wear a hat — even if this is the last time you ever do so. A hat seems to serve as a symbol of respect to the importance of the occasion. A girl or woman should wear a small inconspicuous hat; she should carry a good-looking but not too elaborate bag, and she should wear gloves. A man should wear a hat; he may carry a briefcase (but not a bulging one), and a neatly pressed topcoat.

Grooming for the interview should be perfect. Never skip any detail of grooming when dressing for an interview.

Clothing should be clean and not previously worn since the last cleaning. Be sure to use an effective deodorant and a mouthwash. Carry a clean handkerchief. Wear new hose or socks to reduce the possibility of snags, runs, or holes. Avoid too much jewelry. While tastes of executives differ in this regard, you will never be criticized for wearing too little jewelry. Makeup, too, should be artistic and should be understated.

WHAT YOU CAN DO

Next to your appearance, your interviewer will want evidence of your abilities. The reason your abilities come second is that your appearance is infinitely easier for your interviewer to evaluate. Also, he will read into the neatness of your dress certain estimates of the way you will work. These estimates will be supplemented with questions and, possibly, tests. When questions are asked, general statements of what you like to do, of your interest in people, and so on are of little help. A company wants to hire workers who have proved themselves. You may feel that you have no proof; and, when you seek your first job, you may feel completely inadequate. What you may not realize, though, is that experienced executives understand this feeling; they consider it natural. What they will not understand is any attempt on your part to "gild the lily." If you have had absolutely no previous experience, you must state this frankly when asked. You must not pretend to be something you are not.

An executive is interested. however, in any kind of work you may have done. Although you are applying for office work, the executive will be glad to know about newspaper routes, care of young children, playground directing, leadership in summer camps, manual labor, and many other forms of honest work you may have performed. Vacations spent in worthwhile work tell your interviewer that you have formed desirable work habits.

What You Can Do For a Specific Company

Before you go to any company for an interview, learn all you can about it. Find out what products are manufactured or sold, what services are performed, the location of branch offices in other cities. Ask your librarian for indexes containing this information. You may be surprised to know how much information is available to you. Whether you have an opportunity to display this knowledge is not too important. What is important is the confidence you will gain when you succeed in becoming acquainted with the company.

When you know something about the company, you will be better prepared to display what you can do. First, gather together samples of your work. If you are young and inexperienced, you may not have many exhibits to present. What you do put into your portfolio, however, should be of the highest quality. Depending on the kind of job for which you are applying, you should gather exhibits that will show you are familiar with the type of work done in the company. Actual evidence is much more effective than any unsupported statement you could make.

If you are applying for a stenographic position, you might include in your portfolio the following materials:

1. To show skill:
   2 letters perfectly typed and artistically arranged
   2 form letters with fill-ins
   2 examples of statistical typing
   An example of forms filled in with a typewriter
   A stencil you have cut
   Certificates of proficiency in shorthand and typewriting
2. To show personality traits:
   Clippings from the school newspaper showing activities in which you participated
   Copies of minutes of meetings (you were the secretary)
   Data sheet

If you are applying for a position in the bookkeeping department, you might include in your portfolio:

1. To show skill:
   The journal record of a completed set
   Several invoices, statements, and receipts attractively written
   A copy of your balance sheet that had been selected for class display
   A time test on the adding machine, consisting of section of tape with the record stated
2. To show personality traits:
   Financial statement that you, as treasurer of the student body, issued at a recent meeting
   A letterhead that you designed for school use in a type-writing class
   An issue of the school paper containing art sketches you made
   Data sheet

You can see that almost any evidence of worthwhile activities in school, clubs, or community projects is of interest to the prospective employer. Although such activities may not be directly related to the assignments you will receive on the job, they do show personal qualities that may interest the employer. Samples of your work should be kept from your school classes whenever they appear to be valuable evidence to show when you apply for a job.

There are other bits of information you should have at your finger tips. First, you must know your social security number if you have one. If you don't have one, you should get one before you go for an interview. Second, keep in mind the dates of important events in your life, the names of your former employers, and the kind of work you did in each case.

If you are applying for specialized work, you will need the tools and materials required in case you take tests. For instance, if you are applying for a stenographic position, you should take a shorthand notebook, a pen, a pencil, a type eraser, and a small pocket dictionary in case you are asked to take dictation and transcribe. For all kinds of jobs you should take a pen, a pencil, and a pocket dictionary. You may be filling out forms even if you are not required to take one or more of the many tests now being required by industry.

Take a Deep Breath

No matter how well prepared you may be, the effect will be ruined if you appear for your interview looking as though you just barely made it. Take plenty of time. Allow yourself twice as much time to get to your destination as you would normally require. If you drive, you may have car trouble; if you take a bus or a train, you may have to wait longer than you expected. And, regardless of your means of transportation, always go to your interview alone. Any young person who needs the support of a friend is not mature enough to take a job.

When you go into the reception room of the company, you will give your name and the time of your appointment (and the name of the interviewer if you know it). The receptionist will probably ask you to be seated and wait. Don't be alarmed if there are other people waiting, too. Be friendly, reply to all questions courteously, but do not bother the receptionist or other employees with questions.

Even if you wait for some time, try to relax; think of a pleasant subject. Above all, don't anticipate difficulties when your turn comes to go in to talk with the interviewer. Even with the best of intentions, you may find yourself suffering from stage fright as you walk into a strange office. It may help you to know that stage fright often acts as an aid to the sufferer. "Butterflies" may mean that you are keyed up to a high level of alertness, and your first words to the interviewer will banish your nervousness. In any case, the following suggestions may help you:

1. Stand tall. The first impression you make is certain to be a better one if you stand tall. This does not mean a stiff, military posture. Raise your chest, keep your ears lifted, and your posture will be as it should be. One hazard may happen to you: the employer may be busy when you go into his office. If this should happen, do nothing except stand quietly until he looks up. Don't do anything with your hands as you stand. Putting them in your pockets, moving your handbag from one hand to another, crossing your arms, all advertise that you are ill at ease. Just let your hands hang at your sides. Regardless of how this feels to you, it looks more relaxed than any other attitude you could assume.

2. **Think about something pleasant.** Have you ever had someone ask you to look pleasant as he snapped your picture? And, as you looked pleasant, how did the snapshot turn out? Was the smile you forced a natural one? Probably not, yet this is usually the way any attempt to look pleasant turns out. A better way to achieve the appearance of being comfortable in your surroundings is to think of something pleasant. If you do this, your "look" will follow suit, and it will also appear more natural. Perhaps the best thing to think about is some good point you have noticed about the company. If you are interested, you will look interested — and this is a pleasant sight for the interviewer to see.

3. **What should you say first?** Suppose you have been standing in front of the interviewer's desk for several moments and he finally looks up at you. What should you say? Remember, the employer does not know you; so the first thing you say is your name. In your most natural manner, tell the employer who you are — and use the employer's name. Say, "Mr. Eccles, I am John Cardwell. You asked me to come in this morning." It is pretentious to give yourself any title whatever, so don't say you are Mr. Cardwell or Miss Ellsworth. And don't supply your middle name unless you go by both names. It sounds all right to say, "I am Mary Jo Smith, Mr. Eccles," but to say, "Mr. Eccles, I am John Kennleworth Cardwell," is too much. After you give your name, the interviewer will ask you to be seated and take the interview from there.

4. **What do you do with your belongings?** In cold weather, it is best to leave your outer coat, boots, or other

paraphernalia in the reception room, hanging them up if there is some arrangement such as hooks, hat racks, or closets available. It is decidedly awkward to carry excess clothing into the employer's office. You girls will wear your hat and carry your handbag and gloves. These items you will keep with you. If your bag is large, put your gloves inside it and place the bag upright at your feet. If it is small, hold it and your gloves in your lap. You men should hold your hats in the same way, placing your briefcase on the floor beside your chair. If you are asked to write something, do so at your chair. Do not touch the employer's desk. Don't put anything on it, and don't look at anything on it (letters, contracts, and the like). If you can keep your hands quiet, you will add to the good impression you make. Any kind of activity of the hands, turning a ring, smoothing your hair, touching your face, will show that you are nervous.

What Do You Say?

The employer will lead the interview, but there are a number of directions he may take. Some interviewers ask many questions. When this happens, be sure to answer with enough detail. For example, if an employer should say, "You say your name is John Cardwell," you might answer, "Yes, sir." A more detailed answer is better, however. If you continue, "Mr. Kent from the Central College placement office asked me to see you," this places you more exactly than merely answering in the affirmative could do. This answer, too, will naturally lead into a discussion of your school work, the subjects you liked best, your grades in your major field, school activities, and so on.

It is important that you answer all questions without hesitation. You may be asked why you want to work for this particular company. Such a question is frequently asked, so it is wise to be ready with an answer. If you have a friend who is employed in the company, this is a valid reason. Or you may answer that you are interested in this business (banking, manufacturing, the oil business, or whatever it may be). Another reason may be that you have been a customer of the company and have admired the way they deal with the public. Whatever your reason may be, give it promptly and sincerely.

Controversial questions. Some interviewers make a practice of asking a question or two that is controversial. Such a question might have to do with politics, religion, racial matters, or economics. If this kind of question is asked you, give a mild but straightforward answer. It is important that you refrain from anything that may sound argumentative no matter what your interviewer may say. It is possible that such questions are asked to see if the applicant can remain calm under pressure. No matter what the motive, however, it will be to your advantage if you *do* remain calm. A good mental attitude is recognition of the universality of different opinions.

Your previous employer. You must avoid saying anything negative about a former employer or teacher. Your interviewer will assume that you will be just as likely to knock him and his company to someone else. The reputation for loyalty is built up by saying positive things about former associates of all kinds. An employer who asks about your low grades in some school subject will appreciate your taking the blame. If you say you didn't work as hard as you should, or that you spent too much time on extracurricular activities, you will make a better impression than if you blame your low grades on a poor teacher. Because he dislikes hiring a troublemaker, an employer will avoid hiring a person who whines or knocks. Saying negative things about former associates is one symptom of the troublemaking habit. Be careful that you keep away from any possibility of having the tag of troublemaker applied to you.

What about salary? Should the beginning applicant say anything about salary? In general, it is best not to bring up the matter too soon. Don't ask the interviewer how much the job is worth at the beginning of the interview. On the other hand, you should be prepared with some statement about salary if the question is asked you. What should you say if the interviewer asks, "What salary do you expect?" If you are currently employed or if you have worked recently, you might mention the salary you made or are making, with the qualification that you would expect an advance if you are working. The beginner, however, does not have this advantage. What should you say if you are seeking your first job? In this case, you need not mention a specific amount. You might say you are interested in advancement, but that the interviewer would have more of an idea what the particular job is worth. This statement would open the matter for discussion.

Before you go to your first interview, you should find out what beginning office jobs are paying in your community. Possible sources of information about salaries are your school placement service, the United States Employment Service, and the business teachers in your school. If you should reach the end of your interview and find that nothing has been said about salary, you will have to bring up the subject. You might say, "Could you give me some idea of the salary?" Stated this way, the question sounds reasonable rather than grasping. It should merit a factual reply.

When discussing salary, you should be perfectly frank. Do not say you have been offered some amount if it is not the case. The quickest way to be blacklisted among business-men is to misrepresent facts when applying for a job. If you should be seriously considered for employment, your would-be employer will certainly check on the information you have given him. On the other hand, you should not understate your desires. If you are willing to work for the salary suggested, that is one thing; it is another if you agree to the suggested salary in order to get the job and then regret your decision.

Remember that a business is not a charitable organization. You should not explain why you need a job or why you need a certain salary. The employer is interested in what you can do for the company. It is much better, then, for you to emphasize your abilities and skills, your knowledge of the work to be done, and your interest in the field.

What Do You Do?

In a way, an interview can be a miniature working situation. You may be given a test that simulates the work for which you are applying. If you are asked to take dictation, for example, try to be calm. It is better to go slowly and accurately because hurrying will cause mistakes which, in turn, will make you more nervous. You have been instructed to have a pen, notebook, small dictionary, and type eraser with you when applying for a secretarial position. This is because asking to borrow some needed item during the test session will look anything but efficient to the person conducting the test.

You fill out an application blank. One activity is customary when you go to a firm for an interview; this is filling out an application blank. Again, do not hurry. Take enough time to read each item carefully. Notice if your name is to be written or printed and whether your last or first name is to appear first. Unless you are asked to typewrite the information, the blank should be filled out in ink. Careful reading of each statement will eliminate erasures and strikeouts. You should answer all questions, leaving no blank spaces. If the question does not apply to you, such as military training for most girls, draw a horizontal line in the space provided. This indicates that you have read the question but that it does not apply to you. If you leave a blank space, this could mean that you failed to see the question or that you did not wish to answer it for some reason. Be as neat as you can, both in writing and in keeping the blank free from smudges, wrinkles, and fingerprints. Be extra careful to carry out all directions that are printed on the blank. Some firms consider the ability to follow directions one of the best indications of the applicant's suitability for employment.

You leave promptly. When you have finished taking any tests that are required and filled in the required forms, and when the employer has asked everything he wishes to know, he may indicate that the interview is over. This indication may be a statement, a question, or merely a long pause. You must be perceptive enough to catch your cue, whatever it is, and to act upon it at once. Long, drawn-out leave takings are inappropriate and will do you harm. You should pick up your belongings (such as a briefcase or a handbag), rise, thank the employer for considering you, say good-bye pleasantly, and then go. There is one thing you might make sure of, however. The employer may tell you he will call you in a few days, after he has consulted your references. If he says nothing, you may ask if you may call in a week or so to see if a decision has been reached. In any case, whether you mention the matter or not, following up on a job you want is good strategy.

You follow up. It is courteous to write a short letter of appreciation for the interview. Then, after several days, you may call the employer and ask if he has filled the position for which you applied. If the job is still open, the telephone call may bring your application to his attention; if it is filled, knowing about it at once is preferable to waiting. Some excellent jobs have been won because of persistent follow-up on the part of the applicant. Keeping yourself in the picture is usually to your advantage; but whatever happens, you must not give up. You will learn a great deal from going on several interviews. If you consider each interview as a stepping-stone to the job you want, you will be less likely to try too hard to impress any one employer. Just be yourself; it is the most impressive *you* that you can present.

APPLICATION FOR EMPLOYMENT

Full Name (Print)

Mr.
Miss
Mrs. _____

FIRST   MIDDLE   LAST

Present Address _____ Telephone No._____

STREET AND NUMBER

CITY OR TOWN   STATE

How long have you resided there? _____

Permanent or Home Address _____

STREET AND NUMBER

CITY OR TOWN   STATE

How long did you reside there? _____

Date of Birth _____ Age _____

MONTH   DAY   YEAR

Are you single? _____married? _____widowed? _____

separated? _____divorced? _____

Have you any relatives in the employ of this company? _____

If so, give name, relationship, and position. _____

APPLICANTS SHOULD NOT WRITE BELOW THIS LINE

Interviewed by:	Date of interview	Date applicant available for work
Applicant's Areas of Special Strength and Interest		

Date Employed	Clock Number	Enrolled in Bonus Plan	Classification
Enrolled in Group Insurance	Enrolled in Pension Plan	Blue Cross–Blue Shield Coverage ☐Ind. ☐Fam. ☐Surg.	
Date Employment Terminated	Reason	Consider for Re-employment	

Application blank (continued)

EDUCATIONAL RECORD

SCHOOL	NAME AND LOCATION	NO. OF YRS.	DATE OF GRADU- ATION	SPECIALIZED SUBJECTS
Elementary........				
High or Preparatory				
Trade............				
Business..........				
Correspondence....				
College..........				
Others (Specify)...				

Are you now attending school? _____

If so, give particulars. _____

What office machines do you operate? (Typewriter, Calculators, etc.)

Are you a skilled operator in the use of these machines? _____

Give experience. _____

What experience have you had as a stenographer? _____

What foreign languages do you speak? _____

What foreign languages do you read and write? _____

Application blank (continued)

EMPLOYMENT RECORD

FROM		TO		NAME AND ADDRESS OF EMPLOYER	NATURE OF WORK	SALARY	WHY DID YOU LEAVE?
YR.	MO.	YR.	MO.				

If you are employed at present, why do you wish to leave? _____

May we write to your present employer concerning you? _____
Have you ever been dismissed or requested to resign from any position?

If so, when, where, and for what reason? _____

Are you in debt? _____ If so, how much and for what reason?____

PERSONAL DESCRIPTION

Height _____ | Have you any physical defects or deformities?

Weight _____ | _____

Color of Eyes ____ | Explain fully. _____

Color of Hair _____ | Is your sight or hearing impaired in any way?

Complexion _____ | _____

Do you use stimulants, narcotics, or drugs of any kind? _____

Have you ever been accused of or convicted of any crime? _____
Give particulars. _____

Have you ever had a surety bond canceled or an application declined
by a bonding company? _____ If so, state particulars. _____

Application blank (continued)

PERSONAL REFERENCES

List the names of three persons, other than relatives, to whom we may refer concerning you.

NAME AND ADDRESS	OCCUPATION	YEARS OF ACQUAINTANCE

DEPENDENTS

NAME	AGE	RELATIONSHIP

THE SPACE BELOW IS FOR THE USE OF THE INTERVIEWER:

Application blank (concluded)

Which Job Should You Accept?

If you are well qualified, you may have your choice of several positions. You may be hesitant to accept a position that is available because you may think you can find a better position elsewhere. This attitude may or may not be realistic. If you cannot perform your best work with maximum satisfaction in a particular job, you are wise to discover the fact before you begin work. If you are reluctant to accept an available job because your salary or prestige demands are too great, then you may have to adjust your demands. However, as you want to build a satisfying career for yourself, you should not sell yourself short just to obtain immediate employment. Your goal is to market your services for the best possible measure of job stimulation and challenge, security, appreciation, and other rewards.

In deciding whether or not you will accept a position, the following questions should be considered:

How stable is the firm? Is it just getting started? What are the indications that it will succeed or grow?

What opportunities are there for advancement?

What promotional policies has the firm established?

Do I have educational or personal characteristics that will limit my advancement?

Will I need more education if I remain with the firm? Have I formulated plans for such education?

When a vacancy occurs in a better position, is someone likely to be brought into the firm to fill the vacancy?

What is the reputation of this firm? Within the company itself? Among the personnel? Among customers or clients? Among other people?

What security does the position offer? In times of depression what layoff policy will be followed? Can the employers usually be depended upon to be just and fair? Will the employers keep their word? If sickness takes an employee from his work temporarily, will his job be filled by someone else?

What social security does the position offer for retirement? For unemployment? For sickness and hospitalization? For injury?

Can you offer this firm your trust and your best work?
Will the work be challenging enough during a period of
years?

Do you like the employers and your immediate superiors?

Do you have the aptitudes, interests, and abilities required by this job?

Are there any negative characteristics? Some people
want to avoid night work, travel, and so forth.

In answering these questions, you will have to find sources
of information about labor trends, industrial expansion, technological changes, and other factors. Many books and magazines discuss opportunities for employment and advancement
in great detail.

If You Like the Job

If you like your new position, do all you can to express
your appreciation by doing your best work. You may find
that you can achieve greater satisfaction by growing in the
present position than by competing for advancement. If you
make a decision to grow in the present capacity, you must
constantly try to improve your efficiency. If you have no
ambition to advance or to improve in your present assignment, you will grow stale and become both bored and boring.

Length of service in a single capacity offers opportunity
that is rewarding. By familiarity with the position, you can
obtain more knowledge and skill. You will become more
expert in your duties and will assume more responsibility.
This thoroughness and familiarity may make you more
secure in times of staff reduction. If the human relationships
afforded in the present capacity are pleasant, you may find
that continued work with the personnel will be more rewarding than adjusting to new co-workers.

Some people cannot perform their best work in a competitive situation. By growth in a job instead of ambition
to advance, the stress of competition can frequently be
avoided, and yet a feeling of success can be attained.

TRAIT TRAINING

The sections devoted to trait training in each chapter in this volume are just as applicable to getting a job as they are to behaving on the job. You should review much of what has been said about personality traits when you are ready to apply for work. Some traits, however, may seem especially appropriate for study when the time comes for you to leave your studies and join the labor force. Two such traits are courage and self-control.

Courage

You may picture heroic actions when you think of courage, but there is another definition. For courage is that quality that enables one to remain steadfast under difficulties. Sometimes the latter kind of courage is designated as moral courage. Often the person who is being courageous in this sense is doing so without letting anyone know of his difficulties.

When your parents were young, character was a word that was spoken of as frequently as we now use the word personality. In that bygone day, strength of character was the most important attribute an individual could possess. Character seems now to have gone out of fashion, as least as far as talking about it goes. But because we hear less about courage, strength of character, and nobility does not mean that these traits are less needed. No one can succeed without strength of purpose.

How do you know whether you have courage? One clue is this: Can you do the hard thing, the unpleasant action, that you know is right? The easy way is rarely the courageous way. Another clue is whether you can "stand on your own two feet." People who lean on others, who always ask for help, who are filled with self-pity are not being courageous. Everyone has problems. The person with courage masters his problems; the weak person's problems master him.

It takes courage to admit your mistakes; but once having admitted them, you will find your path smoother. When you cover up your mistakes, you spend far too much time making excuses, blaming your troubles on others, depending on the alibi. If a businessman must admit an error in judgment, he may feel chagrin or may even be punished, but eventually he will be admired for his honest admission. To "pass the buck" may reap an easy way out, but it will also reap loss of respect.

You demonstrate courage by taking responsibility for your errors, by facing irritations without reacting to them, by defending the policies of the firm, by ignoring pettiness and gossip which may involve you, by standing up to be counted for what you know is right. You show courage when you cheerfully perform the difficult, tedious, or unpleasant task when it falls to you. You will be especially courageous if you perform your work with poise, dignity, and patience although conditions at work or in your private life may be distressing. You are courageous when you do not take unnecessary advantage of illness, physical handicaps, or interruptions to avoid work.

The strong person may not be rewarded immediately. You should prepare yourself for the fact that, like the reward for many other positive traits, it is earned after a long period of time. If you advertise courage, after all, you do not really have it. You can demonstrate character, strength, and courage in unobtrusive ways only when the occasion demands that you do so. Eventually, others will know that in a crisis, great or small, they can depend on you.

Self-Control

Another valuable trait is self-control, the exercising of restraint over oneself. This trait is shown best in tranquility, in refusing to become ruffled, no matter what the provocation. Anyone in business who possesses this trait becomes a valuable addition to the firm. This is because emotions are contagious. Hysteria is catching, but tranquility is equally so. Modern business is filled with emergencies, crises, pressures. Someone who can remain calm will act as a human tranquilizer to those about him. To paraphrase Kipling, if you can keep your head when those about you are losing theirs — you will be a real addition to the staff of the firm.

Self-control has another side, as well. Not only must you control negative emotions, but you must see that you act as a self-starter to make yourself do the things you should do. Actually, your success in business will depend to a great extent upon your ability to control your work habits. Innate intelligence is highly overrated by many people as a factor in success. A brilliant mind helps, of course, but it will not insure success. Interest in your work, enthusiasm, work habits, carefulness in checking details — all these play an important part.

You may have observed someone with great talent who was at the top of his profession. What you did not see was the long period of hard work that had gone into this person's career. The axiom that genius is 90 percent perspiration and 10 percent inspiration is true. Even gifted men and women must work hard if their talent and intelligence are to benefit themselves and others; work always requires self-control. In long-range planning, all of us want to work; but doing the job in front of us requires much personal discipline. If a supervisor oversees the work, this outside force helps you to settle down to work. If you have a job you must do without prodding from others, you must have great self-control to work efficiently.

Some of the common ways to put off applying self-control are used by all of us. We get a drink of water; we adjust the ventilation; we become distracted at the slightest interruption and find it hard to pick up the thread again. All of these preparations for work must be forgotten. The best way to start working is to sit down and begin. Get started with a stubby pencil. Save that drink of water for a reward at the end of your first completed page. Adjust the ventilation as a reward for the completion of your second. If you use self-control the first few times, you will form the habit of concentrated effort. With this habit, you will find yourself becoming a much more productive worker.

There is no simple formula for controlling efforts and emotions. By trial and error you will discover ways that work for you. Just remember that practice in self-control builds strength. The following list will provide you with opportunities for practicing self-control. If you find habits in this list which you would like to acquire, begin now to make such habits a part of your own personality.

Ability to work at a task that does not offer immediate interest or pleasure

Ability to work on a fixed schedule, even when you are your own taskmaster

Ability to work instead of participating in pleasant sports or entertainment when the work cannot be postponed

Not waiting until the last minute before beginning a necessary task

Attending to the most demanding duties first, rather than doing the most interesting work first

Conquering evidences of anger, impulses to "tell off" other people, and smouldering resentment

Ability to control giggling, idleness, tears, and visiting

Ability to spend some time alone in quiet work or recreation

Ability to work in the presence of distracting influences—physical discomfort, noise, emotional stress, heat, etc.

Ability to work when weary, even late at night if the occasion demands "the midnight oil"

Expecting oneself to perform assignments, not just satisfactorily, but well

Ability to take correction or criticism without malice, anger, or tears

Ability to tolerate differences of opinion, injustices, and impositions without a display of emotion

Ability to be objective and impartial when working with others, regardless of friendly or unfriendly feelings toward co-workers

Ability not to spend money for something that will give immediate pleasure when the money can provide greater satisfaction in the future

Ability to save some money for emergencies

Ability not to indulge in pleasures that injure the body, mind, or emotions

Ability not to boast, even though there may be cause

Ability to keep confidential information secret

Patience when other people make work difficult

FOLLOW-UP ACTIVITIES

1. It has been said that if you work for two weeks, eight hours a day, as hard as you would on the job, you will get the job. Outline two weeks of activities on a job-finding campaign that would bring this kind of success.
2. How many businesses can you count in your town where you might apply for a job you would like?
3. Survey 10 business firms in your town regarding the future openings for some kind of work that you can do. Present your findings to the class orally.
4. If you had your choice, in what area of business would you like to work? How many such businesses are there in your town?
5. Suppose you were being interviewed today. In the space provided, write the adjective that would best describe the way an interviewer would probably rate you in the following:

Appearance _____   Attitude _____
Approach _____   Temperament _____
Dress _____   Knowledge _____
Hands and face _____   General
Speech _____   Reaction _____

6. Which of the following adjectives would you use to describe the way you meet people during an interview? What can you do to improve your rating?

Lacks ease   Slightly nervous   Averted eyes
Nervous   At ease   Great poise

CASE PROBLEMS

1. If at First You Don't Succeed . . .

Karen Williams is about to graduate from the junior college in her town and has begun her job-getting campaign. On Tuesday morning she mails ten application letters with data sheets enclosed to the leading firms in the area. On Thursday there is one reply. The office manager of Stewart Electronics, Inc. asks her to call for an appointment for an interview. Karen calls and is told to come the following Monday. When Karen arrives, she is told that Mr. McKay has been called out of town for a week. Karen asks if there is someone else she can see, but the receptionist answers that no one else in the firm can hire office workers. Greatly discouraged, Karen goes back to her typewriter and sends out ten more application letters.

1. If you were Karen, what would you have done in this situation?
2. Which would you consider the most effective follow-up in this case, a letter, a telephone call, or a personal call at the office the following week? Why?
3. Why should Karen take the initiative, even though she did not break the appointment?
4. What attitude should Karen take when she sees Mr. McKay? Why?
5. Why is it inappropriate for Karen to show any resentment because of the broken appointment?

2. It Works Both Ways

Dick Bennett is badly in need of a job, as his father has recently had a heart attack and is temporarily unable to work. Dick hears of a job in a box factory and applies at once. He is interviewed by one of the company officers and is given a series of tests. The following day Mr. Daynes, the man who interviewed Dick, calls him and says that he has not been given the job because his test scores were too high. Dick insists that he would be happy to take the job, no matter what the test scores say. Mr. Daynes insists, however, that it is company policy to give routine, repetitive jobs only to applicants of average ability. Dick feels that he has been treated unfairly.

1. Why would such a policy be made? What is its purpose?
2. Do you agree that Dick might not enjoy working at repetitive, monotonous work?
3. What should Dick do now? Is there any place he can go for further advice?
4. What other policies can you suggest for dealing with this problem of repetitive jobs?

3. Make Your Own Opportunities

Dale Evans and Joe Packard are good friends. Both have finished school and are ready to look for work. Both are good typists and both have studied accounting for two years. Joe feels that opportunities are limited in his town and is thinking of moving to a large city if he doesn't hear of an opening soon. Dale has no money to keep himself in a larger city and decides he will have to find something on his own. Consequently, he maps out a campaign. At the office of the local Chamber of Commerce he gets a list of all of the business firms in his town that employ more than two hundred office workers. Dividing the list into geographical areas, he visits ten firms a day. At each firm he either speaks to the office manager or makes an appointment to do so later. At the end of a week, Dale has had five offers of employment.

1. In what ways are getting a job and selling a product from door to door similar?
2. A rule of selling is to see as many people as you can. How does this apply to finding a job?
3. It is not easy to be given a refusal. What attitude can a job applicant take toward a refusal that will help lessen its sting?
4. Are there other job sources Dale did not cover?

4. Salaries and Advancement

June Carlson has applied for several jobs and has gone out on three interviews. In the first interview she found her training was not adequate; in the second, a small office, the salary was excellent; but there seemed to be no chance for advancement. The last interview is most interesting to June. The job is secretary for three doctors. The beginning salary is low, but Dr. Meade (who interviews June) informs her that by the end of the year the office manager, Mrs. Smott, will be retiring and, if June seems capable of filling the job, she might be considered. June is undecided. She dislikes refusing a good salary on what is actually just a chance that she will be offered the office manager's job six months later. She asks for a day to think the offer over.

1. Assuming that you are a friend of June's and that she asks your advice, what would you suggest?
2. Besides salary and opportunity for advancement, is there a third consideration of even greater importance?
3. Is there a possibility that June could be advanced too rapidly? Explain.
4. It is said that slow, steady progress is more likely when the ultimate job is a good one. Do you agree?

5. Are You a Team Worker?

Max Golden has been a brilliant student in high school and college, but he has never shown an interest in athletics or school activities. There are two jobs open in the Peerless Bonding Company. One requires that the individual be able to work with others and prefer this type of work to that done alone. When the head of the firm, Mr. Kenny, interviews Max, he suggests that the actuarial job, requiring no group work, might be the better choice for Max. This suggestion is agreeable to Max, but he wonders how Mr. Kenny was aware of his preference.

1. Do you agree with Mr. Kenny that participation in school activities indicates a liking for people?
2. What jobs can you list that require team effort?
3. Which ones can you list that need no ability to work with others?
4. Which of your lists is the longer? What does this fact indicate?

═══ Chapter 15

Growing on the Job

Graduation days are called commencement for a good reason. Now your real education begins. It is the same when you get a job. Now comes the time for proving yourself. Even the experienced worker needs to learn new procedures and routines when he changes jobs. For the beginning worker the learning process may be more difficult and more time-consuming than the schooling which preceded his appointment. Adjusting to a new job is made smoother, however, when you realize that fairly difficult adjustments are normal to most beginners.

A new job is rarely tailor-made to your abilities and training. This is partly a result of the vast multiplicity of business operations in themselves. Still another factor is the swiftness of technological change. The most modern, up-to-date school cannot possibly keep up with all new changes and inventions in business. While students are learning procedure A, the invention of machine B may be changing the procedure into something else entirely. All you can do under the circumstances is be aware of change, be prepared for it, get the best training and education you can before your employment, and continue learning and progressing on the job.

TECHNICAL IMPROVEMENT ON THE JOB

The first inadequacy you may encounter when you take a new job is in your technical preparation. You may have become proficient on a certain machine, only to discover that your employer has installed another. You may find that the methods, systems, and routines of the new firm are entirely different from those you learned. What should you do?

First of all, keep a learning attitude. No matter how "sold" you may be on the equipment and procedures used in your training or your previous employment, try to adjust to those found in your present job. It will be helpful, also, if you refrain from mentioning how you solved the problem at your former school or on your other job. Like the customer, your boss is always right — at least until you have given the new situation a fair chance.

A learning attitude means that you will be alert for any departure from your present knowledge or training. Suppose your supervisor suggests that you do a certain task in a new way. Pay attention, and ask questions if you have any doubts. Write down and number each step of the new method. Ask that it be demonstrated and see if you can follow the demonstration by trying it yourself. Most supervisors would rather spend extra time with a new employee than have errors appear in his work. Be appreciative of the extra help you receive, too. A considerate employee will find that his supervisors will usually respond with equal consideration and will be glad to help him when he needs it.

In-Service Training

Large firms may recognize the importance of the need for special training for new workers by organizing specific training courses. These may be training at the time of employment, called induction training; on-the-job training when new procedures must be learned or difficulties are encountered; and promotional training.

Induction training is usually required of all new employees, and you should be eager to learn all you can when you have such an opportunity. One vital part of such training is becoming acquainted with the overall business of the firm. Learn all you can about the product your firm manufactures or the service your firm performs. Find out about the extent of its operations and the location of its branch offices. Learning these things will result in an increased interest in your job. You will no longer be an unimportant cog in a huge machine if you realize just how your job fits into the whole.

The second type of on-the-job training may be offered to certain employees who have been transferred from other departments, those employees who lack certain needed skills, and those who are expected to work on new equipment or with new procedures. If such training is given you, welcome the opportunity to learn something new. This alone will set you apart from the other employees, as resistance to change is a common trait. Even if the training involves longer hours, be glad for the opportunity. Learning something new is a guaranteed way of improving your vigor and effectiveness. Take advantage of each opportunity that comes your way.

If, after you have been working in a firm for several years, you should be considered for advancement, you may be asked to take some sort of promotional training. Special training is usually needed before a worker is promoted to a supervisory post. If such an honor should come to you, be aware of the benefits such training will bring you. For example, you may be given help in developing your leadership qualities, in planning your work and the work of others, in developing desirable attitudes, and in evaluating your work and the work of others. This type of training is sure to be helpful to you through all your working life.

Home Study

Another type of self-improvement is optional. Taking advantage of it is entirely up to you. Have you noticed how many courses are available to you through television? Taking advantage of television training may mean arising an hour earlier than usual. Once you have made early rising a habit, however, you will be amazed to find how easy it is. Learning by television may or may not be for college credit as you wish. In any case, though, you should put yourself in a school situation. Take notes. Review the notes just before you begin the next session. If you take one course each year, you will be getting the equivalent of a university course each year, in comfort and at no cost.

Reading has been an educational tool for thousands of self-made business leaders. Regular reading for short periods of time and on one subject is the secret. Decide to become knowledgeable in some area of interest to you. Get a book or two on the subject from the public library. Start reading. That's all there is to it. It will help if you set aside a special time for general reading of this type. Just before retiring is a good time. Fifteen minutes each night (before you turn to your brand of escape reading) spent on a serious subject should greatly improve your education. Good reading has a further advantage, too. Teachers of writing tell us that the best way to increase your vocabulary is through reading and that the best way to learn spelling and punctuation is through reading. Such a rewarding activity should not be overlooked.

College Courses

In some types of businesses, for example, banking and insurance, special courses are offered in local colleges and universities. These courses are for the benefit of employees of such businesses and are supported by banking or insurance associations. College credit may be earned if it is desired. These courses provide a splendid opportunity to the ambitious worker, whether he is a beginner or has been working in the firm for some time.

In addition to prescribed courses, you will find night classes offered at universities and colleges. These classes become more popular each year. In fact, many colleges have an "extended day" enrollment equal to that of their regular programs. As business continues to emphasize automation, communications, accounting, and economics, the college degree becomes more and more essential. If you have not yet graduated from college, extended day courses leading to a college degree will be worthwhile.

Still another kind of self-improvement study can be pursued through correspondence or home-study courses. These have been discussed in describing job preparation, but they are just as helpful as part of your improvement-on-the-job program. As was stated before, the only drawback in working by correspondence is that you must motivate yourself. Developing such self-discipline, however, is in itself a valuable accomplishment.

PERSONAL IMPROVEMENT ON THE JOB

In addition to taking advantage of training opportunities, you should be constantly aware of ways of improving your personal traits. Advancement comes, of course, to those who are doing well in their present positions, but special attention is usually paid to personal traits as well. Preparing yourself personally for advancement means that you plan for advancement, that you brush up on your human relations, and that you learn when and how to speak up.

Planning for Advancement

The best time to plan for advancement is before you take a job. One of the considerations you should weigh is the job's promotion possibilities. A well-established firm may offer more security than advancement. A new firm, on the other hand, may provide rapid advancement to those employees who are promotional material and yet be less stable than an older firm.

If you are serious about advancement, you should study the possible jobs to which you might be promoted. What other skills, abilities, and traits in addition to those you now possess are needed in the new job? Be willing to prepare yourself in these areas before asking for advancement.

Planning for advancement also means that you will develop more dependability Be the sort of worker who completes the assigned task, no matter how dull or unchallenging it may be. If you have responsibilities (such as locking files or doors, or closing windows), never neglect them. Follow the rules and regulations established by the company, such as directions for smoking, taking coffee breaks, turning off lights. Last, and most important, do not blame others for any of your errors. A leader faces up to his own mistakes; he does not make excuses.

Brush Up Your Human Relations Skills

The way you get along with your co-workers will have much to do with your promotional chances. One important factor is your ability to be friendly with everyone without becoming involved in office feuds. It is wise to remain somewhat impersonal and detached at first, as you may not be able to detect factions and dissensions until you become more familiar with the firm. You will be slow to confide with others. Be a listener instead of a confider. Keep the confidences of others, and keep your own confidences to yourself.

Be willing to help others on occasion, but do not permit yourself to be exploited. In every office there are workers who try to find someone to do their work for them. Becoming a party to this sort of thing merely encourages irresponsibility in others. This type of worker is of no use to the firm, and if you should become a supervisor, he would continue to expect favors. A better way to handle this situation is to encourage the "leaner" to do his own work, to stand on his own feet.

A part of your human relations skill must go to keeping yourself in a good frame of mind. When you take a new job, you will probably go through periods of discouragement and dissatisfaction. You may receive reprimands, or you may be impatient with your mastery of the new position. When such times of disappointment come, try especially hard to do your job well. Self-discipline means you will not let your productivity respond to the variation in your own feelings.

Knowing that there will always be difficult times in any job may help you.

There are cases where employees become indifferent to the demands of their jobs or where they are poorly prepared for the jobs they hold. If this should happen to you and someone in authority should point it out to you, your reaction should be one of gratitude. You would attempt to find and correct the source of the trouble. In other instances, however, even well-prepared employees with good work habits and good attitudes feel tense and ill at ease in new positions. If this should happen to you, an understanding of your own feelings may help you.

Psychologists say that many people are too sensitive. If you are sensitive to the point that you feel other people are often sniping at you, criticizing you, or cheating you, you should examine your own feelings. Suspicious people cannot be happy or work easily with others. Self-understanding and self-discipline can frequently relieve this excessive sensitivity and give you a trust in others, enriching all your relationships. Sometimes all you need to do is recognize excessive sensitivity for what it is: self-consciousness or thinking too much about yourself.

Psychologists say that many employees are anxious. Of course, if you are not performing your best work, you may have reason to be anxious. In such a situation *action,* not anxiety, is required. Whatever is bothering you should be studied and remedied. Work habits and attitudes can be changed by a determination to do so; lack of technical training can be remedied through further education and experience.

When the anxious feeling does not seem to be caused by any actual failure, discovery of the reason may be impossible. There are steps you can take, however. You can do the very best work of which you are capable, *not* because you want to appear efficient in your employer's eyes, but because you want to do well. Second, you can make yourself think of something else every time you begin to worry about yourself. Make it a point to say something cheerful and pleasant to someone else when you feel anxiety coming on.

One of the best bits of therapy for excessive anxiety is talking it out with a counselor. Large firms may employ a company psychologist, or they may assign this task to the personnel director. If you can discuss your fears with such a professional, you may be better able to understand your weaknesses and how to overcome them.

Anxiety may manifest itself by worry or by excessive fatigue. Of course, fatigue may be actually merited. You may be getting insufficient sleep; you may be overworking; you may be involved in too many outside activities. If there seems to be no actual physical reason for your fatigue, however, anxiety is probably the cause, and monotony the symptom. If you do find your work monotonous, you might suggest to your supervisor that you rotate with other workers on repetitive jobs. Another suggestion is to change the way you do your work. One successful device is to time yourself on repetitive tasks, trying to cut down on the time taken while you continue to maintain high accuracy. If you can increase the interest and attention you give your work, you may be able to increase your enthusiasm for it.

Another change of pace that helps fatigue is a complete change of activity outside office hours. If you sit at a desk all day, you will benefit from physical activity after work. Bowling, tennis, golf, swimming, and other sports, all contribute to zest for your work and increased efficiency.

Learn How and When to Speak Up

So much depends on speaking — when to speak, when not to speak, what to say, and what not to say — when working for advancement. It is true that sometimes silence is golden. A beginning worker, for example, should be slow to suggest changes in working procedures. Before you make such suggestions, you should study the reasons for the present processes. You might learn from such study why your changes would not be practical at the moment. Suggesting changes just to prove you are alert and up to date is a practice that can only be detrimental to you.

Another time when silence is golden is when you are tempted to criticize another worker or an employer. Idle criticism will only earn you a reputation for being a troublemaker. Oftentimes, too, when you know the reasons for a person's actions, you will recognize that your intended criticism is undeserved. When you do decide to say something critical, it should be said *to* the person involved and not about him.

Think before you speak. There may be times when you have constructive suggestions to make. The first rule is to learn when and where you should express your views regarding the firm, your office, a particular job, process, or decision. Until you can learn the appropriate timing for such expressions, you should say nothing. Even when you know the right time and place for stating your views, you should do so concisely. Come directly to the point. If explanations are essential, organize them in logical form. It may be that your employers will welcome your suggestions. If, however, you find that your superiors have different ideas on the subject, you must abide by their decision. You must never argue or refuse to cooperate. Your superiors are older, wiser, and more experienced than you. In most cases, they have more information than you have.

Asking for a raise. The ideal situation exists when true merit is recognized and need never be called to the employer's attention. If your situation is not ideal, what can you do? Obviously, there is only one answer: You must bring the matter up; you must ask for a raise. All that has been said about timing your speaking applies here with extra force. Before you speak at all, however, you must precede it with considerable thought and study.

First, see if you are justified in asking for a promotion
or a raise. If it appears that you are, make out a good case
for yourself *in writing* — but be objective. What about
your production? Is there a standard for your work in your
office? If so, how does your production compare with this
standard? How many mailable letters do you transcribe in
an hour? How many papers do you file in an hour? How
many customers or callers have you handled without a complaint? What additional preparation have you made since
you were hired? Have you attended extension courses? If
you were to take an employment test at this point, would it
be significantly higher than the one you took when you
applied for your job?

Second, check your attitudes and work habits. Are you
always prompt in arriving for work? Do you work overtime
without complaint when it is necessary? How many days of
work have you missed because of illness? Are you considered
cooperative by your supervisor and your co-workers? When
you finish the work assigned, do you find something else to
do?

Third, ask your employer for an appointment. Of course,
you will not tell him the object of your request. Merely ask
if you may speak to him one of the following days. Mondays
and Fridays are busy days, so it is better to ask (on Tuesday)
for an appointment on Wednesday or Thursday. It is good
persuasion psychology to give your employer a choice of days.
Notice his mood, however, and wait for another week if he
seems busy or worried.

Fourth, if your request for an appointment is granted,
bring your notes with you to your interview. You might
begin your remarks with something like the following:
"Mr. Blank, I have enjoyed my work here very much. As
I was hired two years ago, you may be interested in the progress I have made since then." And then tell him how much
progress you *have* made. If you are confident of your worth,
you will be able to respond pleasantly to any gruffness or

lack of enthusiasm on your employer's part. If he challenges your statements, see that you neither back down nor get on the defensive. Simply and calmly bring up the case that you have prepared. After all, it is merely another employment interview, and you passed the first one!

Fifth, as in other interviews, when you have stated your case, you should thank your employer for the interview and for his time and leave. Go back to your work and be patient. Even if your employer has seemed impressed with your facts, you must not expect your raise to be forthcoming at once. He may intend to grant your request after conferring with other members of the firm. Don't ruin a good case by becoming a nuisance. If you hear nothing about your request after two weeks, you might ask your employer if any decision has been made. Both when asking for a raise and following up, keep your tone friendly but impersonal. Too much emotion has ruined more than one otherwise good cause.

KEEPING YOUR BALANCE

Like the old stock companies of your grandfather's day, the office has its stock characters. These may be recognizable at once, or they may be hiding behind a facade that is entirely different from the real person. This fact is one reason why you should take your time in joining one of the many groups you will encounter. The secret of a successful entrance into a new office is to be pleasant to everyone. Say "Good morning" to the janitor and to the president. Be sure to avoid becoming part of a clique until you have become better acquainted.

Don't React to Office Characters

One of the stock characters you will meet is the office grouch. A beginner may become upset over the office grouch, but remember he is not mad at you. There may be several reasons for his crankiness: his home life; finances; or his responsibilities in the office. If you are pleasant and sympathetic, if you refuse to take his complaining personally, you may make him less of a grouch.

What about the bossy "non-boss"? There is usually one around every modern office. This person criticizes everything you do (and everything others do, too). Remember that this bossy person is mainly dissatisfied with himself. Calling attention to the faults of others is just his way of easing up on this self-dissatisfaction. Pay no attention to the bossy person if he is your co-worker. If he *is* your boss, however, you will help him by paying careful attention to detail and by following his directions as accurately as you can.

The office complainer is more dangerous than these other office characters because complaining is highly contagious. The best thing you can do is politely avoid the complainer. Trying to counter complaints with cheerful, positive statements is useless, because the complainer is interested only in gloom. Whatever you do, don't let the complainer influence your thinking so that you become a complainer, too.

Another dangerous character is the tattletale. You can recognize him by the stories he tells you about other employees. No matter what the provocation, even if he repeats what one of the employees said about you, don't retaliate. A tattletale will go back to this person and repeat what you have told him. Gossip is unwise at anytime, but gossip with a tattletale is positively dangerous. When such a person starts telling you some tale about another person, be polite but firm. Suddenly remember a pressing engagement. There are plenty of your co-workers who will listen to him, unfortunately. The tattletale will leave you alone if you refuse to listen.

The best insurance against office characters is a busy social life outside the office. With the assurance friends of your own give you, you will not be upset by the office tease. You will be able to smile and agree with him good-naturedly, no matter how it really gets under your skin. The office wolf will be less of a menace, too. Remember, in any situation with an office wolf, it is best to be casual. Whistles and the like will be discontinued if you fail to react. The best way to handle the office wolf is to be pleasant but firm, pretend not to hear him, and have a sense of humor that puts him in his proper place; he will soon move on to greener pastures.

Don't become an office character. There is one office character that you may become — the favorite employee. Try to keep such a situation from developing if you can. If, in spite of your efforts, the boss seems to favor you, do everything you can to stay on good terms with the other workers. You must never try to capitalize on such favoritism. Even though your employer may call you Jack, or Mary, or Bill, you must not call your boss by his first name. You will have everything to gain and nothing to lose if you treat all superiors with "distance" — that slight formality that indicates respect.

Another character you must not assume is that of the arguer. It is possible to avoid unnecessary arguments; it takes only two ingredients, relaxation and patience. If someone makes a controversial statement, relax. Feel your muscles go limp. Then wait and listen until you have heard the whole story. Many arguments are merely the result of not letting the other fellow finish his story. Decide to say nothing until your "opponent" has talked for at least three minutes. By that time, particularly if you are relaxed, you will find yourself much less likely to say something rash, something that might hurt the other person's feelings.

Have an Emotional Outlet

An important part of keeping your emotional balance in the business world is having an emotional outlet outside of office hours. Sports provide this outlet for many young people, but everyone does not enjoy sports. To be effective, your hobby must be one that *you* enjoy. There is no definition of a good hobby. Anything you can lose yourself in is good for you. If you have a talent, expressing that talent is the best hobby for you. There can be tremendous emotional release in little theatre productions, amateur orchestras and quartets, painting, photography, or writing.

If you have no talent but have goodwill, you can find just as effective an outlet. Helping the helpless brings greater emotional satisfaction than any other activity. Call your hospitals. Ask if they need someone to read to crippled children. Call your blind centers and ask if readers are needed. In most universities there is a great need for readers for those students who have poor vision. Local rest homes offer unlimited opportunities for bringing happiness to those who may feel they are completely unwanted.

No matter what your business life may offer, you need an outlet that *you* consider rewarding. And don't let someone else tell you that the hobby you have chosen is without value. People's emotions are the most individual phenomena imaginable, and only you can make your choice.

Let Your Personality Grow

No matter how you may feel about your personality right at this moment, you can improve your personal traits. The trouble with many improvement campaigns, however, is that they go the wrong way. Like your hobby, your personality is an individual matter. It won't help you if you try to pattern your personal traits after those of someone else. What you need, instead, is some kind of standard, some indication of personal growth.

There is, of course, no end to personal growth. We will never be totally free from faults. There are a number of standards by which you might judge if you are growing in inner strength and personal warmth. With personal growth as your motivation, you may see measurable improvement in each of the following:

You will be able to judge people correctly, to detect insincerity. You will not be fooled by those who try to impress you with superficialities, with material possessions, with dropping the names of their famous friends.

You will become natural and spontaneous, and you will tend more and more to dislike artificiality in others.

You will be able to forget yourself and do what needs to be done. This means you will become more problem centered; you will not fight the problem to defend your own ego.

You will need more privacy. You will need to be alone to build up your own inner resources; and, because of this, you will be better able to take misfortunes with detachment.

You will be more interested in growing than in attaining some goal. For you, the journey will be more rewarding than the destination. Because of this, you will work to improve in what you are and what you do rather than expect acclaim for what you have done.

The simple beauties of life will become more precious to you. Sunshine, sunsets, rain on the trees, flowers, these simple beauties will bring you joy. In the same way, you will have many acquaintances but not so many true friends. Those you love will grow more precious as the years go by.

You will develop a nondestructive sense of humor. You will not enjoy cruel wit; most of your jokes will be at your own expense rather than that of others.

You will enjoy making things, creating, and inventing. You will look for new ways to do your work to make it more interesting and more enjoyable.

You will become less of a conformist. You will not slavishly follow the latest styles but will develop your own taste. Because your own strength will be more important to you than what others think, you will get along with the world you live in without becoming engulfed by it.

You will make mistakes, but you will be able to accept your own blame and pick up the pieces and go on.

This, then, is a description of the personality that is motivated more by growth than by adjustment. It is believed by many psychologists that this personality is the healthiest and most productive. If these suggestions appeal to you, keeping a score periodically might motivate you to grow in these ways. This method was used by Benjamin Franklin at the beginning of his career.

TRAIT TRAINING

There are some character traits that are particularly applicable to growing on the job. One reason for this is the maturity level at which they usually develop. A young person is nearly always self-centered, but with maturity comes an increase in his ability to be concerned with others. The mature traits, a desire for improvement, social consciousness, and unselfishness, will become evident.

Desire for Improvement

The desire for improvement is a wish to enhance oneself in value or quality. Everyone has vague desires for improvement. With success, however, you become aware of what is involved in achieving greater success and are able to set more realistic goals. For example, the untried schoolboy may dream of handling scores of workers with a word, of swaying great audiences with his eloquence. A businessman who knows what is involved in leading others and who knows the difficulties he is likely to encounter, will set his goals within the realm of possibility. For this very reason, a realistic desire for improvement is usually stronger after the worker has had some success in his work.

A number of studies have been made of successful young people. One such study asked many questions of young people who had succeeded. In their answers, successful beginning workers said they did not expect success to come to them without effort. They stated that nothing comes to those who only wait for it. They believed that successful people must work hard, adjust to life's problems, want to improve, and make a determined effort to become more capable.

You probably know someone who is bitter because success did not come to him. That person may explain that he did all that he was told to do. Unfortunately, however, doing only what you are told to do or meeting the minimum expectations of a job is not enough to bring success.

The successful businessman must go beyond the call of duty. He must do what is expected of him — plus. In adding this plus quality that is needed for success, he must not be aggressive or obtrusive. Instead, he should, in a quiet, confident way, give more thought and work to the assignment. This plus quality has two parts. One part is a desire for improvement; the other is doing something about the wish to improve.

The desire for improvement may be expressed in being proud of the growth of your firm, in watching and helping that growth. If you have this pride, you will also be proud of the amount of work you can do in a certain time. One of the joys of any kind of work is pride in good craftsmanship. This joy will be lost if your main concern is in the hours you work or the wage you earn.

Even after the day's work is finished, you can express pride in your work. Read the newspapers and newsmagazines for items that may affect your firm. Keep in touch with current and local affairs.

A desire for improvement is shown in your attitude toward your work. You will welcome and encourage suggestions from your superiors for doing your work more efficiently. You will be alert to suggestions for improving your work when they come from fellow employees. If someone tells you about an unconscious mannerism you have that is making you conspicuous, you make a determined attempt to eliminate it.

Social Consciousness

The trait of social consciousness means being aware of civic responsibilities and having a desire to further existing institutions. Working for public betterment is one of the hallmarks of an adult person. You know, of course, that business depends on society and that society regulates business. You know, too, that the services of all legitimate institutions have value. You also serve society in your capacity of employee, no matter how humble your position.

When you are called upon to contribute to your Community Fund, the Red Cross, and the various other drives, you are glad to do so. The request usually comes through the business that employs you, and that business is judged by the social consciousness of its employees. If you are asked to work for some civic organization for the general good of the community, you are glad to be of help. When requests for information come to you, you answer them promptly and courteously. You obey the laws of your community; you set a good example to others in your conduct and in your speech.

As you mature in business, you in turn become a leading citizen of the community — one to whom your fellow citizens will turn for leadership. This day will come more quickly if you get the feeling of civic responsibility early — responsibility for those less fortunate than you, responsibility for helping to maintain and carry on the worthwhile institutions of today. Your service to society is a debt you owe in payment for the privileges that are yours.

Unselfishness

To be unselfish means that you are willing to share, to pay attention to the interests of others, and to be generous with your time and talents. The selfishness of business has been the object of humor since business began. All human traits are found in business because businesses are composed of human beings. Yet, while selfishness can be found in business, unselfishness and many other positive qualities can also be found. As an employee, you must be aware of your interests but also aware of the interests of others.

The ability to share is sure to be appreciated by the companies for which you will want to work. All businesses are working hard to create goodwill with their customers and their potential customers. If this same quality is evident among the employees of a firm, it will help them create a good feeling with the public. Sometimes you may see cases where it appears that selfishness is rewarded and unselfishness unnoticed. Such instances do occur, of course, both in business and in all other areas of living. The results of an unselfish attitude toward others will be evident in your personality, however, if you continue this trait. Appreciation of unselfishness may be slow, but it will be sure.

If you have the opportunity, talk with experienced businessmen and women about selfishness and unselfishness in business. You will discover that most people have a basic respect for fair play and unselfishness. Your co-workers will dislike you if you violate these basic values. To be accused of unfairness or selfishness would cost you more than any reward you could attain through pursuing these qualities.

You may express unselfishness by lending or sharing your materials and equipment with other employees when there is a need. You will give information, time, or services when your department is working under pressure. You will work overtime when this is necessary to complete the job on time. When there are unpleasant duties to be done, you will do your share willingly. All of these suggestions are familiar to you. Most of you have grown up with such maxims. All that is necessary is to make them habitual actions.

There is another side of unselfishness, however, that is not stressed; yet it is even more important to the smooth working of the business team. This side is the ability to accept gracefully the praise that is given your superior when you were largely responsible for the work, the idea, or the plan. Developing this kind of unselfishness is not easy. In our fiercely competitive society most of us try to shine individually; we dislike sharing honors rightfully belonging to us with others. Yet an old saying is true: You can get anything done so long as you don't care who gets the credit.

There are steps in developing this cooperative kind of unselfishness. First, you refrain from talking about your high skills, high grades, successes in general. Rather, you help another person to accomplish something and then praise the one you helped. This is the way to begin. After a while you will receive a greater feeling of pleasure from the success of the one you helped than you ever would from your own successes.

From this beginning it is a short step to a glow of pride when others in your department or your company achieve honors in which you had no share. Envy and jealousy — two most unattractive traits — can be eliminated from your nature with this sort of practice. All it takes is practice each day. If you can become the kind of person who is pleased when he hears words of praise for someone else, you will have taken a giant step toward emotional health. Nothing is so destructive to the personality as resentment, and nothing removes resentment more thoroughly than happiness in the success of others.

FOLLOW-UP ACTIVITIES

1. After you have been working for one year, ask a friend to rate you on the following scale. You might suggest that you rate each other. You must both be absolutely objective in your ratings, however. Flattery will get you nowhere! If you can get an honest appraisal, and if you can work on improvement where it is needed, you will be surprised at your progress. The results of this rating should be kept and the same appraisal made a year later. A comparison of the results will show you "how you are doing."

   Check each item from 1 to 4 according to the following rating: 1 — Good, 2 — Average, 3 — Fair, and 4 — Needs Improvement.

Rating

a. Good Grooming _____
b. Cleanliness _____
c. Appropriate Dress _____
d. Dress Suits Your Personality _____
e. Color Combinations _____
f. Posture and Carriage _____
g. Correct English _____
h. Voice and Diction _____
i. Facial Expression _____
j. Poise _____
k. Health _____
l. Vitality and Enthusiasm _____
m. Self-confidence _____
n. Cheerfulness and Sense of Humor _____
o. Friendliness _____
p. Sincerity _____
q. Willingness to Cooperate _____
r. Consideration for Others _____

2. *Helps Toward Growth.* On a form like that below, keep an up-to-date list of suggestions you encounter in your work and in your reading that you think might help you to grow. Check each suggestion that you try out. If you find the suggestion helpful, put an asterisk (*) beside the check mark.

Suggestion	√	*

3. Everyone has a mental picture of himself. Sometimes it is a good likeness, and sometimes it is not. In Column 1, check the statements that correspond to what you think you are like. In Column 2, check the statements you

believe other people think you are like. In Column 3, check the statements that you would most like to be someday.

a. *How I Feel About Myself*	1	2	3
Inferior to most of my associates			
Superior to most of my associates			
Self-confident			
Lacking self-confidence			
Conceited about my achievements			
Conceited about my appearance			
Modest about my achievements			
Ashamed of my appearance			

b. *How I Feel Toward Others*			
Tolerant			
Intolerant			
Friendly			
Unfriendly			
Like to be with others			
Dislike to be with others			
Like most people			
Dislike most people			

4. Psychologists say that we become what we think. As part of your improvement campaign, try keeping an improved mental picture of yourself in mind. Write down the statements from No. 3 that you checked that indicate what you would like to be someday. Visualize yourself as being this way for the next three months. At the end of that time, try this rating again. The results may surprise you.

CASE PROBLEMS

1. Future Dividends

Ted Tyler was employed as one of two bookkeepers in a small manufacturing concern. Mr. Christopher was the manager of the accounting department. Ted found that he could work much faster and more accurately than his fellow employee. He thus had time to spend in doing extra work or in helping the other bookkeeper. Things seemed to go just as well, however, if he took more time with his own tasks. He worked more slowly, therefore, so he would not have to do anything extra.

At the end of the year some special reports and records had to be prepared. A new man, Henry Mack, was employed as an extra bookkeeper for one month. Although his work was temporary, Henry was interested in the job and worked as hard as he could, doing exceptionally well. At the end of the month, when Henry was scheduled to leave, Mr. Christopher became ill and had to resign. Mr. Christopher recommended that Henry be given his vacated post as department manager, and this was done.

1. Do you feel Mr. Christopher was justified in overlooking Ted's seniority in the firm?
2. Do you think Ted had any claim on the position as department manager?
3. In working slowly, what impression did Ted give Mr. Christopher as to his ability?
4. If Ted had worked more efficiently and then spent the extra time in helping the other bookkeeper, would this have gone unnoticed?

2. Giving One's Talents

Mildred Taylor, a talented musician working as a secretary for the Black Company, has been asked to perform at a benefit show to be given by the company to raise money for the Red Cross. All of the employees of the company are participating in the show, performing, helping backstage, providing refreshments to be served after the show, or selling tickets. Mildred feels that she has been imposed upon, as she is asked to play for something nearly every week. She tells the chairman of the show that she would rather give $5 to the fund and be excused from playing.

1. Is it true that talented people are sometimes imposed upon?

2. If Mildred were justified in refusing some of the requests to perform that she receives, where should she draw the line?

3. In considering such requests, should Mildred weigh the purpose for which the performance is to be given?

3. Competition or Cooperation?

John Evans and Paul March are supervisors of divisions in a large company. Both have done well and are being considered for advancement. John has been assigned the job of making a survey of equipment costs in the various divisions. He comes to Paul for the data on his division. Paul gives John the data he needs; but, as he looks over the work John has already done on the study, he discovers a serious error in John's calculations. Paul realizes that if John makes a success of the survey, John will get the promotion instead of Paul. He hesitates about calling the error to John's attention in any case because he does not want to hurt John's feelings by criticizing him. After much thought, Paul decides to say nothing about the error.

1. In thinking about not hurting John's feelings, Paul was "rationalizing," or finding a good reason for doing something he wants to do. Do you think this is a common practice?

2. Can you think of any bad effects that may come to Paul if he lets the error go by?

3. If Paul had pointed out the error to John in a tactful manner and John had received the promotion, would Paul have been hurt, careerwise, in the long run? Why or why not?

4. Why is it always best to take the action that is best for the company as a whole?

4. Nearly Everyone Resists Change

One of your duties as the newly appointed assistant purchasing agent is the supervision of the stock room. In charge of the stock room is Mr. Black, who has been with the company for thirty years. It is he who devised and installed the system of records used in the stock room. This system is now out of date, clumsy, and too elaborate.

A major item of concern is how to get Mr. Black's cooperation in making the change from the old system of records to one that is more efficient.

1. How will you win the confidence of Mr. Black?
2. Write down the opening statement you will make when you bring up the matter of installing a new record system for the first time.
3. Assuming that you win Mr. Black's cooperation, what will you say when Mr. Black makes a suggestion that you feel is not a good one? Give your conversation in detail.
4. The new system is now ready to be installed. What will you say to Mr. Black to help get the system off to a good start?

5. Tell me frankly . . .

Keith Berg has been working as a salesman for the Southern Power & Light Company for three years. During this time he has had only one advance in salary. He sells as much each year as any of the other salesmen; but, while others advance, he remains stationary.

One day he stops one of his fellow salesmen, Grant Daly, who has just received a promotion to district manager. He tells Grant that he knows something is wrong with him or else he would have been promoted, too. He asks Grant point-blank to tell him his faults.

1. What are some of the traits that Keith should possess to be promotable material?
2. If you were Grant, what would you say to Keith?
3. When someone asks for frank criticism, should you still use tact? Why or why not?
4. Psychologically, it is better to impersonalize negative criticism. How would you do this in discussing Keith's faults?
5. Assuming that Keith is pleasant with customers but abrupt with co-workers, how would you tell Keith this fact?

6. In discussing personal traits with another, it is wise to compliment before you criticize. What good quality has Keith shown he possesses by asking for frank criticism?

PROJECTS

1. From your own experience, write a case illustrating one of the traits discussed at the end of each chapter in this volume. Discuss the case in class.

2. From the case problems in this chapter and other chapters, choose one or more for dramatization. One person is to play each character. Act out the solution of the problem before your other class members. Do you feel this is a valuable experience?

APPENDIX SUPPLEMENTARY READINGS

Supplementary Readings

Allport, Gordon W. *Becoming.* New Haven: Yale University Press, 1955.
————. *Pattern of Growth in Personality.* New York: Holt, Rinehart, & Winston, Inc., 1961.
————. *Personality and the Social Encounter.* Boston: Beacon Press, 1960.
American Women. Report of the President's Commission on the Status of Women. Washington, D.C.: U.S. Government Printing Office, 1963.
Anderson, Camilla. *Saints, Sinners, and Psychiatry.* New York: J. B. Lippincott Co., 1950.
Anderson, John E. *The Psychology of Development and Personal Adjustment.* New York: Henry Holt & Co., Inc., 1949.
Bacharach, Bert. *Book for Men.* New York: A. S. Barnes & Co., Inc., 1953.
————. *Right Dress — Success Through Better Grooming.* New York: A. S. Barnes & Co., Inc., 1955.
Baird, Albert C., and F. H. Knower. *General Speech,* Third Edition. New York: McGraw-Hill Book Co., Inc., 1963.
Becker, Esther R., and Richard L. Lawrence. *Success and Satisfaction in Your Office Job.* New York: Harper & Brothers, 1954.
Berrien, Frederick K. *Practical Psychology,* Fourth Edition. New York: The Macmillan Company, 1952.
Bettelheim, Bruno. *Love is Not Enough.* Glencoe, Illinois: Free Press, 1950.
Chase, Stuart. *The Power of Words.* New York: Harcourt, Brace & Co., Inc., 1954.
Cole, Luella W. *Psychology of Adolescence,* Fifth Edition. New York: Rinehart & Company, Inc., 1959.
Coleman, Lester L. *Freedom From Fear.* New York: Hawthorn Books, Inc., 1957.
Cosgrove, Marjorie C., and Irma Unruh. *Discovering Yourself.* Life Adjustment Booklet. Chicago: Science Research Associates, 1957.
Duvall, Sylvanus M. *Art and Skill of Getting Along With People.* Englewood Cliffs: Prentice-Hall, Inc., 1961.

English, Oliver S. *Emotional Problems of Living*. New York: W. W. Norton & Company, Inc., 1955.

Fink, David H. *For People Under Pressure*. New York: Simon & Schuster, Inc., 1956.

——————. *Release from Nervous Tension*. New York: Simon & Schuster, Inc., 1953.

Flesch, Rudolph. *How to Be Brief*. New York: Harper & Brothers, 1962.

——————. *How to Make Sense*. New York: Harper & Brothers, 1954.

Finkelhor, Dorothy C. *How to Make Your Emotions Work for You*. New York: Farrar, Strauss & Young, Inc., 1952.

Fromm, Erich. *The Art of Loving*. New York: Harper & Brothers, 1956.

Giles, Lambert L. *Charting Your Job Future*. Chicago: Science Research Associates, 1957.

Hiltner, Seward. *Self-Understanding*. Charles Scribner's Sons, 1962.

Hodnett, Edward. *The Art of Problem Solving*. New York: Harper & Brothers, 1955.

——————. *Art of Working With People*. New York: Harper & Brothers, 1959.

Horney, Karen. *Our Inner Conflicts*. New York: W. W. Norton & Company, Inc., 1945.

Hovland, Carl I. *Communication and Persuasion*. New Haven: Yale University Press, 1953.

Ingram, Karl C. *Talk That Gets Results*. New York: McGraw-Hill Book Co., Inc., 1957.

——————. *Winning Your Way With People*. New York: Whittlesey House, 1948.

Johnson, H. Webster. *How to Use a Business Library*, Third Edition. Cincinnati: South-Western Publishing Company, Inc., 1964.

Keily, Helen J., and R. G. Walters. *How to Find and Apply for a Job*. Cincinnati: South-Western Publishing Company, Inc., 1960.

King, Eleanore. *Guide to Glamour*. Englewood Cliffs: Prentice-Hall, Inc., 1957.

Laird, Donald A. *Sizing Up People*. New York: McGraw-Hill Book Co., Inc., 1951.

——————. *The Technique of Getting Things Done*. New York: McGraw-Hill Book Co., Inc., 1947.

Landis, Judson. *Building Your Life*. Englewood Cliffs: Prentice-Hall, Inc., 1954.

Lasser, Jacob K., and Sylvia Porter. *Managing Your Money*. New York: Holt, Rinehart, & Winston, Inc., 1962.

Lee, Irving J. *How to Talk With People*. New York: Harper & Brothers, 1952.

Liebman, Joshua L. *Peace of Mind*. New York: Simon & Schuster, Inc., 1946.

Lyle, Guy. *I am Happy to Present (A Book of Introductions)*. New York: The H. W. Wilson Company, 1953.

MacGibbon, Elizabeth. *Fitting Yourself for Business*, Fourth Edition. New York: McGraw-Hill Book Co., Inc., 1961.

Maslow, Abraham H. *Motivation and Personality*. New York: Harper & Brothers, 1954.

McKinney, Fred. *Psychology of Personal Adjustment*. New York: John Wiley & Sons, Inc., 1960.

Meerless, Joost. *Conversation and Communication*. New York: International University Press, 1952.

Menninger, Karl. *Love Against Hate*. New York: Alfred A. Kopf, Inc. (Paperbound), 1959.

——————. *Man Against Himself*. New York: Harcourt, Brace & Co., Inc., 1956.

——————. *The Human Mind*. New York: Alfred A. Kopf, Inc., 1945.

Overstreet, Harry A. *The Mature Mind*. New York: W. W. Norton & Company, Inc., 1949.

——————. *The Mind Goes Forth*. New York: W. W. Norton & Company, Inc., 1949.

Overstreet, Bonaro W. *Understanding Fear in Ourselves and Others*. New York: The Crowell-Collier Publishing Co. (Pocket Edition), 1962.

Peale, Norman V. *The Power of Positive Thinking*. Englewood Cliffs: Prentice-Hall, Inc., 1954.

Reik, Theodore. *Listening With the Third Ear*. New York: Grove Press, 1956.

Reilley, William J. *How to Get What You Want Out of Life*. Englewood Cliffs: Prentice-Hall, Inc., 1957.

——————. *Successful Human Relations*. New York: Harper & Brothers, 1952.

Ryan, Mildred. *Clothes for You*, Second Edition. New York: Appleton-Century-Croft, Inc., 1954.

Saul, Leon J. *Emotional Maturity*, Second Edition. New York: J. B. Lippincott Co., 1960.

Seabury, David. *Art of Living Without Tension*. New York: Harper & Brothers, 1958.

Stratton, Dorothy, and Helen B. Schleman. *Your Best Foot Forward*. New York: McGraw-Hill Book Co., Inc., 1955.

Thomason, Calvin. *Human Relations in Action*. Englewood Cliffs: Prentice-Hall, Inc., 1948.

Tillich, Paul. *The Courage to Be*. New Haven: Yale University Press (Paperbound), 1959.

Vanderbilt, Amy. *Complete Book of Etiquette.* New York: Doubleday & Co., Inc., 1963.

Wertheimer, Max. *Productive Thinking.* New York: Harper & Brothers, 1959.

Weschsler, David. *The Range of Human Capacities,* Second Edition. Baltimore: The Williams & Wilkins Company, 1952.

INDEX

≡ INDEX

A

Ability, discover your own, 10
Achieving success, 4
Adaptability as a trait in business, 145
Advancement, planning for, 267
Apparel, harmonizing colors in men's, 70
Appearance, 65
Application blank, filling out an, 247; illustration of an, 249–252
Application letter, 222; essential points in preparing, 225; illustrated, 227
Applying for a job, 209
Appreciation as a trait in business, 195
Arranging the interview for a position, 237
Attitude, 3, 21; business, 186; eliminate negative, 37; friendly, in selling, 142; positive, 19; positive work, 5

B

Balance, keeping your, 273
Behavior problems in business relationships, 35
Behavior, related to service offered in an office, 160
Business attitude, impersonal, 186
Business behavior, basic needs, 17; goals in, 7; grammar in, 98; mannerisms in, 166;

principles underlying, 31, 32; reasons for training in, 3
Business contacts, techniques employed in, 183
Business introductions, 191
Business psychology, in office, 159; in selling, 141
Business relationships, behavior problems in, 35; impersonal nature of, 186
Business situations in which tact must be displayed, 104
Business success, 3; factors in achieving, 9
Business traits, adaptability, 145; appreciation, 195; basic, 26; courage, 255; courtesy, 117; desire for improvement, 278; foresight, 228; generosity, 148; gratitude, 196; happiness, 197; honesty, 151; initiative, 149; judgment, 167; loyalty, 28; morality, 168; neatness, 164; punctuality, 118; responsibility, 170; self-control, 326; self-judgment, 230; social consciousness, 279; sympathy, 103; tact, 104; thoroughness, 229; unselfishness, 280

C

Callers, practice in greeting, 174; practice in turning away, 174
Career versus marriage, 188
Care, of the hair, 81; of the skin, 80

297